The Marriage You Want

Moving beyond Stereotypes for a Relationship Built on Scripture, New Data, and Emotional Health

SHEILA WRAY GREGOIRE AND DR. KEITH GREGOIRE

BakerBooks

a division of Baker Publishing Group
Grand Rapids, Michigan

Published by Baker Books
a division of Baker Publishing Group
Grand Rapids, Michigan
BakerBooks.com

Printed in the United States of America

Library of Congress Cataloging-in-Publication Data
Names: Gregoire, Sheila Wray, 1970– author. | Gregoire, Keith, 1969– author.
Title: The marriage you want : moving beyond stereotypes for a relationship built on scripture, new data, and emotional health / Sheila Wray Gregoire and Dr. Keith Gregoire.
Description: Grand Rapids, Michigan : Baker Books, a division of Baker Publishing Group, 2025. | Includes bibliographical references.
Identifiers: LCCN 2024033537 | ISBN 9781540903761 (paper) | ISBN 9781540904683 (casebound) | ISBN 9781493449057 (ebook) | ISBN 9781540905093 (audio)
Subjects: LCSH: Marriage—Religious aspects—Christianity.
Classification: LCC BV835 .G737 2025 | DDC 248.8/44—dc23/eng/20241002
LC record available at https://lccn.loc.gov/2024033537

Cover design by Kat Lynch

Baker Publishing Group publications use paper produced from sustainable forestry practices and postconsumer waste whenever possible.

25   26   27   28   29   30   31   7   6   5   4   3   2   1

Contents

Introduction   7

Balance

1. The Unity You Want   17
2. The Teamwork You Want   44

Affection

3. The Friendship You Want   63
4. The Passion You Want   83

Responsibility

5. The Partnership You Want   113
6. The Dependability You Want   142

Emotional Connection

7. The Understanding You Want   163
8. The Closeness You Want   185

Conclusion: Creating the Marriage You Love   215
Appendix   218
Acknowledgments   224
Notes   227

To Tammy and Steeve:

We love you. Thank you for being in our corner,
and for having the marriage everyone wants.

Introduction

When we were dating, we hated saying good night. Our relationship started when we were in university (and we married as students too!), and that good-night ritual usually stretched out over several hours. One of us would reluctantly say, "We really need to get to sleep," and the other would agree, but then we would hug some more or kiss some more or just hang on to each other for dear life because we didn't want to part. We longed for the day when we would never have to shut the door on our beloved to brave the cold weather, walking back to a lonely apartment in the middle of the night, ever again.

Now that we've been married for over thirty years, what we appreciate about marriage is a little different. Someone to laugh with about all your kids' idiosyncrasies and your grandkids' antics. Someone to go hiking with, to give you a backrub when you can barely move, to hug you through the griefs of life. Someone who loves you, knows all your quirks and inside jokes, and still rests their head on your shoulder.

We all want a marriage to someone who feels like home. We all want a safe space combined with a passion that won't burn out. But how do we get that?

The fact that you picked up this marriage book means that you care about two things: First, you want your marriage to be that passionate and safe space. Second, you also want to glorify God. In the church, those two things have often been linked—if you're married, the way you glorify God is by having a good marriage. Perhaps that's why we Christians really love marriage books! We love reading about marriage, flocking to group studies on marriage, and thumbing through marriage books in premarital counseling. That's likely why, on Amazon, an outsized proportion of the top twenty-five books on marriage are actually from Christian publishers!

Yet despite all the attention we pay to marriage, many Christians are not experiencing the marriage they dreamed of when they walked down the aisle. Every day, my (Sheila's) inbox fills up with messages from yet more people telling me how they've read "all the books" and tried so desperately to put them into practice but have failed to see thriving in their marriage. How is this possible? If we have God's eternal truth for life and we're talking about marriage all the time, why aren't all of us doing well?

I have been blogging about sex and marriage since 2008. I've written multiple books, and every year I publish hundreds of blog posts, the equivalent of seven more books. For the first part of my career, I thought the answer to the marriage problems I kept hearing about was to provide more teaching. So I worked constantly, teaching about how to have great sex, how to love sex, how to increase your libido. But people kept having the same issues. No matter how much good teaching I gave, and no matter how much I pointed to the truth, many were still stuck.

What was going on?

In January 2019, I had the catalyst that helped me answer that question. It was a Friday afternoon. I had a migraine and I was trying to procrastinate, so I was scrolling what was then called Twitter. There, I happened on a debate over whether women's primary need is for love or respect—referring to the thesis of one of evangelicalism's bestselling marriage books. I remembered that I owned that book but had never read it.[1] I had been writing about marriage for over a decade, but I made it a practice not to read other marriage books for fear of inadvertently plagiarizing.

I figured, "They love Jesus, I love Jesus, so we must all be saying the same thing!" But that day, procrastination triumphed over fear, and I flipped to the sex chapter.

My whole world spun as I read one piece of horrible advice after another. It bafflingly told wives, regarding sex, "If your husband is typical, he has a need you don't have,"[2] and encouraged a wife to "minister to her husband sexually . . . as unto Jesus Christ."[3] Excuse me? (And ick!) It explained that sex was about a husband's physical release, and if the husband didn't get physical release, he'd come under satanic attack.[4] Nothing about intimacy. Nothing about the fact that a wife should feel pleasure too. If this was what people were reading, no wonder they were still having issues! My team and I began to suspect that the trouble in Christian marriage and sex advice isn't an absence of good teaching as much as the presence of bad teaching that has gone completely unchallenged. Our team started reading other bestselling books on marriage, and we noticed two interesting differences between the advice given in most Christian books versus the advice given in more general-market books.

First, the main point in Christian books was always simple: You need to commit more.

- *Never say "the d-word" (divorce).*
- *Nail the back door shut.*
- *You don't marry the right person; you become the right person.*

Commitment is often portrayed as the panacea that can solve everything, and lack of commitment as the poison that causes marriages to end and passion to fade. But how is "never say the d-word" supposed to get you to the point of actually feeling like your marriage truly is your safe space? It can't. And we want you to know up front: We're not writing this book to convince you to stay in a marriage you hate. We're writing this book to help you create a marriage you love.

Second, Christian books seemed to have an allergy to data. In most bestselling secular marriage and self-help books, you find authors referencing studies of actual couples to show you why they believe what they do about what goes into making a great relationship. Christian resources, on the other hand, tend to present lots of ideas about what the author believes will make your marriage great based on their interpretation of the Bible, but surprisingly little in the way of real-world evidence. For example, on the secular side, Emily Nagoski's bestselling sex book *Come as You Are* includes 177 peer-reviewed references plus dozens of others. In contrast, Stephen Arterburn and Fred Stoeker's evangelical bestseller *Every Man's Battle*, which has sold four million copies in the series, has not a single one. Even the old evangelical classic *The Act of Marriage* by Tim and Beverly LaHaye has only one, and it's from an anatomy textbook.[5]

To some evangelicals, this seems to be a point of pride, painting this as an either-or proposition: Either you do marriage "God's way" (i.e., based on one's personal interpretation of Scripture), or you do it the "world's way."[6] But can't we believe Scripture and also believe the evidence of our own eyes? To put it in the words of Galileo, should we "feel obliged to believe that the same God who has endowed us with sense, reason, and intellect has intended us to forgo their use"? If Jesus is *the* truth (John 14:6) and God has revealed himself in creation (Rom. 1:20), then what we see in the world that God has made and what we see in Scripture should line up. If they don't, the answer isn't just to cling to our particular interpretation of Scripture and ignore reality. When someone seems to be teaching us from Scripture something that doesn't line up with the truth that God baked into his creation, we should remember what Jesus said:

> Likewise, every good tree bears good fruit, but a bad tree bears bad fruit. A good tree cannot bear bad fruit, and a bad tree cannot bear good fruit. Every tree that does not bear good fruit is cut down and thrown into the fire. Thus, by their fruit you will recognize them. (Matt. 7:17–20)

If we're trying to decide what advice is actually good for our marriage, Jesus tells us the answer: Look at the fruit. This book is for couples who want to take marriage to the next level by giving up pat answers and having the courage to see what actually works.

What Does the Fruit Say?

Our motto at Bare Marriage (home of Sheila's blog and podcast) is that we teach what is healthy, evidence-based, and biblical. For the last few years, our team has been up to its eyeballs in data, trying to discover whether common evangelical teachings are increasing marital and sexual satisfaction or decreasing them. We started by surveying 20,000 women. We followed that up with a study of 3,000 men, and then with another study of 7,000 women looking at how women's experiences as teens impacted them as adults. We compiled the results of all this research (as well as many other peer-reviewed sources) into Sheila's previous books, including *The Great Sex Rescue*, *The Good Girl's Guide to Great Sex*, *The Good Guy's Guide to Great Sex*, and *She Deserves Better*. Since their releases, many have told us how our approach—listening to the evidence while staying true to Christian principles rather than trying to force the data to fit with theological preconceptions—has been so freeing and helpful to them.

Those books dealt primarily with the sexual aspect of marriage, and most were written primarily for women either by Sheila alone[7] or by Sheila and her team, including Rebecca Lindenbach (our oldest daughter) and our statistician, Joanna Sawatsky (who joins us for this book too!).[8] Keith joined Sheila to write *The Good Guy's Guide to Great Sex*,[9] and in this book, Keith, a physician, is adding his insight as well. We needed both of us because we wanted to tackle not just sex but something more fundamental: the marriage itself. We wanted to write a book about marriage that was healthy, evidence-based, and Jesus-centered. We wanted to show that data and Jesus can go together! As you read this book, you'll see results from our various surveys and from other peer-reviewed studies that point to what creates not just a good

11

marriage—but a great marriage.[10] And in addition, just for this book, we did something unique: a matched-pair survey. Surveying 1,370 couples, plus another 5,000 individuals, we asked respondents to complete a comprehensive survey that took around 30–40 minutes. When couples took the survey, we were able to match their answers—though each spouse wouldn't be able to see the other spouse's answers. Those couples helped us figure out which teachings actually brought the best results, and the answers may surprise you—because sometimes they look quite different from the advice given in many evangelical marriage books.

Let's Get Back to Bare Marriage

In August 2022, I (Sheila) rebranded my blog. I felt the old name, *To Love, Honor and Vacuum*, didn't reflect what the blog had become. When I originally launched it, I was writing to women who felt more like maids than wives and mothers, and I focused on organization, parenting, and self-care. But over the years, it had morphed into something else. I had made sex my main topic of conversation, yes, but I had also been addressing what I called "toxic teachings" that took people away from the life that Jesus wants for us.

We decided our new name would be Bare Marriage. That had a convenient sexual connotation that worked for our brand, but it also had a secondary meaning that is more fundamental: It suggests stripping things away that aren't needed to get to the heart of what Jesus wants. It's about true authenticity, which requires vulnerability, not masks. We believe that we will only be able to create fulfilling and God-honoring marriages when we have the courage to stop asking, "How can we make this marriage look right?" and start asking, "How can we truly feel united, connected, and intimate?"

That's what we want to do in this book. Instead of addressing the question, "How can I stop feeling lonely in my marriage?" we're going to ask, "Why do you feel lonely in your marriage? And what can you do about it?" Instead of addressing, "How can

I increase my libido?" we'll ask, "Why don't you want sex very much? What's going on that's lowering your libido?" If you're feeling distant, let's figure out why. If you're feeling overwhelmed and tired, let's work on a solution. If you're going through a sexual drought, let's find an actual water source.

We'll start with the foundation: a proper balance. Let's put Jesus back on the throne so that we're focused on him, and let's make sure we're tending to the foundations of a strong relationship. After that, we'll turn to the two foundational ingredients that build a great marriage—affection, including passion for one another, and sharing responsibility so we work as true partners. We'll finish with emotional health and connection, that "safe" feeling that we're all aiming for.

Together, those four elements spell BARE:

Balance
Affection
Responsibility
Emotional Connection

We're going to debunk and strip away the advice that doesn't work and point you to what it takes to truly thrive in marriage. We're going to treat you like whole people who want and need healthy relationships, and that's exactly what you deserve.

So, let's look at how to help you thrive!

Balance

Using Your Unique Giftings and Strengths to Act
as Partners Running toward Jesus Together

CHAPTER ONE

The Unity You Want

During our premarital counseling, our pastor pulled a black Sharpie out of a drawer and sketched a triangle on a piece of paper. Holding it up in front of us, he encouraged us to imagine this triangle representing our marriage. God was at the top, while each of us resided in our own corner at the bottom. Drawing arrows pointing to the Creator, he assured us that as we moved closer to God, we would also move closer to each other.

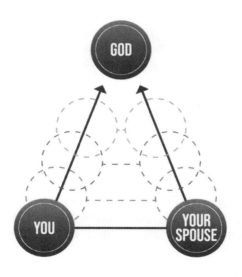

As soon-to-weds who were very zealous in our faith, we ate it up. It perfectly encapsulated our dream: Each of us follows hard after God, and we end up closer together as a couple! I (Keith) even had my wedding band designed with two diamonds flanking a cross to show that Sheila and I would always look to Jesus in our marriage and that he would unite us. That has largely been the story of our marriage. Through good times and bad, our faith has tended to draw us closer to each other, to make us both better people, and to bring health and wholeness in ways that neither of those two young kids pledging vows to each other could have imagined.

At the start of this book, we want to put first things first. What does it mean to run after Jesus? Well, the Bible tells us that our relationship with God is a personal one. We call God "Abba, Father" (Rom. 8:15). We recognize the Shepherd's voice; he leads us and we follow (John 10:27). We are to run the race, looking to Jesus, who is the author and perfecter of our faith (Heb. 12:2). And as we do that, we're transformed into his likeness (Rom. 8:29), which means not trying to get power and authority over others but instead living a life of service (Matt. 20:25–28). It means having the same mind that was in Christ, who took the form of a servant (Phil. 2:5–8).

And then Jesus himself told us what was most important: We love God with all our heart, soul, mind, and strength, and then we love our neighbor—including our spouse—as ourselves.

That's really all it comes down to. We treat our spouse as we would want to be treated, and we live a life of service within our marriage. Can you see how, when you do that, you also grow closer to each other? When we're listening to Jesus' voice, and we're loving and serving each other, marriage is going to be awesome.

There. That's it. It's really that simple! That's how the triangle works.

Until, that is, unhealthy teachings from church or our culture stretch that triangle all out of shape. What was simple suddenly becomes complicated. And we don't like complicated! So, let's see how things can get all bent out of shape, and how we can get back to what's simple again.

Stretching the Triangle: When You Don't Get to Just Be You

Why did you fall in love with your spouse? Likely because they were so totally unique, someone so special that you hadn't found anywhere else. You weren't going to marry *any* woman or *any* man—you wanted to marry *this* woman, *this* man. That's called love! And because you are both unique individuals, your marriage will be unique as well—and it will leave its unique mark on the world.

We know that God has special things planned for each of us—from before the very foundation of the world (see Eph. 2:10). And that calling can be expressed through your marriage. For years, our partnership blessed our small community, which was drastically short of pediatricians.[1] Keith spent many days (and nights!) working crazy hours in the local hospital, covering calls for neonatal and pediatric emergencies. Sheila held down the fort and looked after the kids while starting her writing career. Our unique giftings and interests also allowed us to lead medical mission trips to Kenya. And now God's given us the privilege to teach about marriage. Your unique gifts are all part of how God can bless his creation through you, not just as individuals but as a couple. God has a unique calling on your marriage too. And it depends on each of you showing up with your personalities, your strengths and gifts, your interests. You can't have a thriving marriage if one of you is holding back or trying to be someone you aren't.

But what happens if, instead of being told to run after Jesus in our own unique way, with our own unique gifts, we're told that we have to fit into a mold that wasn't meant for us? Instead of being Jessica and Diego, or Michael and Ashley, or Mandy and Timon, we're pressured into being MAN and WOMAN. Now, in your marriage, you may naturally fit into more stereotypical roles, and that's fine! We are not trying to replace one stilted, inflexible way of doing marriage with another. But one of the pivotal ideas we want you to grasp is this idea of balance.

Balance is the ability to make adjustments to keep yourself stable while your situation changes. Think of a tightrope walker.

If the wind blows them to the left, they better be pretty quick to lean to the right! In the same way, balance in marriage requires us to adjust to circumstances rather than plowing ahead with the same strategy no matter what the challenge. Gender roles are a perfect example of how things can go wrong, because too often they sacrifice adaptability and replace it with inflexibility. Rather than trying to live up to what someone else says you should be, you'd be so much better off focusing on *what actually works for you both*.

Consider an imaginary couple: She's super organized and loves doing finances, while he's allergic to spreadsheets. They love their kids, but getting down on the floor with them causes her to feel an overwhelming desire to check her phone notifications, while he savors building endless towers of blocks and drinking the imaginary tea their daughter hands him. This couple goes to a marriage conference where they are taught that stereotypical gender roles are God's prescription for every marriage. He hears that, as a man, he needs to take leadership, step up to the plate, and get a handle on the finances and that, as a woman, she needs to remember that her main role in life is to stay home and be the primary caretaker of the children. If they put this into practice, would this couple thrive? Of course not! Everything would be an added struggle as they play to their weaknesses rather than their strengths. They would be trying to follow someone else's idea of what a marriage should look like rather than figuring out what works for *them* based on how God created them—to say nothing of the needless shame and confusion they would feel from not fitting into an arbitrary mold being foisted upon them.

The teaching that there is only one way to be a man or woman goes against the many varied examples in Scripture and against the uniqueness and variety God demonstrates in creation. Consider how many Christian men's groups teach that "all men are warriors." For some reason, the example always given is William Wallace (specifically as portrayed by Mel Gibson in *Braveheart*). Why not choose an example from Scripture? Likely because if we searched Scripture, we would see the many godly men of the

Bible who were not warriors, and furthermore, we'd find that David, the Bible's most famous warrior, was a sensitive poet who played the harp, wept openly, and danced like no one was watching. None of that fits the cherished stereotype, though, so we turn to Hollywood instead. And don't get us started on how our modern evangelical concept of biblical womanhood completely ignores women in the Bible who ran businesses (see Prov. 31:24), called out their husbands when they were being fools (see 1 Sam. 25:25), and drove tent pegs through the skulls of their enemies (see Judg. 4:21).[2] When we take cultural stereotypes, baptize them as "biblical," and direct others to emulate them, we're treating stereotypes as if they're equivalent to God's will for our lives. Stereotypes are not reliable guides, and when we follow them, our triangle stretches out of shape! We lose our balance because somebody has put a big, unnecessary weight on one end of our balance pole, separating us from ourselves, our spouses, and even God. How can we be truly known, after all, if we aren't even free to be who God made us to be?

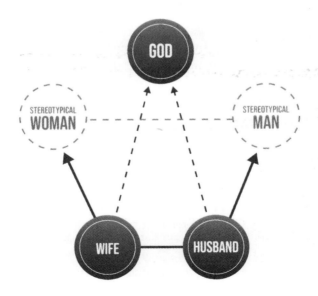

If It's Only "Sometimes True," Then It's Not "Always True"

For some reason, evangelical marriage advice really seems to love gender stereotypes. The titles of the bestselling books in that category reflect this: *Love & Respect*; *His Needs, Her Needs*; *For Women Only*; and *For Men Only*. Men and women are often portrayed as two different species that can barely understand one another. But are these stereotypes helpful—or even accurate? After all, there's a world of difference between saying women or men *tend to be* like this or that and saying they *should be* like this or that. My (Sheila's) father and grandfather were both very tall men, but they inherited that from my great-grandmother, not my great-grandfather. My great-grandmother was 5′11″, which is taller than 99% of women today—let alone in the late 1800s when she was born! Her husband, on the other hand, was a modest 5′7″, but scientists weren't banging on their door, trying to figure out how this could possibly be. We instinctively understand this basic truth about statistics when it comes to something obvious like height: Just because men on the whole are taller than women on the whole, it does not mean that all men are taller than all women.[3]

Social scientists call this the concept of overlapping bell curves. If you take a trait that is variable within the population and plot it on a graph, most people fall somewhere in the middle, with fewer and fewer people falling at the increasingly extreme limits. This graph makes a bell shape. In the exact middle of the bell is the mathematical average of that population. For many traits, men and women have different bell curves, *but these curves tend to overlap*. And here's another interesting fact about things that are distributed on bell curves by gender: Often there's more difference *within* males and *within* females than there is between the *average* man and the *average* woman. This is part of the way that God made us and is normal (no pun intended for you stats nerds).

One of the things that we found in our survey of 20,000 women, for instance, is that in about 57% of marriages, the husband has the higher sex drive. However, we must never forget that in many cases the opposite is true. In 43% of marriages represented in our

22

original study, the wife had the higher sex drive or they had similar drives. Yet when resources blithely state "men have higher sex drives" without the caveat that there is overlap between men and women, it can leave higher-drive wives and lower-drive husbands feeling like freaks.

Similarly, most Christian resources suggest that men are visually stimulated and women aren't. In fact, research increasingly shows that women are neurologically just as visually stimulated as men; they've just been conditioned out of responding to it.[4] But even if the general trend were true, it would be much more responsible to say that men tend to be more visual than women but that there is significant overlap than to say (as too many of our Christian resources do) that men are visual in a way that women will never understand.

Plus, gender stereotypes don't even apply to the majority of couples! Consider the idea that men's orientation to the world around them is based on thinking, while women's is based on emotion. One of the four scales on the Myers-Briggs Type Indicator (MBTI) measures people's preference for feeling versus thinking. A compilation of 58,000 people's results on this inventory found that 56.4% of women scored as "feelers," while 73.3% of men scored as "thinkers."[5] In both cases, the MBTI results support the stereotype. But let's go back to middle school math for a second. If you know the chance of *A* happening, and you know the chance of *B* happening, how do you find the chance that *A* and *B* will both occur at the same time? You multiply them together! For any given couple, then, the chance that he's a thinker and she's a feeler is 73.3% multiplied by 56.4%, which is only 41.3%.

Think about that for a moment: *Every single sermon, marriage talk, or marriage book you've ever encountered that assumed the wife is emotion-oriented and the husband is logic-oriented does not apply to 58.7% of couples.* And even if a majority of couples did fit the stereotype, it would still be more helpful to simply talk about the value of understanding each perspective. Attaching male and female labels doesn't provide any additional help when the stereotypes fit and adds tremendous confusion when they don't. It complicates what should be simple—you're allowed to be who God made you to be! So how about we stop talking about stereotypes and just look at how to properly express your needs and preferences—and how to understand your spouse's needs and preferences—in your own unique marriage? That's what we're going to do throughout this book. And then you'll be able to live out God's unique purposes for you as a couple, not as a stereotype.

Love Your Spouse as Yourself

Jesus tells us that we are to love our neighbor as ourselves (Matt. 22:39). And your spouse is your neighbor! Marriage, then, involves loving two people: yourself and your spouse. To live out those unique purposes, you both need to show up in the marriage.

We become unbalanced when loving our spouse and loving ourselves are not held in proper tension. Sometimes we may forget our spouse is our neighbor and ignore or dismiss their needs and preferences. That clearly goes against Jesus' teachings and will hurt your relationship, but let's also not make the opposite mistake and think it is a virtue to ignore and diminish our own legitimate needs and preferences. Yes, Christian teaching emphasizes that we are to be selfless and care for others. But it is not the whole truth. Jesus' command to "love your neighbor as yourself" contains an implicit assumption that a certain amount of love for ourselves is normal and important. Your spouse matters, but you matter too! A marriage in which only one person matters is not a thriving marriage because it's not a true partnership. Suddenly your triangle looks like this, with one spouse dwarfing the other:

We knew a couple who lived out this dynamic. Colleen married Bill when she was in her early twenties, and he was a decade older. Bill was a steady, loyal man, bringing home a good paycheck and striving to make his wife's life easy and stress-free. Colleen, though, tended to see him as wimpy and criticized him frequently. To reduce tension and keep the peace, he tended to give in whenever she made demands, even if they were unreasonable. He became almost invisible in the marriage and also to his children. Instead of standing up for himself, he accepted her treatment because he wanted to keep her happy.

Two decades into the marriage, Colleen got bored and left, claiming that Bill was emotionally unavailable. The kids, who were mostly young adults by this point, were left reeling. But as they now navigated a relationship with their dad on his own, they felt like they were meeting him for the first time—and they discovered how interesting he was. After his retirement, he even moved in with one of his children to help with the grandchildren, and in many ways is living his best life today, surrounded by people who genuinely appreciate him.

Colleen let herself become the focus in the marriage, and Bill went along with it, thinking that was how he should love her. Instead of creating harmony, it left Colleen unable to respect Bill and Bill feeling unloved and unappreciated. Some of us, like Bill, need to be challenged to show up more in the marriage (more on that in chapter 7). And some of us, like Colleen, need to be challenged to take the spotlight off ourselves. Your spouse is not an extension of you. Your spouse is a unique individual just like you are. Show up in your marriage—and give your spouse room to show up too.

The Tiebreaker Question (aka The "He Decides" Shortcut)

Another way that one spouse can dwarf the other is in how they handle decision-making. Often, in Christian circles, that responsibility is placed on the husband. When the couple disagrees, he gets to decide what to do. But if he has the final say, then his opinions, for all practical purposes, matter more than hers. While it may not be the intention, this means that the wife's responsibility is to follow her husband rather than following God directly. We've replaced a partnership paradigm with a power paradigm.

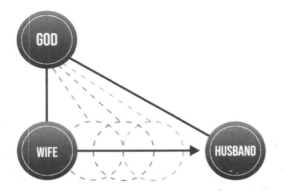

Pastors, authors, and marriage speakers often present this "husband as decision-maker" model as necessary and inevitable: "Without someone to break ties, you'd always be at an impasse! How else will you find agreement if someone doesn't have veto power?" While they may treat this as a "mic drop," our stats, as well as our experience, tell a different story.

In our study of 20,000 women for *The Great Sex Rescue*, we found that most couples (78.9%) make decisions together—even the ones who say they believe the husband should have the final authority—and these marriages do well. However, in marriages in which the husband actually made the decisions for the family, even if he consulted with his wife first, the couple was 7.4 times more likely to divorce. Ours is not the only study to show that the best way to ruin your marriage is for someone to try to be the boss. World-renowned marriage researcher John Gottman discusses in his book *The Seven Principles for Making Marriage Work* how difficult marriage can be for couples with a religious belief that the husband is supposed to have authority. His solution is that those husbands need to learn to ease up and share power with their wives. And if they don't? "Statistically speaking," Gottman tells us, "when a man is not willing to share power with his partner, there is an 81% chance that his marriage will self-destruct."[6]

Unilateral decision-making in marriage is always a net negative, whether it's the wife who decides or the husband.[7] But in many Christian circles, it's actively taught that a husband having authority to make unilateral decisions is a good and godly thing. Now, we are not going to provide a comprehensive argument of how Scripture actually teaches mutuality in marriage. First, others have done a great job of that elsewhere.[8] Second, our specialty is data, so we'd simply like to compare the fruit of deciding together versus deciding unilaterally with the husband serving as the tiebreaker.

When a couple believes that they are true partners, then the expectation is that, when they disagree, they'll be able to work it out. It's assumed that unity and solidarity are the bedrocks of the relationship. When disagreement comes, that expectation motivates the couple to hone the skills they need to bridge the gap so that both feel heard and valued.

But what happens if a couple believes that the husband should serve as tiebreaker? Such a couple will assume that sometimes disagreements are intractable. When disagreements hit, she may default to, "This must be the time I'm supposed to submit," or he may default to, "I'm supposed to step up and decide for us." This short-circuits the entire process of working through the problem using your own individual insights and perspectives, let alone waiting on God together. Not to mention, many people may move to these positions at the drop of a hat. But every time a couple chooses this shortcut and fails to truly wrestle through a problem, they deprive themselves of the opportunity for growth while also confirming their expectation that intractable disagreement is normal. Eventually, they can't even see how it would be possible to live out marriage without a tiebreaker.

Not only does this shortcut stop couples from growing; it makes women feel unimportant and overlooked in their marriages. Our data show that in marriages with collaborative decision-making, women are almost three times more likely to report feeling heard when the couple has a disagreement.[9] And in marriages in which

Why a Tiebreaking Vote Isn't Benign

Which member(s) of the couple is (are) affected if they go into marriage believing that men get to have a tiebreaking vote in marriage? Does belief from one spouse affect marital and sexual satisfaction outcomes for both?

Our survey results showed a fascinating pattern: Women's belief in the presence of a tiebreaking vote negatively affected the marital and sexual satisfaction outcomes for nearly every outcome we measured. But it also made their husband's marriage worse. When women believed in a male tiebreaking vote, their husbands reported lower sexual satisfaction.

he holds final decision-making power (even if he consults with her first), a wife is 11.8 times more likely to say that her opinions don't matter as much as her husband's.

Is it possible for marriages to function without an arbitrary tiebreaker? Absolutely, according to both our surveys and our focus groups. Here are the strategies the people we interviewed say they use in their marriages:

- We take a few days to pray about it separately, and then we talk about it again.
- We shelve it for a time and then return to it later.
- We talk to other people to get their opinions.
- If one of us has more expertise in the area, we tend to go with what they think.
- If one of us would bear more consequences of the decision, then they get to decide.
- We yield to the person for whom this might have a negative impact.

Do you see the balance in these approaches? Healthy couples do end up deferring to one or the other, but it's not rigidly always to the husband by default. They defer *for a reason*, and that reason

Figure 1.1

What happens if you believe when you get married that one spouse has a tiebreaking vote?

To interpret these data, use the following: If [I / my spouse] believed when we got married that men should have the tiebreaking vote in marriage, then [I am / my spouse is] [#] times more likely to say that _____.

■ **Effect on husband**   ■ **Effect on wife**

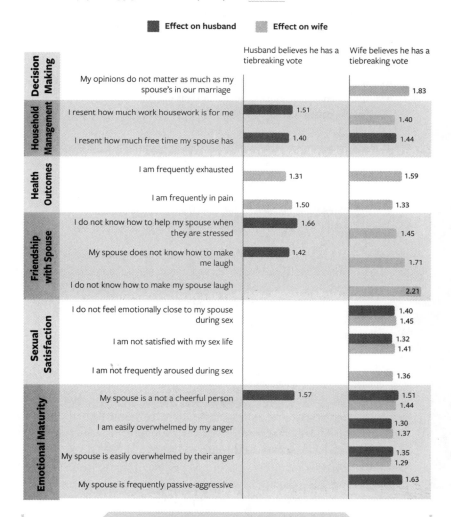

		Husband believes he has a tiebreaking vote	Wife believes he has a tiebreaking vote
Decision Making	My opinions do not matter as much as my spouse's in our marriage		1.83
Household Management	I resent how much work housework is for me	1.51	1.40
	I resent how much free time my spouse has	1.40	1.44
Health Outcomes	I am frequently exhausted	1.31	1.59
	I am frequently in pain	1.50	1.33
Friendship with Spouse	I do not know how to help my spouse when they are stressed	1.66	1.45
	My spouse does not know how to make me laugh	1.42	1.71
	I do not know how to make my spouse laugh		2.21
Sexual Satisfaction	I do not feel emotionally close to my spouse during sex		1.40 / 1.45
	I am not satisfied with my sex life		1.32 / 1.41
	I am not frequently aroused during sex		1.36
Emotional Maturity	My spouse is a not a cheerful person	1.57	1.51 / 1.44
	I am easily overwhelmed by my anger		1.30 / 1.37
	My spouse is easily overwhelmed by their anger		1.35 / 1.29
	My spouse is frequently passive-aggressive		1.63

KEY TAKEAWAY: Belief that one partner gets to have a veto bears bad fruit, even years later.

changes based on the specific circumstances of each particular situation. Just like our tightrope walker, you adjust left or right based on circumstances. Here's how one of our readers explains it: "We tend to let it fall to our strengths. There are some things that I just trust my husband's expertise over and some things where he trusts mine. It isn't about winning an argument but about trust. I can't think of a single argument that we couldn't get on the same page after real discussion and logic." When you both show up to your marriage, and one spouse isn't dwarfing the other, then you can defer to the strengths God has given each of you.

Another reader says,

> If it's not a major life decision (like a vehicle or appliance purchase, etc.), we defer to the one who cares more or has more of a vested interest in said decision. When we bought our dishwasher, he was working 40+ hours/week and I was a stay-at-home mom, so I was the one using it more. So my choice carried more weight. He is the resident computer geek, so I tend to defer to him and his ability to troubleshoot when choosing electronic devices. We haven't really been at an impasse over major life decisions in over twenty-five years of marriage. We came to our marriage as whole, individual people with our own relationship with God, and so we trust that He is going to put us both on the same page. I'm a major logic person, and my husband trusts that I have thoroughly weighed, researched, and (usually) overthought all the options. On the flipside, I trust his discernment and intuition that I am sometimes lacking. It all somehow works out for us.

In over two decades of marriage, this reader, like the vast majority of Christians, has never needed her husband to make the final decision simply by default. We've been married for thirty-two years, and we've never needed Keith to break a tie because we've always worked it out. That's how most people operate. And that's a good thing, because an arbitrary tiebreaker is not only unnecessary; it's actively harmful. When people don't feel that their opinions have as much weight in their marriage as their spouse's, marriages suffer.

Figure 1.2

How does not believing your opinions are equal with your spouse's affect marriages?

To interpret these data, use the following: If [I / my spouse] believe(s) that our opinions are not equal in our marriage [I am / my spouse is] [#] times more likely to say that _____.

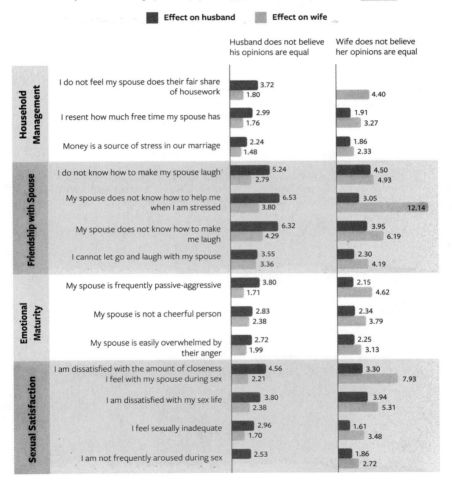

KEY TAKEAWAY: Marriages suffer when either spouse's opinions matter less than the other's.

One of the fun things about a matched-pair study is that we can look at how things one spouse believed impacted the other spouse. When one spouse does not feel their opinions are equal to their spouse's in their marriage, their marital and sexual satisfaction is lower . . . and so is their spouse's. When a husband and wife value each other's opinions, though, balance is restored and marriages thrive. Respondents who said they feel their opinions

Figure 1.3

How does believing your opinions are equal with your spouse's affect how you describe your marriage?

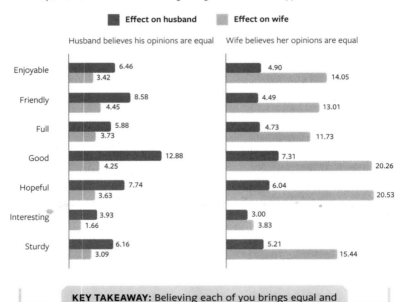

To interpret these data, use the following: If [I / my spouse] believe(s) that our opinions are equal in our marriage [I am / my spouse is] [#] times more likely to describe our marriage as [descriptor].

One of the scales we used in our matched-pair survey, which we conducted for this book, was the Couples Satisfaction Index (CSI).[10] The CSI includes seven questions, which asked respondents to describe their marriage using a choice between opposites.[11]

■ Effect on husband   ■ Effect on wife

Husband believes his opinions are equal   Wife believes her opinions are equal

	Husband: Effect on husband / Effect on wife	Wife: Effect on husband / Effect on wife
Enjoyable	6.46 / 3.42	4.90 / 14.05
Friendly	8.58 / 4.45	4.49 / 13.01
Full	5.88 / 3.73	4.73 / 11.73
Good	12.88 / 4.25	7.31 / 20.26
Hopeful	7.74 / 3.63	6.04 / 20.53
Interesting	3.93 / 1.66	3.00 / 3.83
Sturdy	6.16 / 3.09	5.21 / 15.44

KEY TAKEAWAY: Believing each of you brings equal and valuable perspectives to your marriage bears good fruit.

matter as much as their spouse's were more likely to describe their marriage with positive adjectives—and this effect was greater for women than for men.

Collaborative decision-making leads to a sense of teamwork. We found that 40.98% of women report that their spouse is always or almost always willing to hear them during disagreements if they come to a decision collaboratively, compared with just 10.73% if he makes the decision after they talk it over.[12] Things are even worse if one spouse makes unilateral decisions without discussing the matter first. Without collaborative decision-making, women especially are more likely to feel unheard. That's downright dangerous to marital flourishing. When someone feels their spouse is always willing to really hear what they want to communicate during a disagreement, only 0.75% of them have second thoughts about their marriage. In other words, basically none. But when someone feels their spouse is never willing to hear them? Then 51.7% have second thoughts—more than half![13] And women are far more likely not to feel heard in arguments when we teach that decision-making should rest in the husband's hands since his opinion, in practice, trumps hers.[14]

The harmful effects of a husband serving as tiebreaker don't stop as we arrive at the bedroom door either. While there is no statistically significant change in men's sexual satisfaction if they make unilateral decisions, their wives don't fare as well and are 3.8 times more likely to be dissatisfied in their sex life.[15] This makes sense: When the way you do marriage primes the couple to consider his opinions above hers, that can transfer to the bedroom, too, where his pleasure is prioritized and hers is not. Your decision-making style can impact far more than just how you handle conflicts.

Placing the responsibility for decisions on the husband doesn't just hurt the wife; it also hurts the husband. Mary Bell, the mom of one of our longtime readers, recently shared in an article her own experience of following the "husband as authority" model of marriage and how that affected her husband too. She and her husband married at twenty-three with stars in their eyes, determined to do marriage "God's way," which they thought meant

How Do We Measure Marital Satisfaction in This Book?

We were fortunate to be able to incorporate question sets from previously validated surveys into our survey for this book. Other researchers tested the questions, made sure they work as intended, and developed scoring rules so that new researchers (like us!) could use the same scale.[16]

We used four scales to measure marital satisfaction:

1. the Relationship Flourishing Scale (RFS)[17]
2. the Couples Satisfaction Index (CSI)[18]
3. the Trust in Close Relationships Scale (TCRS)[19]
4. the Kansas Marital Conflict Scale (KMCS)[20]

Throughout this book, you'll find various charts and graphs in which we used these scales to investigate how different actions, choices, and relational styles affect different aspects of marital satisfaction. We used the Relationship Flourishing Scale as our default but also looked at how each item affects the other scales and included those findings in the endnotes.[21]

These scales measure marital satisfaction in different ways—but they also tend to paint a very similar picture. When a social scientist develops a new scale investigating some aspect of marital satisfaction, they will test to see if the results of the new test correlate with results from other instruments. Focus groups and interviews might also be involved to make sure that a question is actually measuring what the researchers want it to measure.

Here's what researchers find: Scales correlate. *A lot.*

And that is what we found in our survey too. When marital satisfaction improves, so does marital flourishing. When conflict resolution happens in a healthier way, trust improves. Feeling connected is associated with better conflict resolution habits. And on and on. Invest in one area, and the payoff can be wide reaching.

that her husband led, and she followed. This worked well for a while, until they had a special needs son with many behavioral issues. She writes,

> Our carefully constructed Christian life began to fall apart. His behavior was so challenging that our church asked us to not bring him anymore. Devastated, we stopped attending, and many of our church friends dropped us. My husband felt humiliated that he could no longer act in leadership positions in the church because he did not "have his children under control" (1 Tim. 3:4–5);

Figure 1.4

How does decision-making style affect marital satisfaction?

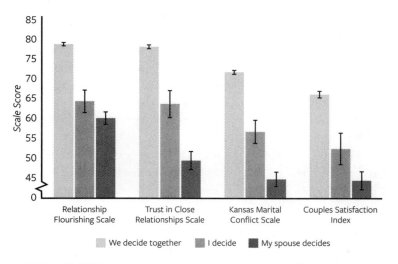

We found that for both men and women, collaborative decision-making is associated with the highest marital flourishing and relational trust. But if decision-making is lopsided, there are winners and losers. Spouses who make unilateral decisions don't fare as well as those who make collaborative decisions, but they fare better than those who have unilateral decisions made for them.

KEY TAKEAWAY: Collaborative decision-making leads to the best marital outcomes.

he withdrew from our family and focused on his work, where he could feel competent.[22]

Even though Mary had a background in research and psychology and was able to learn what behavioral techniques could help her son, her husband often resisted her input, interpreting their son's behavior as a challenge to his authority rather than as a sign that he wasn't able to process his environment. The marriage was in trouble—until they started to question the fundamental belief that family was supposed to be about hierarchy. They began to believe that it was okay to treat marriage as a genuine partnership where each could contribute their unique giftings, including Mary's training and insight into her son's condition.

Mary explains that they started to realize how the theology they were taught "pits the interests of wives and husbands against each other. If the wife's role is to always defer to her husband's superior authority, it undermines her confidence in her own abilities and competence, fostering fear and resentment. If the husband is the sole, final authority in a family—and if he must be always in 'control' of that family—then any problem in the family is ultimately his failure. Fear of failure fosters insecurity and authoritarianism in husbands."[23]

Her husband was becoming a shell of a person under this need to have his family "under control." But once he realized he could give it back to Jesus and stand by Mary's side, knowing that it wasn't all up to him? They found harmony again.

Instead of focusing on following what the husband wants, marriages flourish when the couple stands arm in arm together, running wholeheartedly after Jesus. Men, you don't need to bear the burden for the family alone. It's not good for your wife, and it's not good for you. And women, speak up! Your opinions and giftings matter too. If you both use your talents and giftings, you'll maintain balance and adjust to whatever comes your way, but if you prioritize one spouse over the other, you'll be trying to balance on that tightrope with one hand tied behind your back. Be a team as you follow Jesus together, and you'll find that's what leads you closer to the marriage you actually want.

What If the Triangle Gets Stretched out of Shape?

Think back to elementary school for a moment and imagine your teacher drawing different triangles on the blackboard. Remember learning about equilateral triangles, where all the sides of the triangle are the same size? That's the type of triangle our pastor was talking about when he said, "Aim for God, and you'll end up closer to each other." But equilateral triangles aren't the only kind of triangles. Let's say one person is trying to move closer to Christ and their spouse, but the other person is running in the opposite direction. Then your triangle gets super stretched. You may be closer to God, but farther away from your spouse. You're not working with an equilateral triangle anymore; you're a scalene triangle. And when it comes to our marriage triangle: equilateral GOOD, scalene BAD.

There are basically three types of people who read Christian marriage books. First are those who are excited to learn about marriage, either because they're about to get married or they're doing a small group study or they just really enjoy reading Christian self-help books. There's nothing particularly wrong with the relationship; they're just always on the lookout to improve. Second are those who may have a few issues that need work in the relationship but are both invested in working them out. We really hope you're in one of those categories.

But we also know some of you are reading this book because you're desperate. Perhaps your marriage has not turned out to be the blissful partnership you envisioned. You're lonely. You're dealing with betrayal or anger or even just chronic indifference. You may even be facing a spouse's emotional, physical, spiritual, or sexual abuse. People in abusive relationships often don't realize it because one of the characteristics of abuse is that it's very confusing. Often, the abusive spouse tells you that you are the problem and you need to fix things—and too often our church culture repeats this mantra. Abuse is then framed as a relationship problem that you should fix.[24] Now you're left hoping to find the magic formula that will make your spouse realize how they are hurting you and stop it.

The first balance concepts we looked at were "happy" ones—how to build a marriage where we each thrive as we do what we are uniquely called to do and feel cared for, while we go through life as partners, chasing after Jesus together. But there's another aspect to the triangle analogy that is just as vital to understand: If your spouse doesn't want to be your partner, doesn't show care for you, and is actively hurting the marriage—you can't do much about that. Two of you together decided to get married, and two of you together keep that marriage strong. One of you can't do it on your own.

Here's a foundational truth the triangle illustrates: You can move up and down your own segments of the triangle, between you and God and between you and your spouse, but you can do absolutely nothing to make your spouse move closer to you or closer to God. No matter how frantically you move along your side of the triangle, you can't change their position or direction. Only they can decide what they will or will not do.

Unfortunately, the evangelical church has sold tens of millions of books whose main message is that if you just pray hard enough, your marriage can be healed from infidelity, abuse, workaholism, addictions, and more.[25] Inspirational anecdotes may be given, such as a woman who spent forty years praying in her difficult marriage to a bad man, whom her friends and family were telling her to leave (this is basically a description of an abusive marriage). But the takeaway? She prayed hard enough, and he became a Christian and all their problems were solved![26]

What these anecdotes don't tell you is the terrible impact on the lives of children growing up in a home with a destructive parent.[27] And they certainly don't tell you the far more common scenario—the people who prayed just as hard, but their spouses never repented, never changed. Teachers who present only the miracle and fail to warn people of the reality of what happens in the majority of cases are being deceptive and dangerous. Yes, we know from Scripture that God can affect circumstances: He can soften and harden hearts; he can speak to people. But God also restricts what he does for one simple reason: He has baked free will into the world, and he gives us agency over our lives. He allows us to choose whether to serve him or not, whether to love him or not. And the price of freedom means that people can choose not to do the right thing. No matter how hard we pray. No matter how much we abase ourselves. No matter how much we love, give, or sacrifice. People can choose addiction, abuse, affairs. And if your spouse does this, that is not on you.

Holding up miraculous transformation stories as if they are formulas turns the burden for the marriage on its head. While one spouse may be doing something to destroy the very fabric of the marriage, it now becomes the fault of the spouse who wants the marriage to work because if they just prayed harder, forgave more, or had more sex, then supposedly things would change. Tremendous destruction has been wrought by this faulty theology based on a faulty reading of Scripture that values the institution of marriage over the people within that marriage.

Those who abuse, those who fail to offer even the slightest care for the relationship, those who continue to engage in addictive behaviors, and those who do not control themselves sexually are not acting as Christians. They have effectively declared through their actions that they have abandoned their marriage since they have not cared emotionally or physically for their spouse. Abuse, adultery, addictions, neglect—all of these break the covenant of marriage through abandonment. Yes, we can influence our spouse, and we'll talk a lot about how to do that throughout this book. But we can't make a malicious spouse repent or love us. We can't make them change. The best we can do is show grace while we enact appropriate boundaries.

The triangle paints a lovely picture of marriage, in which two people matter and God is at the center. But remember that you're responsible only for your part of the triangle. We hope this book will give you a glimpse of what a healthy marriage looks like and clarity on where your marriage stands. But if you're reading this book to try to change a destructive marriage, that is a burden that is too big for you to carry. Please seek help from people who will enable you to embrace the freedom that Jesus wants for you.[28]

Thankfully, most of you will never have to experience that kind of relationship. For most of you, the biggest issues will be getting over the psychological effects of those faulty teachings we talked about earlier in the chapter. Some of you may need to ditch the false sense that caring for yourself is sinful and embrace a relationship where each of you genuinely learns to balance your own needs and your spouse's. Some of you need to drop the crushing weight of gender stereotypes that you've been carrying and learn to be okay with actually being who God created you to be. And some need to step out into a marriage in which you run hard after God as equal partners, each being strong when the other is weak. Let's look at how to put all of that into practice as you work as a team.

Do Men Need Respect, While Women Want Love?

This idea was popularized by Emerson Eggerichs' bestselling book *Love & Respect*, and he defended his thesis using a survey question from Shaunti Feldhahn that was published in her book *For Women Only*, in which she asked four hundred men, "Would you rather feel (1) alone and unloved or (2) inadequate and disrespected?"[29]

Seventy-four percent of men chose "alone and unloved," which she and Eggerichs use to promote the idea that men prefer respect over love. Interestingly, Feldhahn never asked women this same question.

Feldhahn and Eggerichs seem to have assumed that because men answered one way, women would answer the other. When psychologist Shauna Springer gave the same question to women, she found that women answered the same way as men.[30] No gender difference.

More problematic, though, is that the question is methodologically flawed. It uses what is called a "double-barreled" question set, where people are asked to choose an answer that contains more than one element. Since the word pairs are not synonyms, one cannot know if the respondent is reacting to "alone" or "unloved," or to "inadequate" or "disrespected."

We overcame this problem in our survey by presenting respondents with all four words and asking them to put them in order from worst to not so bad. Here's what we found people ranked the worst:

Figure 1.5

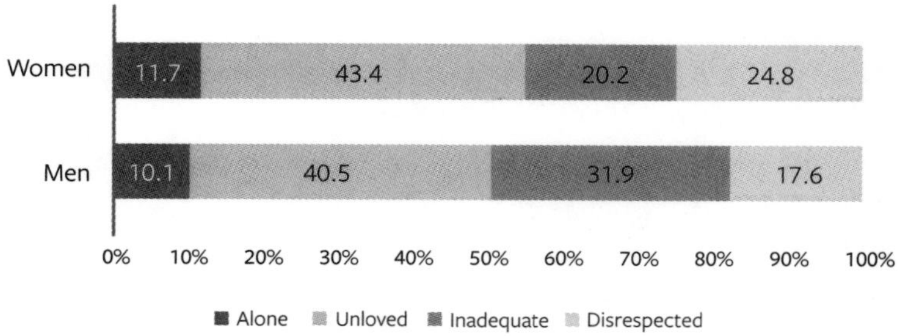

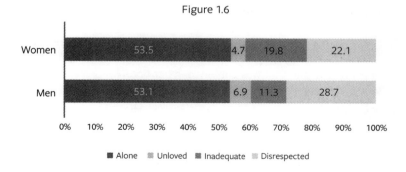

And here's what they decided they could most easily live with:

Figure 1.6

Overall, our study found tremendous similarity in how men and women ranked all four possibilities. These were the key takeaways:

- Men and women both want most of all to be loved.
- It's actually women who value respect most heavily. Men more frequently value not feeling inadequate.
- For both men and women, marital satisfaction was slightly higher if they chose "unloved" rather than "disrespected" as the phenomenon they would least like to experience,[31] so teaching that men most need respect goes against both data and best practices for marital flourishing.

We also asked our survey respondents to tell us whether they believed when they got married that "men need respect in a way that women can never understand." We took a look at how believing this in the past affects marriages today.

Figure 1.7

How does believing when you get married that "men need respect in a way that women can never understand" affect your Relationship Flourishing score today?[32]

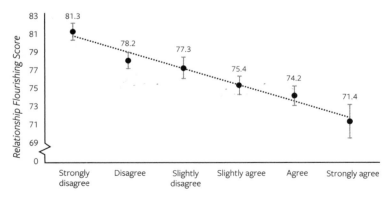

Agreement before marriage that "men need respect in a way that women can never understand"

Figure 1.8

What happens if you believe when you get married that "men need respect in a way that women can never understand"?

To interpret these data, use the following: If [I / my spouse] believed when we got married that "men need respect in a way that women can never understand," then [I am / my spouse is] [#] times more likely to say that _____.

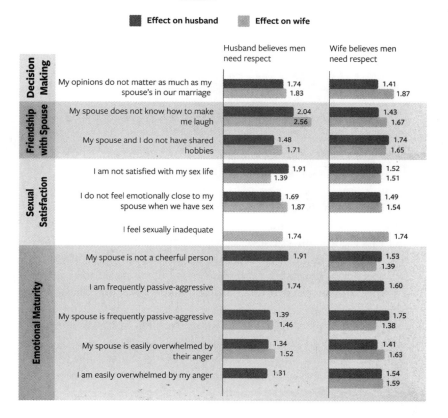

Discussing whether you'd least like to be alone, unloved, inadequate, or disrespected may be an excellent conversation topic for hour seven of a cross-country road trip, but we have to agree with Springer that the idea that "men need respect and women want love" is a faulty premise—and a shaky foundation for a marriage.

CHAPTER TWO

The Teamwork You Want

Several years ago, I (Keith) decided to memorize the Sermon on the Mount as a personal exercise for spiritual growth. Somehow word got out, and I was asked to do a dramatic recitation from the front of the church, which added a whole additional layer of "I'd better get this right!" Since it was such familiar material, memorizing the actual words wasn't the hardest part. Instead, remembering what order everything went in kept tripping me up. Many of the transitions seemed arbitrary, and one especially stuck out like a sore thumb: Right after warning about the dangers of judging others, Jesus immediately goes on to say, "Do not give what is holy to dogs, and do not throw your pearls before swine" (Matt. 7:6 NRSVue). My first thought was to shout, "Hold up, Jesus! How am I supposed to know who is a 'swine' if I'm supposed to suspend judgment about people?"

The Christian faith is full of such tensions, and living within these tensions is an essential part of the Christian walk. "To everything there is a season" (Eccles. 3:1 NKJV), and learning to recognize what season you or your spouse is in is part of maturing in Christ. The same is true for marriage advice. Advice that works well for one marriage may be disastrous in another. For instance, telling people to put their spouse's needs ahead of their own may be highly beneficial to a marriage characterized by mutual good-will but may be pouring gasoline on fire in a marriage character-ized by coercive control.

That's why you won't find many one-size-fits-all answers in this book. Instead, we want to try something we believe is a wiser approach. Rather than giving simplistic answers to complex ques-tions, we want to teach you guiding principles you can apply to your own individual situation. The Christian lingo for this is "discernment." Pat answers tell us to follow a particular formula and things will work out, regardless of the particularities of your situation. Discernment, on the other hand, calls us to apply an underlying principle to the situation, but how that truth should be applied will depend on the circumstances.

So far, we've talked about how to *see* yourselves as partners, where you each matter and where your strengths and giftings con-tribute to who you are as a couple. Now we'd like to turn to how you *act out* that partnership. As you read this book, we want to ask you to think of marriage as a team enterprise. You are teammates working toward the same goal. You are partners who need to look out for each other. Imagine having a marriage in which instead of asking, "What can my spouse give me?" you ask, "How can we create the best team ever?" The answer's not always obvious. It needs discernment. But the results are worth it! Let's look at how to foster this teamwork mentality.

Teamwork and Compromise Don't Always Go Together

One of the most common pat answers about marriage is that com-promise is the solution to any problem. But what if the concept of compromise needs nuance?

Let's look at an example of a typical couple Sheila hears from on the *Bare Marriage* blog.[1] Brad and Gabriella have been mar-ried for just over nine years and have welcomed three children, but their marriage has been struggling for a while. Brad recently confessed to Gabriella that earlier this year, he quit a porn addic-tion that had had a hold on him since his early teens but that he had kept secret from her. Brad knows what he did was wrong, but he hopes she will forgive him and even be proud that he has (in his words) "overcome." Instead, Gabriella feels betrayed, and their sex life—which was already on life support—has disintegrated to almost nothing.

Brad is desperate for Gabriella to forgive him and show up in the bedroom again, so he arranges for them to see the pastor, who he hopes can convince Gabriella to put the past behind them. As they pour out the story to the pastor, Gabriella hopes for sympathy. Instead, the pastor seems to wholeheartedly agree with Brad's perspective. Doesn't Gabriella realize that her body belongs to her husband? The pastor demands to know how she expects Brad to continue to have victory over porn if she "deprives" him in the bedroom. Gabriella, in tears, explains that even if she could summon the desire, she is so incredibly busy with their three kids and her job as a nurse that she is simply exhausted, and most days, sex is the last thing on her mind. The pastor suggests they compromise: Gabriella should make herself more available sexually to Brad, and Brad should help out with the children so that both can get their needs met in the marriage.

This pastor pulled out the "find a compromise" pat answer: Gabriella gives Brad more sex (which Brad wants), while Brad gives Gabriella more help with the kids and the housework (which Gabriella wants). That may look like balance to many people, but *compromise only works if you're already on an equal playing field*. Gabriella and Brad, however, are not. And to explain why, we'd like to introduce you to the concept of foundations and frills.

Balance Requires Differentiating Foundations and Frills

When teaching about priorities, speakers often use a common object lesson, and chances are, it's familiar to you. They bring a big glass jar up to the front of the room with some gravel, some sand, and some big rocks. If you want everything to fit in the jar, what do you have to do? Put the rocks in first, then the gravel, and only then do you pour in the sand. If you fill the jar with sand and gravel first, those rocks won't fit. The moral everyone's supposed to take from this is that you need to attend to the big priorities first if you want to enjoy everything else too.

All too often in marriage, one person is trying to fit all the rocks into the jar while the other person is fussing over how the jar doesn't have enough of their favorite gravel. That's where discernment comes in. Feeling like you aren't getting your needs met in marriage does not always mean that your spouse isn't doing enough. It could be that you're focusing on gravel while they're trying to deal with the rocks. We need to be able to figure out what issues in our marriage are rocks and what issues are gravel. Both may be important, but they need to be cared for in the right order. In this book, we're going to call those things foundations and frills. Some things are foundational to marital health, and some things are frills that you want to enjoy (and that we'd love for you to have too—just in the right order!).

The Marriage Hierarchy of Needs

If you've ever taken Psychology 101, you'll be familiar with a concept called Maslow's hierarchy of needs. Abraham Maslow, an American psychologist writing in the mid-twentieth century, conceptualized human needs like a pyramid. Basic ones, like food, water, and safety, form the bottom—the wide part—of the pyramid (that's right—another triangle analogy!). Lining the middle of the pyramid are things like love, sex, and friendship. At the top of the pyramid we have self-esteem, recognition for our efforts, and self-actualization (finding our purpose in life). The point of Maslow's hierarchy was a simple one: You can't meet the higher needs, like self-actualization, until the lower ones are met. No one is worried about sex if they're being chased by a bear.

We'd like to propose in this book that there's a marriage hierarchy of needs, too, and that it looks something like this:

THRIVING (ACTUALIZATION)

Pursuing passions and callings, feeling known and accepted, true sexual expression

LIVING (SOCIAL)

Building into relationships, creating comfort and ease in other areas of your life, sexual connection, feeling loved and valued

SURVIVING (PHYSIOLOGICAL)

Paying the bills, getting food on the table, taking care of basic needs, caring for kids' basic needs, caring for basic household tasks, an absence of pain in relationships

MARRIAGE HIERARCHY OF NEEDS

In marriage, each of us is spending our time and energy in one of those three tiers. In tier 1, we're in basic survival mode, caring for basic physiological needs like food, shelter, and rest. We're just trying to keep our head above water: making sure there's money for food and rent, caring for children's basic needs, making sure we get some sleep. When you're spending your emotional and physical energy in this tier, there's not a lot of time for fun or for building relationships; you're barely getting by. Our daughter Rebecca calls this marriage tier "acting like a good roommate." A good roommate pays their rent on time, cleans up after themselves, tries not to make life harder for you, and is considerate. But that's about it. Spouses in this tier just focus on caring for basic needs without hurting each other. For some of us, life is so stressful, that's really all we can manage right now. But it is the bare minimum; all of us should at least be "good roommates" to our spouses.

Then there's tier 2, the social one, where you're focusing on things that can make life more enjoyable. Your marriage relationship takes center stage here because there's room for it. You're able to make time for and enjoy sex. You're focused on creating a more comfortable home and a sustainable life. You're finding a church that you enjoy, friends that you enjoy, even a job that you enjoy. Then, finally, we move to tier 3 and we start thriving. Your relationship is a source of strength in your life, your job is taken care of, and now you're able to focus on what you feel called to do, both individually and as a couple. You're able to pursue hobbies and things that bring you joy in life. You're living out your passions. And that, in turn, creates a marriage where you feel absolutely loved and accepted, and your sexual life becomes true sexual intimacy and expression.

To arrive at tier 3 of marriage, you need to travel together. One of you should not be enjoying some of the benefits of a higher tier until both of you have all the benefits of the tier below. But that doesn't always happen. Sometimes in marriage one person gets to enjoy some perks of a higher tier while the other is stuck lower down. Your marriage, however, exists on the lowest tier that either of you occupies. If one of you is barely surviving, focusing on meeting basic needs and having no time to yourself, while the other is pursuing a passion, your marriage isn't thriving. It's in survival mode.

Are You in the Same Tier?

With that in mind, let's return to Brad and Gabriella and see how the principle of balance would help us to better figure out their issues. Brad is asking for increased sexual frequency in exchange for helping with the children. Sexual frequency is at least a tier 2 (we may even argue a tier 3) issue, but caring for your children is tier 1. Brad has been neglecting his basic tier 1 duties, but his wife is being asked to provide all of tier 1 and more for him. Is it fair or proper that he should expect the frill of increased sexual frequency as a reward for finally attending to what should have been his foundational responsibilities all along?

Looking for a quick compromise without asking which desires are foundational and which are frills can end up heaping more pressure onto someone who is already doing too much while having their foundational needs go unmet. On the other hand, once the foundational issues are addressed for both spouses, often the frills naturally follow! Imagine if, rather than asking for more sex, Brad realized that Gabriella was living in tier 1, running ragged with the kids, barely sleeping, but also dealing with the trauma of his porn use and the threat that he would return to it if she didn't give enough sex. Imagine if he realized that his job right now was to get down in the trenches with her so that he could support her, stop hurting her, and lift them both up. Then, once Gabriella had some breathing room, once Brad had proven over time that he was trustworthy, once she was free from coercion and threats, their relationship could become strong, and sexual desire could grow again. But if Gabriella gives him the sex he wants now because she feels coerced, that will inevitably destroy intimacy and actually make sex worse for both of them in the long run. Their marriage can't improve until Brad realizes his actions (pressuring Gabriella for sex, not caring for the kids and the household) are pushing Gabriella into survival mode while he tries to enjoy an easier life.

We should always ask ourselves, *Am I choosing to enjoy benefits of a higher tier while unintentionally pushing my spouse down to a lower tier?* It's awfully easy to do! You overspend on things that you may think your family deserves, but it pushes you further and further into debt, and then your spouse has to work longer hours. You don't spend your time wisely, and your spouse—who is already overworked—has to accomplish what you've failed to get done. Sometimes it's even just a lack of consideration for our spouse's experience. What if you are an absolute cat lover and desperately feel called to rescue seven cats? You bring them home in an excited frenzy and set them up with their litter boxes while filling your living room with cat trees.

Unfortunately, your spouse works from home and is allergic to cats. All day, your spouse is popping antihistamines in between dumping litter boxes while you gaze at the framed photos of each of your seven cats, regaling your grade 3 classroom with stories of Murphy's latest antics. Meanwhile your spouse has to juggle phone calls with clients while finding ways to muffle the sounds of Murphy scratching up Buttons. Plus, for some reason, your spouse is starting to smell like ammonia. You're living in tier 3 with your passions, while you've pushed your spouse down to tier 1. Not okay.

Has Entitlement Taken Root?

There's a word for thinking that we deserve a perk, even if it costs our spouse something: *entitlement*. Nothing we have seen kills a marriage faster than entitlement. Entitlement enters a marriage any time one person believes they deserve frills without having to build the foundation. Entitlement is the feeling that what you believe you are owed in your marriage outweighs any needs your spouse has. And often, you feel you are owed these things even without effort.[2] Rami Tolmacz, an Israeli psychologist who has done groundbreaking work measuring entitlement in romantic relationships, explains it this way: "People characterized by an excessive or exaggerated sense of entitlement feel free to do anything they want and believe they deserve to have their needs and wishes satisfied regardless of others' feelings, needs, and rights."[3]

You do not marry so that you do not have to work—or so that you get to do significantly less work than you did before. You are supposed to be partners in your marriage. No one is entitled to someone else working harder in the marriage than they do. This concept is found throughout the New Testament:

- Jesus told us to love our neighbors as ourselves—so we should not expect them to do more for us than we do for them (see Matt. 22:39).

51

- Paul said we should each carry our own load—that is, look after ourselves the best we can without expecting others to do it for us (see Gal. 6:5).
- Paul said if we don't work, we shouldn't eat—meaning that we're not entitled to someone else's labor (see 2 Thess. 3:10).

But most people, when they're in marriages in which the other person is putting in more effort than they are, don't actually agree that they're not putting in enough effort. They're not seeing the situation clearly because entitlement is like tinted glasses: It colors everything you see.

Erin felt a strong calling to homeschool her children (a tier 3 desire). She wanted to raise her kids in the fear of the Lord, where their schooling could focus on Scripture and incorporate God's principles in everything. But when Erin and her husband, Clark, married, they faced tight finances. Clark installed air conditioners and furnaces, and though it brought in a decent income, it was very difficult to save for a down payment on a house. They were renting a small home, and every month they were going a bit more into debt. When the kids arrived, the situation started to snowball. They were already struggling to get by on one income, but Erin was continually buying curriculum and new educational toys because "the kids needed them." The math curriculum alone was almost $500 per child, but Erin insisted this was necessary because she wanted to provide the best Christian education for their children. She signed them up for expensive homeschooling co-ops and overnight Christian camps. Meanwhile, Clark was growing more and more stressed. He finally sat Erin down and told her, "The credit card bills are getting out of control. We need you to work." Clark truly loved Erin and was doing his best; he just felt the finances couldn't be ignored. But Erin felt like Clark was going directly against God, didn't have enough faith, and was betraying his promises to her as her husband.

As former homeschooling parents ourselves, we can empathize with Erin's desire to homeschool. But while providing your children an education is a foundation, doing it specifically by homeschooling—let alone with the most expensive curriculum—is a frill. It's gravel, not rocks. It's tier 3, not tier 1. Clark was focusing on the tier 1 issue of balancing their books, but Erin interpreted the situation as Clark harming her by denying her something that she had felt was fundamental to her identity. That's the particularly pernicious aspect of entitlement: The entitled person ends up treating their spouse unfairly while actually believing that *they* themselves are the victim. If they do not get this thing they feel entitled to, then they feel as if a great wrong has been done to them and that they are justified in not caring for foundational issues in the marriage. And while it is easy to judge Erin, if we're honest, we have to admit that we all can be a little bit entitled. That's why we've got to remember the marriage hierarchy of needs and try to take off the tinted glasses and judge ourselves fairly.

Proverbs 20:23 says, "The LORD detests differing weights, and dishonest scales do not please him." The Levitical law says, "Do not use dishonest standards when measuring length, weight or quantity. Use honest scales and honest weights" (Lev. 19:35–36). What's the deal about weights? Back then, people would sell their produce, like grain, and use the income to buy what they needed. The merchant would have a set of scales, and on one side they would place standard weights (like pounds or kilograms, although they used different measures in those days). Then they would pour the grain, or whatever else was being sold, onto the other side of the scale until the scale was in balance in order to measure how much money was owed. What would happen if the grain merchant had a dishonest weight? They could make a profit by cheating their customers! God wasn't happy about that. We have to weigh and measure things fairly. When we give what we want more weight than what our spouse wants, or think that we deserve more than our spouse does, we're not using fair weights and measures.

Another interesting finding from our matched-pair survey: If one spouse believed their opinions didn't matter as much as their spouse's, their spouse was 2.8 times more likely to *also* believe that their opinions didn't matter as much as their spouse's! Now, it could be that entitled people are just more likely to marry entitled people. But there's also a dynamic to entitlement that makes this more likely. Think back to Erin and Clark for a minute. If we were to ask them, "Do your opinions matter as much as your spouse's?" they both would likely answer no. But there's a difference. Erin would answer no because she felt entitled to something that Clark couldn't give her and was ignoring Clark's legitimate requests, while Clark would answer no because Erin truly was ignoring his opinions. When one spouse is entitled, they actually do value their spouse's opinions less—but they also often unfairly accuse their spouse of the same thing.

When Nancy married Joey, they were head over heels in love, each sure that they had found their soulmate. They had met at their church's college-and-career group and hit it off immediately. Nancy felt swept away. Joey was kind. He treated her well. He prayed with her. As a lawyer, she knew she had the better paying and more stable job but figured that with time Joey would find his niche. Yet somehow that niche never really materialized. Joey kept trying to get his band off the ground while earning money as a stagehand for several other acts. He spent most of his time practicing—and spending large amounts of money on expensive instruments.

This arrangement seemed acceptable for the first three years of marriage, but when Nancy hit thirty, she really wanted to start a family. She worried about how she would ever be able to take time off since Joey wasn't providing an adequate income for the family. And he was so often on the road that he wouldn't be able to be relied on to care for the children either. Whenever they talked about it, Joey explained that he just needed a few more years to get established. He needed Nancy to support him. But Nancy was wondering who was going to support the family.

If we truly are a team, then we must balance being true to ourselves (as discussed in chapter 1) with being true to our marriage partnership. Our passion shouldn't add to our spouse's load. Our spouse should not have to live in tier 1—sacrificing security, peace of mind, and sleep, let alone having children—so that we can enjoy some benefits from tier 3.

Our Individual Passions Have to Come Second to Our Marriage

Most entitlement issues revolve around one person living out their passions at their spouse's expense. This dynamic is understandable. Your passions can seem like your very identity! If you give them up, who are you? But once you're married, it's not just about your own passions anymore. It's about creating a life that allows *both* of you to thrive, not one of you to thrive at the other's expense. The apostle Paul writes in 1 Corinthians 7:32–34,

> I would like you to be free from concern. An unmarried man is concerned about the Lord's affairs—how he can please the Lord. But a married man is concerned about the affairs of this world—how he can please his wife—and his interests are divided. An unmarried woman or virgin is concerned about the Lord's affairs: Her aim is to be devoted to the Lord in both body and spirit. But a married woman is concerned about the affairs of this world—how she can please her husband.

In context, he is saying that if you're single, stay single if you can, because you'll be able to devote yourself wholeheartedly to the Lord. That is not possible to the same extent when you're married because you will be (very appropriately!) concerned about caring for your family and pleasing and loving your spouse. Here's our take on this passage: *If you're married, it's not fair to your spouse for you to live like you're single.*

Preacher and writer A. W. Tozer was so dedicated to God that he lived a life of simplicity, taking public transit, never buying new clothes, and spending hours face down in prayer every day. This wasn't a difficult life for him to live, but it significantly burdened his wife, Ada, as she tried to wrangle seven children on the subway to go grocery shopping or walk them in the snow to church. He always put ministry before family and left his family broken in his wake. He died fairly young, and his widow remarried. When asked about her two husbands, Ada replied, "Aiden loved Jesus. Leonard loves me."[4] Ouch.

Figure 2.1

How does feeling you are part of a team with your spouse affect how you describe your marriage?

To interpret these data, use the following: If [I / my spouse] believe(s) we are a team in our marriage [I am / my spouse] is] [#] times more likely to describe our marriage as [descriptor].

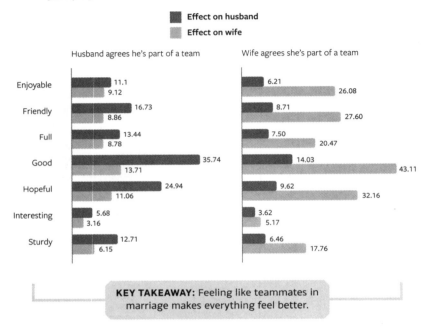

KEY TAKEAWAY: Feeling like teammates in marriage makes everything feel better.

An Entitlement-Free Partnership

How do we get out of this entitlement mindset? We adopt a team-mate approach! One 2023 study looking at couples in which one person felt a high degree of entitlement found that couple satisfaction went up and conflict went down when, instead of getting into fights about who was going to get their needs met, they focused on the needs for the relationship and cooperated.[5] In other words, they identified the rocks together and then figured out how to get them into the jar.

Figure 2.2

How does feeling you are a part of a team with your spouse affect marital and sexual satisfaction?

To interpret these data, use the following: If [I / my spouse] believe(s) that we are a team in our marriage [I am / my spouse is] [#] times more likely to say that _____.

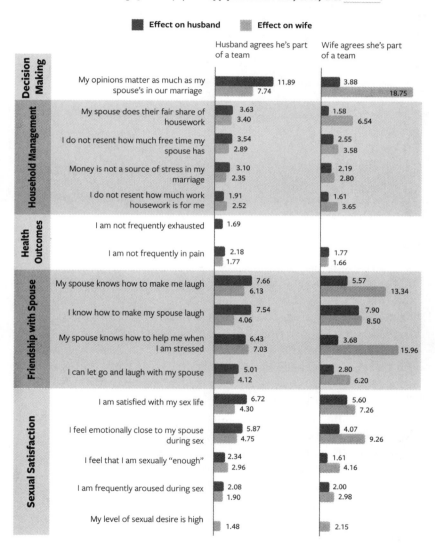

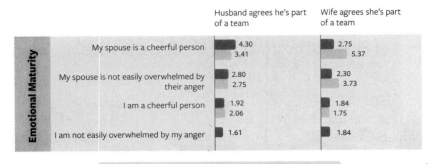

		Husband agrees he's part of a team	Wife agrees she's part of a team
Emotional Maturity	My spouse is a cheerful person	4.30 / 3.41	2.75 / 5.37
	My spouse is not easily overwhelmed by their anger	2.80 / 2.75	2.30 / 3.73
	I am a cheerful person	1.92 / 2.06	1.84 / 1.75
	I am not easily overwhelmed by my anger	1.61	1.84

KEY TAKEAWAY: Feeling like teammates is a key part of building the marriage you want!

Teams are only as good as their weakest member, so teams have to watch for those who are struggling. Taking the teammate approach means choosing to truly see your spouse, even when you're upset. How are they coping? What's their mood like? Are they in survival mode? Are they struggling more than you are? Do you have more free time to pursue what you want than they do? Are they stressed about basic things, like money or housework, that you're ignoring? Proverbs 3:27 says, "Do not withhold good from those to whom it is due, when it is in your power to act." Instead of focusing on what you want, focus on how you can help your teammate get out of survival mode and start really living. And when you do that—when you get down in the trenches with your spouse in the areas where they are having difficulty—you'll find that many hands make light work. It's so much better to raise both of you up on that pyramid than for one of you to live on a higher tier at the expense of the other.

Imagine truly working together, bringing all your individual talents, skills, and passions to the relationship for the benefit of the relationship, rather than seeing yourselves in competition with each other. Can you throw away the idea that marriage is meant to provide you with an easy, pain-free life in which you get to pursue all your individual dreams and passions while someone else takes care of you and instead embrace the adventure of having a true partner to walk through life with? That's the foundation of how you create a relationship where you both thrive and become more Christlike every day.

And that attitude is going to impact every aspect of your marriage. It's going to affect your sex life, how you choose to spend time together, how you handle the division of labor in your home, how you resolve conflict. And, if you act as a team in those areas, you're going to make it safe for your spouse to open up and get vulnerable, to achieve that emotional connection we all crave.

It's all about teamwork. Now let's get down to the nitty-gritty of how you act as a team in the different areas of your marriage.

Are You Entitled?

It can be difficult to see and accept that we are acting from a place of entitlement. Take some time (and a deep breath!) and ask yourself these questions (or talk through them with your spouse):

1. Am I expecting my spouse to provide a result rather than invest their effort and time? Examples might be expecting my spouse to cook just like Mom does or expecting my spouse to bring home a certain income.
2. Do I have more chances to sit down and do nothing than my spouse does?
3. Am I significantly less tired than my spouse is? Do I get more sleep than my spouse?
4. Do I have more time to exercise, pursue self-care, see friends, or pursue hobbies than my spouse does?
5. If there's an unforeseen emergency (kids get sick, furnace breaks down, car needs to go in for repairs, etc.), do I expect my spouse to figure it out? Or do we discuss ahead of time who is in the best position to deal with unforeseen circumstances?

6. If a child is fussing, are we equally likely to tend to that child? Or do I assume my spouse will take care of the child?

7. Do I make plans that involve being out of the house when I would normally be home without checking with my spouse first (especially if we have kids at home)?

8. When we have company, does my spouse get up and serve me and the guests, and does my spouse clear the table and clean up, or do we do it equally?

9. Am I expecting my spouse to give me an orgasm without me attending to my spouse's needs for emotional safety, rest, or downtime?

10. Am I expecting an orgasm even if my spouse doesn't get one? If my spouse says no to sex, do I treat my spouse worse or punish them in some way?

There's another kind of entitlement that is especially destructive—feeling entitled to be in control of the relationship and one's spouse. When some people don't feel in control, or when they experience vulnerability, they feel as if their spouse is actively and deliberately hurting them. They can then build up all kinds of narratives in their minds about why it's okay to try to control their spouse because they feel as if *they* are the victim since they are entitled to never feel vulnerable or out of control. Control might look like constant criticism and ridicule, the silent treatment, violence, withholding money, punishing the children, cutting a spouse off from friends and family, or withholding any kind of positive interaction unless they get absolute deference and abasement. If entitlement flows into power and control, this isn't safe. Please call a domestic abuse hotline or see a licensed therapist (see the appendix for more suggestions).

Affection

Finding Joy and Passion in Being Together

CHAPTER THREE

The Friendship You Want

In TikTok land, there is much debate as to what the cutest thing in the animal kingdom is. Is it baby pandas hurtling themselves down slides? Baby humans tasting lemons for the first time? Woodland hedgehogs snuffling under leaves? As far as we're concerned, it's none of the above. Sea otters win, hands down, simply because of this amazing habit: When they sleep, they cozy up to a beloved, lie on their backs in the water, and hold paws. Yep. Sea otters sleep holding paws so that when they wake up, the current won't have drifted them away from each other. That's a serious level of cuteness right there.

But it also gives a great marriage lesson: Otters remind us that the natural state of life is to drift apart, so if you're going to stay together, you need to be deliberate. There will always be currents that threaten to pull away at your connection—busy schedules, in-law troubles, work worries, studying for qualifying exams. In the midst of that, how will you fight the drift?

We've talked about balance, how we prioritize each other in marriage, and how we prioritize our responsibilities. Now we're going to turn to the other aspects of marriage, starting with the one that we're all likely most excited about: affection, or building your relationship and enjoying being together.

A few years ago, I (Sheila) traveled to Atlanta on a speaking engagement with my friend and manager, Tammy, where we visited the Martin Luther King Jr. Memorial. I cherished reading the words on the monuments and breathing in the history. But it was simultaneously a difficult, disappointing day because I was having this tremendously important experience and Keith wasn't with me. Over and over again, I kept thinking, *This would be so much better if Keith were here.* Affection in marriage is this pull to do life together, to have a witness to your life, a partner on the road. Most likely, affection is what sent you heading to the church to say your vows (or what's sending you in that direction soon).

Feelings of affection and closeness, though, come after you have invested time in showing someone, *I care, you matter to me,* and

Figure 3.1

Does it matter if we talk in the car?

We asked couples, "On a scale of 1-10, if you and your spouse have an hour to drive and chat, how do you feel about your relationship afterward?" (1=very distant; 10=highly connected).[1] We then looked at how those results correlated to the Relationship Flourishing Scale.[2] This chart shows a classic "dose-dependent response" effect, which you'll see throughout this book: The more you enjoy spending time together in the car, the more your marriage flourishes. Every step up in connection helps build a stronger marriage overall.

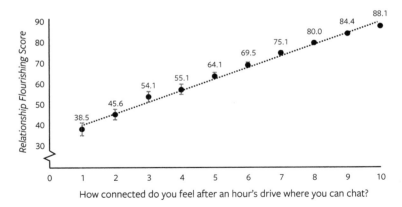

How connected do you feel after an hour's drive where you can chat?

KEY TAKEAWAY: Enjoying each other's company is a great foundation for a thriving, flourishing marriage.

I have fun just being with you! While most of us start marriage with an abundance of affection, sustaining affection over time isn't automatic. We have to invest time in building our feelings of closeness.

The Relationship Flourishing Scale and Time Spent as a Couple

The Couples Satisfaction Index (CSI) includes two questions about spending time with your spouse. We found that enjoying each other's company and having fun together are both strongly correlated with having a high Relationship Flourishing score. To put it more simply, playing Mario Kart together after the kids go to bed can absolutely be part of building a strong marriage.

Figure 3.2

How does having fun with your spouse and enjoying their company affect marital flourishing?

Was there a difference in the average Relationship Flourishing score depending on how often respondents had fun with their spouse or enjoyed their spouse's company?[3]

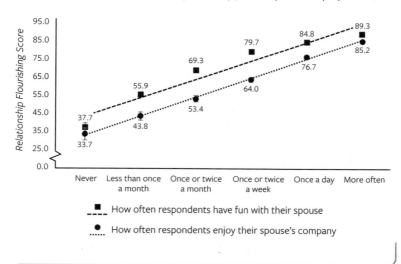

65

Don't Make Things Harder Than They Need to Be

We can already feel some of you getting panicky. Sure, you want to feel close, but you know that usually when you hear someone talk about how important it is to spend time together, it's going to be followed by a long list of things you need to start doing, on top of what you're *already* doing. Nope, not here. Being intentional does not necessarily mean you need to add any big thing to your to-do list. You don't need a weekly date night or a weekend away every few months (though those can be fun!). Most of us already have less money and time than we'd like, and affordable, safe babysitters are in short supply. Instead, we'd like to invite you to simply rethink how you do normal life. Otters don't add an extra step to keep from drifting; they just sleep differently. They'd need to sleep anyway, so when they sleep, they sleep in a way that keeps them together. The quest for affection and connection can be the same for you too. Our motto for you, as you read this chapter, is a simple one: *Don't make things harder than they need to be.*

No one gets married and says, "I really want to stop spending time together." It's just that the date nights and the things you did together to connect before marriage are often harder to fit into a life that gets dominated by work and chores and kids. So, how do we hold on to the activities that keep affection common in our marriage? Well, when things are natural and fit into your daily schedule, they get done.

In his runaway bestseller, *Atomic Habits*, James Clear explains why it can be so difficult to do the things we care about and truly want to do and also how *we can actually start doing those things.*[4] Why is it so hard? Because our brains can only focus on a few things at a time. Therefore, we naturally gravitate toward habits because they remove the need for thought. We are more likely to do things if we don't have to think about them, so the more we form habits, the easier it is to get things done.

When we're tired and stressed, we tend to turn to the easiest thing available that lets us escape—streaming, video games, our phones. The problem is that these things usually don't leave us feeling any more energized when we turn them off. So why do we turn to them? Because they don't require thought; they're easy. How do you make new and more productive habits easy? Bundle new habits with old habits so they become part of the old habit. Want to start walking more? Add it to a routine you already have, like "have dinner, clear the table, turn on the dishwasher." Now add "then go for a walk." When our kids were babies and we were living in downtown Toronto, we started the routine of going for a walk in the evening after dinner. We'd bundle the kids in the stroller and head outside because it was often the easiest way to get to talk uninterrupted. The kids were occupied, and we could just chat (while getting a little bit of exercise!).

Each day has key moments when affection can most easily become a habit: when you say goodbye in the morning, when you connect after a workday, and perhaps most importantly, when you turn in for bed. In most homes today, though, after dinner is over, various family members separate to their own screens—either the computer or the TV or the video game system.[5] She may be on her iPad, and he's playing video games. Eventually somebody gets tired and heads to bed, but the other person doesn't follow for several hours. This is quite a historical anomaly. We still remember the days before the internet, when people all tended to turn in together at one of three times: after the evening news, after the hockey game, or after Johnny Carson's monologue on the *Tonight Show*. Nowadays, though, there's nothing signaling to you, "It's time to go to bed."

Even if you do head to the bedroom at a decent hour, people do not sleep well when they turn in right after being in front of a screen. A 2022 study found that for roughly every five minutes you spend on your smartphone in bed, your sleep can be delayed by four minutes, and every ten minutes of smartphone use in bed can cause your total awake time to increase by nine minutes.[6] Using your phone in the bedroom is highly associated with worse sleep—and keeps you from connecting too.[7]

As a pediatrician, I (Keith) often have parents come to my office for help with their kids who aren't sleeping. The first thing I ask them about is evening screen exposure. The second is about routine. Setting up a routine so that the child knows what's coming and has that transition between daytime and nighttime helps them wind down. Maybe the routine looks like a snack, bath, story, song, prayers, kiss good night. Why not do the same thing in your marriage? Let's say that you have to get up at 6:30, and you want at least seven and a half hours of sleep. That means getting to sleep at 11:00 p.m. So ideally (in a perfect world without kids who aren't sleeping or massive work that needs to get done), you can start your own routine together by turning your screens off by 10:00. Maybe you get a snack together, have a bath together, read a chapter from a book out loud, read the Bible, pray through a daily

What Are the Benefits of a Shared Bedtime?

We were gobsmacked when we found out how big an impact shared bedtimes have on Relationship Flourishing scores (see figure 3.3).[8] We also found that couples who share a bedtime have more frequent and more pleasurable sex (see figure 3.4). Women who go to bed at the same time as their husbands "at least most nights" were 38% more likely to always or almost always orgasm than women who go to bed at the same time as their husbands only "some nights" and 67% more likely than those who "rarely to never" do.

Let's step back and think about two things shared bedtimes do for couples. First, you have dedicated time to connect while you wind down to prepare for sleep, and second, you are in a situation in which, should you desire it, sex can easily happen. Does this mean that every couple who doesn't share a bedtime is doomed? Of course not! Many couples simply can't go to bed at the same time due to shift work or other factors (babies, anyone?). If that's your situation, consider setting aside another time for that same low-key connection opportunity that you would have if you shared a bedtime. You may also need to be more diligent about planning opportunities for sex at other times during the day (or night)!

Figure 3.3

How do shared bedtimes affect Relationship Flourishing scores?

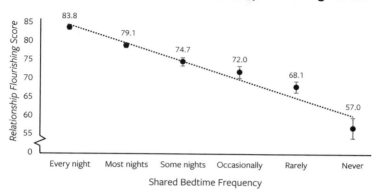

Figure 3.4

How do shared bedtimes affect sex frequency?

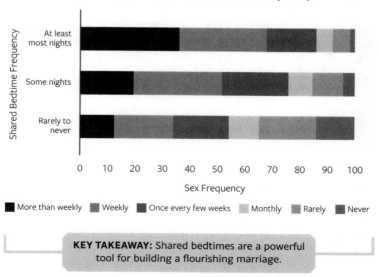

KEY TAKEAWAY: Shared bedtimes are a powerful tool for building a flourishing marriage.

liturgy, or just talk about your highs and lows of the day and what you're doing tomorrow. Whatever seems like a good transition to you! What's important is that one thing follows another, which follows another, which leads to sleep. By setting up a routine that you do together at bedtime, not only will you sleep better, but you will also grow affection and defeat drift. Just like the otters.

Just Do Life Together

Connecting as a couple is one of those foundational "rocks" that every relationship needs. But how do you care for that foundation while balancing all your other commitments? The fitness world has a concept for when people are trying to get in shape that they call "joining the gym of life." Instead of heading to the gym, turn your daily life into exercise by doing things like biking instead of driving. In the same vein, we can do life together in ways that don't add extraordinary amounts of extra time but keep us feeling connected as a couple. Our friends Lisa and Gary had three boys whom they dutifully put in hockey (here in Canada, it's practically the law). Life with practices and games was really busy, so they took the "divide and conquer" approach: Lisa would go to the rink on Mondays and Wednesdays and Gary on Tuesdays and Thursdays, and they'd each get a few nights off. The only problem was that a few weeks into this glorious new schedule, they felt as if they hadn't seen each other at all. So the next week, they all piled into the car together for two of those nights, thermoses of hot chocolate in hand, so they could shiver together on the bleachers and talk while their sons played.

Spending "low-grade" time together has been shown to have a positive effect on your relationship, even when you are not communicating about anything specific.[9] If we create a marriage where "us" time is more often the default, then affection will have more time to blossom. Can you cook dinner together, with one chopping and the other stirring? Can you do chores together on Saturday mornings or even grocery shop together? Sure, time alone is still important (and Lisa and Gary did still give each other some nights off). But when we can be in the same room, chatting, as a natural part of our daily rhythm, then those times when we "do things that are deeply meaningful to us as a couple"[10] come more naturally.

Honor Bids for Connection

The first two episodes of "Don't Make Things Harder Than They Need to Be" were about forming good habits. Now let's turn to something that is equally small but vitally important—bids for connection. Marriage researcher John Gottman talks about how each marriage has an emotional bank account. When couples turn toward each other and connect positively, "they are building up savings that, like money in the bank, can serve as a cushion when times get rough, when they're faced with a major life stress or conflict. Because they have stored an abundance of goodwill, such couples are less likely to teeter over into distrust and chronic negativity during hard times."[11] Gottman found that in healthy marriages, the ratio of these positive interactions (deposits) to negative interactions (withdrawals) is 5:1. In unhappy marriages, the ratio is 0.8:1.[12] Think about the implications of that! It's not that unhappy marriages lack affection or good times. Rather, in order to feel emotionally close and safe, an almost equal ratio of positive and negative interactions *is simply not enough*.

Here's the good news that Gottman also found: Making those deposits is not difficult. You simply need to learn to respond well to "bids for connection," or signals your spouse gives you that they are reaching out and would like to engage with you. Here's what bids may look like:

- Your spouse sighs or makes some gesture revealing how they're feeling.
- Your spouse brings you a coffee or does some small thing for you.
- Your spouse enters the room where you're sitting.
- Your spouse smiles at you.

71

- Your spouse asks you for something.
- Your spouse touches you.

In order to respond to these bids, we have to recognize them—which means we can't live totally in our own world. We have to actively pay attention to one another. In fact, actively paying attention is one of the big things that separates "marriage masters" from "marriage disasters" (Gottman's terms, not ours, but they're awesome!).

Let's think through a few "bids." Imagine you're watching Netflix, and your spouse places a cup of coffee beside you. Smile and say thank you while looking them in the eye. Or better yet, get up, give them a kiss, and then go back to your show. This way you communicate, "I know you did something nice for me, and I appreciate it." Or how about this bid? You're making dinner, and you hear your spouse come in the door. Do you walk to the door and greet your spouse, or do you keep doing what you're doing and ignore them? Or maybe your spouse is sitting beside you, and she takes your hand. Do you smile at her, continue to hold her hand, lean toward her? Or do you pull your hand away to grab your phone?

What if your spouse gives a bid for connection and you don't feel that you can give them what they want right then? For instance, your spouse says something like, "Hon, I'd love to do something together tonight. What do you think?" and you're staring down a pile of paperwork you need to get done before work tomorrow, or you're just exhausted, or something else is preventing you from engaging with your spouse. You can make this potentially negative situation into something positive: "I truly wish I could. I love doing X with you! I just can't tonight. But can we put it on the calendar for Tuesday?" Responding to a bid to connect doesn't have to be a grand gesture; it can be as simple as acknowledging what they said. The point is to communicate to your spouse, "I notice you. I value you. I like being with you."

Taking Advantage of the Power of Two

And now for our fourth installment of "Don't Make Things Harder Than They Need to Be": Marriage increases your chances of achieving goals in your life by giving you a partner to cheer you on and keep you accountable.[13] For our stats analyzer, Joanna, that looks like her and her husband, Josiah, stretching for twenty-five minutes every night to deal with Josiah's back pain. He has to do it anyway, but deciding to do it together says, "I value you, and your well-being matters," and it makes it more likely to happen. Plus, it's something that helps Joanna too. (She finds she falls asleep much more easily now!) For us it means watching ballroom dancing lessons online a few nights a month so that when we take a vacation or attend a wedding, we can wow everyone with some amazing moves! For other couples, it may mean watching financial planning YouTube videos at night so that you can figure out how to get out of debt together and make plans for the future.

When you're trying to build something into your life that matters but is hard to do, these "better together" challenges can build companionship and teamwork. They can also become times when we get to focus on "just us." Because, while we want affection to come naturally and easily, sometimes we do need to intentionally carve out specific times when we concentrate on each other. Let's turn to that next.

Finding "Us" Time

Shared laughter is one of the best signs of a healthy marriage. A study out of the University of North Carolina in 2015 puts it like this: "The proportion of the conversation spent laughing simultaneously with the romantic partner was uniquely positively associated with global evaluations of relationship quality, closeness, and social support."[14] The more you laugh together, the closer you feel to each other. Laughter is associated with play, and play can make you feel better and increase your satisfaction with your marriage.[15] A commonality we found in the happy couples we spoke with in our focus groups was how much they talked about play. One woman said, "I want to have fun with my playmate. Whether that's board games, card games, making art, participating in hobbies, etc., I think it's important to learn how to play and have imagination. To dream. To think about future plans. Even if they're very small."

Here's the mind shift that we want couples to take away: Spending time together is far less about the actual activity that you do together and far more about the meaning that you both attach to it. When we asked couples, "What does quality time look like for you?" the answers we got were as different as the couples we talked to. Some were adamant that it had to be getting a babysitter and having weekly date nights out, while others were quite content to stay at home and do puzzles together. As one couple told us, "Marriage is the art of being allowed to be boring together." The activity wasn't important; feeling connected and having low-stress time to talk naturally was what mattered.

Quality time doesn't only count when it's just the two of you either. Spending time together with people you love or sharing experiences getting to know others can also grow your connection. For us, the two people in the world we most like spending time with are our daughters. Some of our happiest memories as a couple were spent with two smaller humans in tow. As one couple told us, "Our kids are hilarious and sweet, and we enjoy them together." Quality time doesn't have to mean taking a challenging pottery class together. It can be as simple as playing Ticket to Ride with your kids or having another couple over for dinner. The question to ask is not, *Are we spending enough time and money just the two of us?* but rather, *Are we creating memories in which we share experiences that matter and feel connected?*

One way to spend quality time together that has been shown to be beneficial to marriage is participating in your spouse's hobbies.[16] Keith is absolutely psyched about being outdoors (and especially about looking for birds) and we have a lot more time for that now than we did when the kids were at home. When we're out hiking, looking for a red-tailed hawk or an indigo bunting, we're also talking about the grandkids, our future plans, or any number of other issues that are on our hearts at that moment. And we tend to laugh. That doesn't mean that your spouse has to love your favorite thing. My (Sheila's) favorite thing is knitting, and I do not expect Keith to learn to knit (though I do expect him to let me explore yarn stores when we're traveling), just as he doesn't expect me to show up at a swamp at 5:00 a.m. to watch for a Virginia rail and her chicks.

Sometimes you want to spend time together, but as James Clear points out, our brains naturally gravitate to the place of least resistance. If you're not careful, you may end up turning to your Netflix queue or other low-stress habits and letting time slip by in ways that fail to connect you with your spouse. So be deliberate! One couple who differs significantly in what they enjoy doing (one is an active introvert; the other is a more experience-oriented extrovert) told us this: "We talked about it and decided to make a list of activities we can do at home together that we both enjoy that don't involve screens. Some are high energy and some are low energy, some are emotionally connecting and some are just light, fun, and restful. This has been really life-giving for us and has helped prevent us from going on relational autopilot at home."

Sarah, one of our longtime blog readers, lost her husband to cancer three years ago, leaving her a widow when she was only forty. Every Thursday night, they would have a date night together. She told us, "He was sick with cancer for five years, and we would still have date nights in hospital beds and infusion chairs. It was something we prioritized, and I can't tell you the mix of emotions I have every time it's a Thursday. Three years later and Thursday nights still bring all the feels. In itself, that time together was rarely profound. Often it was spent in our own kitchen while we had the kids in their rooms. The key was we loved being together." He passed away on a Thursday night while she was holding his hand. Yet she has all those Thursdays, including the last one, where he made it clear to her, week after week, "I want to be with you because I love you."

When There's a Chasm, Not Just Drift

In some marriages, a chasm grows between you that you can't seem to bridge, no matter how hard you try. You find yourself walking on eggshells, trying to identify the patterns that set your spouse off—but they're not always clear. One night they'll be upset because you wanted them to spend time with you and that felt like pressure, and don't you understand how much stress they're under? The next night they'll be upset because you're doing your own thing and ignoring them, and don't you know how disrespectful that is?

This dynamic is typical of abuse in marriage, but it often goes unrecognized at first. People married to abusers often can't figure out what's going on because they're trying to be loving and kind, but their spouse keeps getting upset with them. Fighting the drift requires two people to fight it. Building intimacy requires two people who are committed to the relationship. You can do everything you can to build a marriage, but if your spouse refuses to pick up the shovel and help, and instead keeps picking up a sledgehammer to knock down what you're trying to do, that is not on you. Please seek help from a domestic violence hotline or a licensed counselor to talk about next steps (see the appendix for more help).

Building Affection with God in the Picture

Remember how we used the triangle analogy to teach that when we grow closer to God, we also grow closer to each other? Well, it's true! Our study, echoing many others, showed that shared religious experience increases bonding and makes you enjoy your marriage more. When you're dedicated to running after Jesus, sharing that precious purpose can grow your feelings of connection and intimacy on every level.

When we were first married, we led the youth group at our small church. Over the years, we've led other youth groups, taught Sunday school, led medical and humanitarian mission trips, and coached church activities our girls were involved in. Serving

How Does a Healthy Church Affect Marriage?

Respondents who had a church family they could rely on were 77% more likely to have an above average Relationship Flourishing score.[17] Church attendance is also correlated with increased Relationship Flourishing Scale scores for both men and women. We've published an article in *The Sociology of Religion* on the benefits (and downsides) of religiosity,[18] and the more we look at the data, the more pro-church we are.[19]

Having a church family was also very strongly correlated with having people to mourn with and rejoice with (see Rom. 12:15) as we navigate the ups and downs of life.[20] Compared to those who can rely only on their spouse for support in hard times, those who can count on their spouse and a lot of other people were 2.15 times more likely to have an above average Relationship Flourishing score.[21] When we did the same analysis looking at having people to rejoice with, those who had a lot of other people to celebrate with in addition to their spouse were 2.42 times more likely to have an above average Relationship Flourishing score.[22] While being able to talk about life's joys and sorrows with our spouse has the biggest effect on Relationship Flourishing scores, having other people to turn to in addition to one's spouse *was also correlated with higher Relationship Flourishing scores*. Having a village is good for everyone.

Now, there's a caveat to this. Our studies have also shown that when churches teach toxic things about marriage and sex and those teachings are internalized, church attendance can actually hurt one's self-esteem and affect other aspects of their life, including their marriage.[23] Other studies have also shown that the health benefits that both men and women get from attending church disappear for women if that church is structurally sexist.[24] We know that many people have been traumatized by unhealthy churches. Sometimes church seems too emotionally dangerous, and you just have to take a break.

When church is healthy, it's such a positive force in marriage. For those who have been hurt, we hope you can eventually find a village where you feel embraced and accepted—and safe.

together has created so many shared experiences, both challenging and satisfying, that have strengthened our bond to each other and to God.

When it comes to God and marriage, the advice that is stressed the most often revolves around prayer and devotions. For many people, these activities come with built-in land mines. Some couples were raised thinking that unless you pray out loud and do family devotions every night, you're not really a Christian. If that's what you enjoy doing and it grows your relationship, by all means continue! But not everyone enjoys highlighter-and-commentary-type Bible studies. And turning your relationship with Jesus into a giant couples' to-do list can add a level of resentment and dissatisfaction to your marriage (and your faith!) that is truly unwarranted.

How can you incorporate more low-stress prayer and Bible time into your life? Prayer is more likely to happen if it's routine (tending to happen at the same time every day), if it's for a specific purpose, and if it's relatively easy to do. So add prayer to something you already do. Pray over your children's beds (or cribs!) at night as you tuck them in; pray as you part in the morning. Just kiss, join foreheads, and say a quick prayer. Or take your spouse's hand right as the alarm goes off in the morning or as you've turned out the light at night. If praying still feels awkward, buy books of prayers. That's not cheating; it's helping you align your hearts together.

Here's a finding we had about the impact of prayer in marriage: Unsurprisingly, praying together increases marital flourishing.[25] But here's the cool thing: It had a larger effect when emotional intimacy was low. Among couples who found sharing what was on their hearts difficult, when they were at least able to pray together, their marriages did better.[26]

When we pray together, we create a space where we can acknowledge what's important to us and talk honestly about our fears, feelings, or deep longings. When couples have difficulty sharing because of childhood wounds, or anything that makes vulnerability difficult, prayer seems to serve like training wheels. When we open up emotionally to God with our spouse, it causes us to feel more emotionally connected, which in turn builds a marriage that flourishes. And that's not even considering the power of the Holy Spirit!

Prayer isn't the only spiritual activity that builds your connection to each other either. We found that frequently talking about spiritual things with your spouse was even more strongly correlated with Relationship Flourishing scores than frequent prayer was.[27]

Bringing God into your marriage helps your marriage. Yay! But sometimes our assumptions about how this is supposed to be

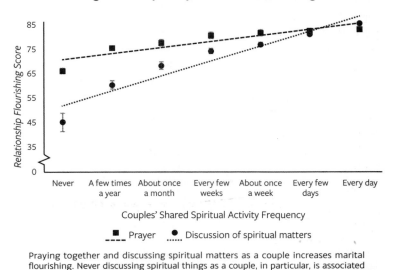

Figure 3.5

How do praying together and talking about spiritual things as a couple impact marital flourishing?

Praying together and discussing spiritual matters as a couple increases marital flourishing. Never discussing spiritual things as a couple, in particular, is associated with lower marital flourishing.[28]

KEY TAKEAWAY: Connecting spiritually as a couple strengthens your marriage and your faith.

done create unnecessary difficulties. Many couples end up stymied because of the idea that the husband must be the one to initiate Bible reading or prayer since he is supposed to be the "spiritual leader"—even though that phrase never appears in Scripture. Women often hold back, thinking it's ungodly if they suggest something spiritual because that's supposed to be the husband's role. Sure, women can initiate date nights or hobbies or suggest something fun for a family outing, but if they initiate something to do with Jesus, they feel they would be usurping the husband's place. If the most important part of your life is the one thing you can't share, then you're doing it wrong.

We had to go back in time to find another study that looked at the role of "spiritual leader" and how that impacted the marriage. The 1996 Religious Identity and Influence Survey[29] found that only 58.5% of men and 34.0% of women who believe in a husband's hierarchical role as spiritual leader actually lived out that belief.[30] And there was no statistically significant difference in marital satisfaction for men[31] based on who leads regarding spiritual matters.[32]

Our daughters were both involved as teenagers in Bible quizzing, a competitive program in which students memorized entire books of the Bible and were quizzed on them. They both had more than a dozen books memorized word for word by the time they graduated high school. The idea that in order to marry properly they would need to marry someone who knew the Bible better than they did was ridiculous. It simply wasn't going to happen. But they could (and did!) marry men who were running after Jesus and allowing their character to be shaped by Jesus, even if they couldn't tell you exactly what Paul said about Andronicus and Junia in Romans 16.

Honoring where each of you are at spiritually is part of balance in marriage. At different points in your marriage, it's likely that one of you will feel God more personally, while one may feel God is more distant. This is a chance to care for one another. When one of you feels like initiating prayer or starting a devotional, go for it! It could be that your strength can help your spouse get through a distant phase—while in a few years that may reverse.

When Drift Happens Anyway

We promised at the beginning of this chapter that we wouldn't add a lot to your calendar; we'd just try to take what you're already doing and help you do it in a way that stops drift rather than ignores it. But some people reading this chapter will still find it too hard. They'd love to have a bedtime routine together, but they're never home together because of shift work or because of distance work. They'd love to have a hobby together, but with work and kids' activities, they have no time to breathe, let alone anything else. They'd love to laugh more with their spouse or pray more with their spouse, but they have no time because of how busy life is. Some of that may be due to marriage dynamics, which we'll address in the next few chapters. But sometimes life is just hard—or even unsustainable. You're operating in that tier 1 surviving level of the marriage hierarchy of needs, and you have no time or energy to give to the relationship.

Hard is okay when there's an end in sight. When we raised our babies, for many weeks Keith clocked over a hundred hours at work as a pediatric resident. Sheila would pack the kids in their stroller, pop a cooked dinner in Tupperware, and trudge the few blocks to the hospital, hoping Keith could grab ten minutes to eat with her and the kids before following up on the next lab test or answering the next page. It only worked about half the time. We were both exhausted. But we were able to power through *because we knew it would end*. We could not have kept going permanently that way.

Bebo Norman was a tremendously successful Christian musician in the early 2000s, writing hits that often played on Christian radio and touring internationally. In 2013, at the age of forty, he announced his retirement. He spent some time as a stay-at-home dad and then retrained to become a physician's assistant. Even though he had a career and was successful in a way that many

Christian artists only dream of, he ultimately wanted to be home with his family and able to enjoy them. And he made that happen.

As difficult as it may be to make a change, if the pace of your life is not sustainable long-term, you need to make a change now before the change that you can't control happens to you. If there are things in your life that will end badly if you keep going in this direction—like a job that is sucking the life out of you, expenses in a city that mean you have to work much harder or commute longer than you want to, or shift work that makes you chronically exhausted—then rethink how you do things long-term and think as creatively as possible. Put into practice whatever you need to in order to have a sustainable life, no matter how difficult or "out of the box" it may seem.

At the end of the day, you want to be able to snuggle up to your spouse and say, "I'm so glad that I get to spend my life with you. I had fun with you today." Whether that happens automatically or as a result of intentionality, it adds such sweetness to your life. And at the end of that day, you may also want to snuggle up and do something else. So, let's turn to that aspect of affection next!

CHAPTER FOUR

The Passion You Want

You shouldn't prioritize sex in your marriage.

That's pretty wild coming from someone who has dedicated her life to writing books about sex, isn't it? Well, we've crunched the numbers, and here's a much better idea: *Prioritize the ingredients that make for great sex, not the frequency of intercourse*. To use the words from our "Balance" section, instead of working on frills like frequency, work on the foundations. If we focus on frills, we may end up making sex worse, but if we focus on the foundations for great sex, frequency tends to take care of itself. And honestly—when sex is great for both of you, it's also awesome for your marriage. Great sex feels wonderful. It relaxes you. It even helps you sleep! And it makes you feel connected. It can be playful and fun. You can laugh and be silly and then just a few minutes later be in ecstatic passion. It's no wonder that women with a great sex life are 5.8 times more likely to have above average Relationship Flourishing scores and men are 3.4 times more likely to.

But the "great" in great sex is an awfully important word because often our definition of sex omits what makes it great. Imagine that a talking head shoved a microphone in your face on the street corner and asked you on the spot, "What's the definition of sex?" What would you reply (assuming you didn't run away screaming)? Most of us would hem and haw and then say something like "Man puts penis into woman's vagina and moves around." Think about the implication of that definition, though. When we talk about how sex is so important in marriage, but our definition of sex is merely intercourse (an act that tends to always result in his climax but not usually hers[1]), then we're saying it's vitally important that certain body parts line up in certain ways so men reach orgasm.

Chances are, growing up, you were taught that this particular way of connecting body parts was going to be just awesome in the right conditions. Put a ring on your finger, and sexual fireworks would follow! But Sheila constantly hears from Christian couples who tell a different story. Despite all the promises, sex has not lived up to the hype. And they wonder if it ever will.

We want better for you than being stuck with obligatory one-sided intercourse that ultimately does little for either of you, or empty sex during which you don't connect, or even infrequent sex that leaves both of you feeling bored. Your sex life can be so much more than that! Whether you're about to walk down the aisle (we hope we caught you early) or it's been years of sex not being what you hoped for, we want to go back to first principles, starting with the assumption that sex is meant for both spouses in a marriage. If you really believe God meant sex for both of you, then when sex is only working well for one of you—or neither of you—rather than "powering through," you'll stop and ask, "What do we need to do differently to make this great for both of us?" And we believe the answer is to remember the threefold, nonnegotiable foundations of sex: It's intimate, mutual, and pleasurable for both. Let's look at each of these.

Sex Is Intimate

The first explicit reference to sex in Scripture is Genesis 4:1, where we read, "Adam knew Eve his wife, and she conceived" (NKJV). People sometimes assume the word *knew* is a euphemism, as if the Bible writers (and God himself) were afraid of using direct language, but we think it signifies something quite profound. The Hebrew root of the word *know* is the same as the word David uses in the Psalms when he cries, "Search me, O God, and *know* my heart" (Ps. 139:23 NKJV).

Sex is more than just body parts joining. It's a deep knowing, a deep intimacy, in which you feel seen as well as wanted. In sex, you're naked, not just physically but also metaphorically. The masks come down, and you're seen in a way that is utterly personal and profound. You're vulnerable in a very good way! When sex is truly intimate, it can be one of the most life-giving parts of your marriage; you finish breathless, not sure where you end and your spouse begins, intertwined, smiling, and at peace. You sleep better. You smile more the next day. Little things don't bug you as much. Life is good! But intimacy is the key. Sex can only increase marital satisfaction to a point; a great relationship influences sexual satisfaction far more.[2]

One of our favorite studies on sex that we found in academic literature came out of Croatia and looked at the sexual satisfaction of 315 couples. They discovered that it wasn't just sexual factors that led to the best sexual satisfaction. Emotional intimacy, having fun together outside the bedroom, sharing decision-making, and marital quality were also responsible for being happy with one's sex life.[3] A great marriage feeds a great sex life, but sex on its own cannot create a great marriage. In fact, when sex lacks intimacy, it can be destructive to a marriage. In our survey for *The Great Sex Rescue*, 16% of women stated their primary emotion after sex is feeling used.[4] For them, their marriage would actually feel closer if they never had sex because the experience of sex was a net negative.

Good sex must involve connection. When I (Sheila) was creating my orgasm course, we scoured peer-reviewed literature to find out what made sex best for women. Can you guess what one of the most consistent predictors was of women orgasming during sex? Kissing during sex.[5] The key to great sex is not trying a different position every night; it's not becoming more acrobatic; it's not dressing up or playing games or having a suitcase full of toys you hide in a drawer you hope no one ever rummages through. The key to great sex long-term in your marriage is not being hotter but being closer.[6] Healthy sexual play results from a safe, fun marriage. It doesn't create one.

How Porn Use Wrecks Intimacy

Porn is one of the biggest roadblocks to intimacy, decreasing both marital and sexual satisfaction.[7] Our studies found that 50% of evangelical married men, and significantly fewer evangelical married women, currently consume porn, even if it's only intermittently or rarely, with younger men consuming it most often.[8] The vast majority of porn users under forty-five started watching porn before marriage, so it's a habit that they developed early and brought into the relationship. Porn use isn't caused by a spouse not having enough sex or hot enough sex, despite what some pastors or marriage "experts" may say.[9]

Early porn use can set a person on a negative sexual trajectory. Watching porn tends to be paired with masturbation, so porn use is associated with increased dopamine hits, feelings of euphoria, and stress release. Often, porn use, especially if initiated young, becomes a maladaptive tool for self-soothing and emotional regulation.[10] When someone's feeling bored, insecure, angry, resentful, lonely, or ashamed, it's easier to turn to porn to numb those feelings than it is to deal with what is causing those feelings in the first place. Unfortunately, this often spirals into a shame cycle, where the more someone uses porn, the worse they feel about themselves, so the more they turn to porn to self-soothe—and the cycle starts all over again.[11]

Not only does porn harm your marriage; porn is one of the largest drivers of human trafficking. Even so-called "consensual porn" is often created by those with sexual abuse in their backgrounds. Is this truly consensual or a trauma response? Haley McNamara, director of the International Centre on Sexual Exploitation, warns that no one can assume consensual porn is actually consensual. After numerous scandals regarding sexual assault materials (including child sexual abuse materials) being uploaded

Figure 4.1

How does porn use affect Christian men's sexual satisfaction?

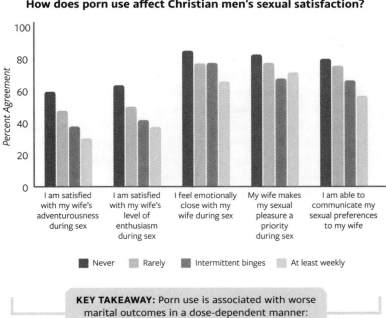

KEY TAKEAWAY: Porn use is associated with worse marital outcomes in a dose-dependent manner: Problems get worse with more porn use.

to "consensual" porn hubs, she writes in *Newsweek*, "It's time to face reality: the pornography industry is not committed to, and not capable of, sufficiently stringent 'consent verification' methods to keep sexual abuse content off its websites."[12] From a justice perspective alone, porn simply cannot be tolerated.

The good news is that most people who use porn will stop—if they want to and are willing to put in the work. But quitting porn involves more than just deciding not to consume pornographic material anymore. It means accepting responsibility for the porn use, not placing the responsibility for continued sobriety on one's spouse, and quitting the objectified view of sex and your spouse. We have heard from too many wives whose husbands have supposedly quit porn but now demand sexual release constantly to keep them from falling into temptation. That's not quitting porn; that's clinging to the same unhealthy view of sex but redirecting it toward your spouse. Sex with your spouse is not methadone for your sex addiction because sex and porn are polar opposites.[13] One says, "I want to know you," and the other says, "I want to use you." Until you get over the "I want to use you" part, you'll never see sex properly or experience real intimacy, and your spouse will keep feeling dehumanized.

The key to getting over porn is learning to deal with the underlying wounds, fear, and shame that drive you to porn, while confronting the feelings of entitlement to sex that porn has fueled. Defeating porn takes not just willpower but rather vulnerability and authenticity. Licensed counselor Dr. Andrew Bauman writes frequently about the effects of porn, especially on men. He points out that we can't defeat porn until we are able to live in authenticity and truth:

> Fantasy is an escape from what is real. Whether it be difficult emotions, such as stress, anxiety, or depression, or just the pain that genuine relationship inevitably brings, fantasy relieves those struggles for a moment. While healthy relationships live in the truth, pornography helps bolster a life of fantasy that is difficult to undo. Fantasy brings relief but does not bring restoration. . . . For relationships to remain thriving and true, both partners must be committed to voicing complaints, hopes, and desires, and living into what is most true.[14]

We'll talk in chapter 8 about how to develop that kind of authenticity, but counselors are increasingly finding that the key to defeating porn is not "white-knuckling" it and trying harder but rather becoming vulnerable to trusted friends, counselors, and your spouse. When you do the work to become authentic to those around you, then the pull to porn, which often grows out of shame, diminishes.

The Pornographic Style of Relating

Even outside of porn use, the unhealthy adoption of what Bauman calls the "pornographic style of relating" can ruin intimacy by affecting how we see each other and how we see sex. Think about how our language treats sex as if it's a commodity—something outside of both of you that you *get* (or, God forbid, *take*):

- "I need more sex."
- "How do I get more sex?"
- "How to have hot sex."

In this mindset, for sex to be hot, it has to be something you take for yourself, not something that flows from relationship. A pornographic style of relating sees sex as an entitlement that is about conquest and taking rather than intimacy, so intimacy becomes almost a turn-off rather than a turn-on.

This pornographic view of sex can sneak in without us even realizing it. For example, we've had men unironically ask us, "How do I get my wife to have sex with me? I do the dishes and I do housework, but she still isn't interested!" This cheapens what is meant to be an intimate expression of love between two people by making it into something transactional, a payment for services rendered.

Acts of service to each other can certainly stoke desire in the right setting, but doing dishes or vacuuming does not magically turn your spouse on. In fact, if the higher-drive spouse does these things *because they want sex*, they're almost certainly guaranteed to turn their spouse *off*. Nobody wants to feel like sex is the payment they give their spouse for doing chores a decent human being would likely be doing already. Instead, when studies show that men doing more housework results in them getting more sex,[15] the reason is something more basic: Those men are showing with their actions that they want to be a good partner in the relationship. And good partners make sexy partners! When you do life together, when you care for each other, when you serve each other, desire tends to flow.

Negative Associations with Sex

When sex doesn't feel intimate, though, it does not mean your spouse is necessarily doing anything wrong. If you're one of the 20% of women or 5% of men who have been victims of child sexual

89

assault,[16] or one of the many who have been victims of sexual assault as an adult, sex can feel threatening and depersonalizing, even if you have the gentlest, most caring spouse in the world. Many sexual assault survivors struggle with traumatic triggers that hinder intimacy. Other people grow up with shame over sex because of how it was taught to them as children or teenagers or because of negative teachings about sex that they've internalized as adults. And then there are the regrets and shame we may feel because of past relationships.

When we don't face our sexual stories, those stories have a habit of showing up anyway. Instead of intimacy and play, we feel shame. We may try to avoid sex entirely or go to the other extreme and use it as a way to regulate our own emotions or combat insecurity. Instead of being able to be known and fully ourselves, we use sex to hide. If you have a story that is causing sex to become a veiling rather than an unveiling, please see a licensed counselor, or read more about how our negative stories about sex can become foundational.[17]

Sex Is Pleasurable for Both

Did you know that in Song of Solomon, the book of the Bible dedicated to sex, the woman actually speaks more than the man?[18] And she's enjoying herself immensely! The Bible depicts sex as something a woman wants that feels great for her too.

That's the ideal. But it can't become reality until we address the orgasm gap. In our study of evangelical marriages, we found that 95% of men say they almost always or always reach orgasm in a given sexual encounter, while the equivalent percentage for women is just 48%. That leaves us with a 47-point orgasm gap. To understand the implications of that, we invite you to imagine (as we explained in *The Good Guy's Guide to Great Sex*) a world where it is widely taught that to feel loved, women need to go out to dinner once a week:

> Picture a couple, Tracey and Doug, who tries to live by this. One Tuesday night our intrepid couple heads to a restaurant. They order appetizers, a main course, and a dessert.

What's the Narrative You've Heard about the Main Problems in the Bedroom?

We're going to lay out a "story" about sex using the data from our matched-pair survey. As you read, consider: Does this sound familiar to you? What is the conclusion you would draw from this information?

Men and women both have higher marital satisfaction if they have sex at least once a week. Respondents who report high sexual desire are more likely to have high marital satisfaction.

Figure 4.2

How do marital satisfaction and sex frequency affect each other?[19]

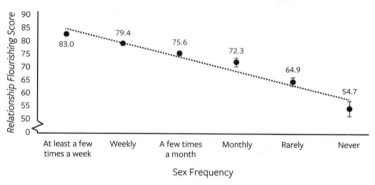

Figure 4.3

How do marital satisfaction and sexual desire affect each other?[20]

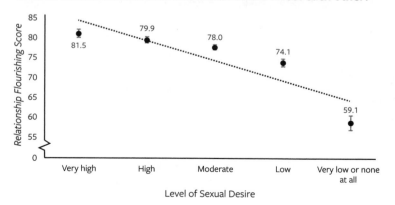

But when sexual frequency is low, men and women report very different things about their levels of sexual desire.

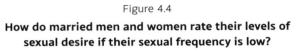

Figure 4.4

How do married men and women rate their levels of sexual desire if their sexual frequency is low?

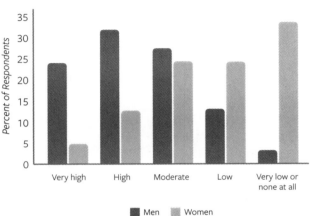

Looking at these charts, there seems to be a simple culprit when sex isn't happening—*women don't want sex enough*—and thus a simple solution to most sexual problems—*women need to have more sex.* When sex isn't happening, it's clearly usually the woman's fault!

But what if these charts aren't telling the whole story?

When we look at women who have low or very low sexual desire, more than 85% of the time we found a *very understandable and valid reason* by asking three simple questions: Is she orgasming every time they have sex? Is she feeling intimate with her husband while they have sex? Is she having pain-free sex?

If we can explain more than 85% of low sexual desire with those three questions, how likely do you think it is that we could explain the rest if we brought in other libido killers, like a spouse's porn use, betrayal trauma, mental load, exhaustion, or abuse?

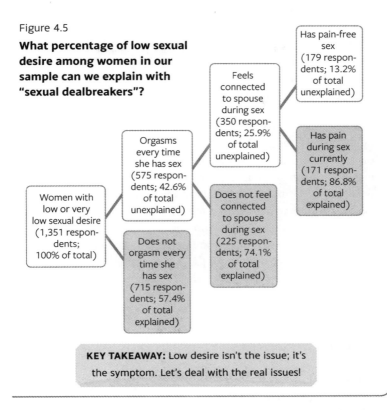

Figure 4.5

What percentage of low sexual desire among women in our sample can we explain with "sexual dealbreakers"?

Women with low or very low sexual desire (1,351 respondents; 100% of total)

Orgasms every time she has sex (575 respondents; 42.6% of total unexplained)

Does not orgasm every time she has sex (715 respondents; 57.4% of total explained)

Feels connected to spouse during sex (350 respondents; 25.9% of total unexplained)

Does not feel connected to spouse during sex (225 respondents; 74.1% of total explained)

Has pain-free sex (179 respondents; 13.2% of total unexplained)

Has pain during sex currently (171 respondents; 86.8% of total explained)

KEY TAKEAWAY: Low desire isn't the issue; it's the symptom. Let's deal with the real issues!

The waitress arrives with Tracey's appetizer—a steaming bowl of cheese and broccoli soup. Tracey finishes it and declares it delicious. But nothing comes for Doug. Then Tracey's steak arrives. Doug's still wondering where his appetizer is, but Tracey starts slathering the butter and sour cream onto the baked potato and takes a bite of the steak with peppercorn sauce and asparagus. She declares it scrumptious.

Now Tracey is finished with her steak, and the waitress heads toward the couple again. In front of Tracey she places a steaming, luscious molten lava cake. Tracey squeals in delight as she scoops some out. Just as she's down to the last few spoonfuls, the waitress finally arrives with Doug's chicken wing appetizer. Doug's ecstatic, and he digs in, eating one quickly, and then another. But before he can get to his third one, Tracey stands up, ready to go home.

"Dinner was amazing," she declares as she heads for the door. He follows behind her, glancing at the uneaten chicken wings still on his plate, while Tracey says, "I love doing this with you!"

Imagine that Doug and Tracey faithfully do this every week for ten years. How do you think Doug will feel about eating at restaurants?[21]

When it comes to sex, wives deserve more than a meager offering of chicken wings. Yet the response to Christian women with low libidos has historically been to tell them, "Don't deprive your husbands," instead of asking the question, "What's actually in this for women?" Think about this: How many sermons and books have you heard prioritizing the frequency of sex? Now, how many have you heard telling men to make sure their wives reach orgasm? (Pause for crickets.) If we stopped seeing sex as one-sided intercourse and started seeing it as something that is meant to be pleasurable for both, we would be appalled by the orgasm gap. At the very least, we would no longer be surprised about why many Christian women seem to have such low libidos. People tend to enjoy things that are enjoyable, but if something is not that enjoyable to begin with, trying to make it better by adding obligation to it is simply absurd.

You Can't Cheat Biology

Women were designed for incredible pleasure. Why else did God specifically give women a body part with no other purpose? The clitoris has even more nerve endings than the penis does.[22] Plus, women are capable of multiple orgasms. No refractory period for her! She can keep going, while he often needs up to an hour before things will work again. Why is it, then, that pleasure and desire are so elusive for many women?

A 2022 study from the University of Toronto found that a woman's first experience with sex can change the course of her sexual story.[23] When a woman experiences an orgasm with her first sexual encounter, her desire level is likely to be equivalent to her partner's. But when she doesn't? Her libido is likely to be a lot lower. If sex doesn't feel great, her body learns "this isn't for me." But if sex *is* great, then her body learns "this is something I really enjoy!"

Figure 4.6

How does her orgasming every time affect how men and women describe their marriages?

To interpret these data, use the following: If [I / my wife] orgasms every time we have sex, then [I am / my wife is] [#] times more likely to describe our marriage as [descriptor].

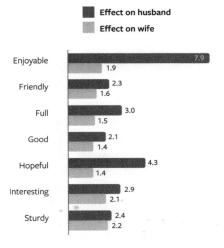

Women who orgasm every time they have sex are more likely to describe their marriage with positive words—and so are their husbands!

KEY TAKEAWAY: When she orgasms every time the couple has sex, they both savor their marriage overall.

This doesn't mean that you're doomed if your first sexual experience was bad; it just may mean that you both have to do some work to give her body a new message. But we can't expect to create a good sex life in the future if we're currently continuing to give her body negative messages about sex.

One of the most frustrating types of comments I (Sheila) get on my blog are ones like this one:

> We've been married for seventeen years, and we're great friends and great partners. The sex life is what's holding us back. I love my wife and I desperately want her to love our sex life. We have

sex about twice a week, but I can tell she's just tolerating it. I keep asking what I can do to make it better for her, but she just lies there and doesn't say much. I know she's not really into it, and I know she's just trying to make me happy, but I hate pity sex. I want her to know what an orgasm feels like, but if I try to make her feel good, she rushes me and tells me to get it over with. I feel like she's still thinking about the kids! I wish she could let go and let herself feel pleasure.

Let's dissect this. He wants her to feel pleasure, but even though she doesn't, *he's still been having sex with her a couple of times a week for seventeen years*. One has to ask, how much does he really want her to feel pleasure? What they're doing isn't working, but instead of stopping and addressing the issue, he's still using her body for one-sided release. The more someone is used like that, the more damage has to be undone later!

How do we bridge the orgasm gap? Learn to love foreplay—it's overwhelmingly related to her likelihood of orgasm. Our studies found that of the women who do reach orgasm with their husbands, only about 39% do so through intercourse alone. Most need other stimulation, and most find other routes to orgasm more reliable than intercourse. When we treat intercourse as the main, or even sole, essential component of sex, we devalue the activities that tend to bring women pleasure.

That's why we need to stop thinking of sex as just intercourse and start thinking of it as sexual play that we do for each other that brings pleasure to each other. In our surveys, we asked men whose wives frequently reach orgasm if they do enough foreplay. Ninety-four percent said yes. But when we asked the men whose wives *didn't* reach orgasm frequently, 71% still said yes. *And so did 52% of the women*.[24] How can a majority of both men and women think he's done enough when she doesn't get to the destination? It may be because we think that if she doesn't enjoy sex, it must be because she's broken—because we assume that the way men tend to approach and experience sex is the standard. After all, men tend to reach orgasm through partnered sex faster than women, and men tend to have a higher felt desire for sex. Take these two factors together, and it can seem as if men are the more sexual ones. When what works for him doesn't work for her, we may assume that she's just lacking something—rather than accepting that our bodies work differently.

An understanding of the sexual response cycle can help us see that she's not broken or less sexual if she requires different stimulation than he does. Physically, our bodies go through different stages as we move toward orgasm, and it looks roughly like this:

Excitement is when you are getting warmed up or "turned on." During arousal, the body seeks stimulation in the more erogenous zones. Plateau is the phase when things stabilize at peak arousal until you finally orgasm, then have resolution. Most men progress through these stages fairly automatically, and each phase looks like more of the same. For women, though, each stage looks different, and the stimulation that's needed to get her to the next one differs too.

Sex manuals and magazine articles talk about the vital importance of clitoral stimulation but rarely talk about the importance of timing to this stimulation. Men wanting to please their wives dutifully head right for the clitoris, but if she's not even excited yet, instead of feeling arousing, it feels invasive, like a pap smear. She then assumes her body is broken because it doesn't want what it's "supposed" to want, he's baffled, and they figure that she just isn't that sexual a person.

But if she takes a while to warm up, that doesn't mean she's deficient or just doesn't like sex. Instead, the couple should respect the sexual response cycle. Start with things that build excitement, like giving a massage, kissing, or soft touching on nonsexual areas like the nape of the neck or the inside of the arms. Don't move on to genital areas until she's actually aroused. Focus on her pleasure,

The Unfairness Threshold with Sex

Figure 4.7

How does not orgasming every time affect women's marital flourishing over the course of their marriage?[25]

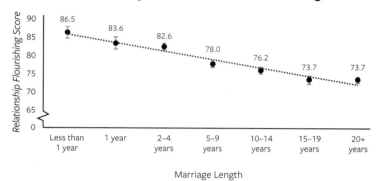

KEY TAKEAWAY: When women don't orgasm every time they have sex, it doesn't affect them very much at the beginning of their marriage. But over time, marital satisfaction takes a hit.

not his. Let her know that there's no expectation that he's waiting for her to hurry up so that he can climax. Have her focus on what her body wants next and what part wants to be touched, and find ways to communicate that to him (even if it's just to move his hand or moan when he gets it right!).

Above all, remember that if she isn't finding sex pleasurable right away, don't assume her body is deficient. She is capable of orgasm. Spend some low-key time exploring and getting to know her body without expecting orgasm for him. That way she learns that her body can respond—and what it takes to make her respond. If a woman's body has been experiencing for years that "sex isn't for me," it may take a while for a new story to rewrite the script.

Remember that unless you deliberately do something different, nothing will change. And our study showed that women can't go on having sex that isn't pleasurable forever. It's like there's an invisible unfairness threshold that's passed, somewhere around year fifteen of marriage (and it shows up in many areas, not just sex, as you'll see throughout the book). At the beginning of marriage, when sex isn't working that well, it doesn't necessarily affect her sexual satisfaction that much. But over time it takes its toll. People can put up with something unfair for a while, but they can't put up with it forever. Focusing only on his pleasure can be a recipe for a sexless marriage.

When Sex Hurts

Most of us were taught that sex is painful for women the first time (we need to get rid of this narrative; if she's aroused enough, any pain usually won't register that much!). But what we weren't taught is that some pain goes far beyond normal—and for evangelicals, this is especially common. Evangelical women suffer from sexual pain disorders, like vaginismus, at over twice the rate of the general population. In our surveys, roughly 23% of evangelical women experienced vaginismus, with 7% finding penetration impossible. Around 27% have also experienced pain with sex postpartum.[26]

Why do evangelical women have it worse? Our studies have been groundbreaking in discovering some of the key factors. We believe much of it boils down to toxic messages common in evangelical circles that the body interprets as trauma. When women are taught that they are obligated to have sex if their husband wants it, the message given to women is "You don't matter; he has the right to use you whenever he wants." Even if her husband would never want to give her that message, if she grew up in church hearing it, vaginismus is more likely to ambush her on the wedding night. And if she grew up hearing that she had to cover up so as not to be a stumbling block to boys, she also has a much higher chance of experiencing vaginismus. She has been taught that her body puts her at risk of objectification and assault, and so her body can tense up to protect itself, even if, consciously, a woman doesn't want this to happen.

Another big factor contributing to sexual pain is the way that evangelicals frequently handle the wedding night. When you wait to have intercourse until the wedding night but then rush to it that night because you're supposed to, her first experience with intercourse is often one in which she feels unaroused and pressured. The most common word we heard in our focus groups to describe honeymoon sex was "bewildering." It's no wonder that pain disorders are more common.

Please don't push through with sex if it's painful. That will only reinforce the body's feeling of "this is something threatening" and exacerbate the problem. You deserve to enjoy intimacy, and no one

Rethinking the Honeymoon

At marriage, 95% of our male respondents, but only 64% of our female respondents, had ever had an orgasm. And while the majority of men and women (81.9% of men and 67.1% of women) knew by the time they were adults that women could orgasm, most couples who waited to have sex until they were married did not ensure that she had an orgasm before trying penetrative sex for the first time. The first time she has consensual sex can set the trajectory of a couple's sex life together, but that first time isn't going that well for many Christian couples.

Looking at couples who waited until marriage for sex, we asked whether their spouses brought them to orgasm before attempting penetrative sex. Here's the breakdown:

- In 41.1% of couples, neither partner had brought the other to orgasm before they tried penis-in-vagina (PIV) sex.
- In 25.5% of couples, both partners had brought the other to orgasm before they tried PIV sex.
- In 24.9% of couples, only the husband had been brought to orgasm by his partner before they tried PIV sex.
- In 8.5% of couples, only the wife had been brought to orgasm by her partner before they tried PIV sex.

That means that 50.4% of men had been brought to orgasm by their spouse before penetrative sex, but only 34.1% of women had. The person who needs other forms of stimulation to reach orgasm and who needs to be aroused and relaxed the most for intercourse to work well is the person most likely to be ignored, while the one who orgasms easily is more likely to be catered to. Something is going wrong!

Looking at these same people who waited for marriage for consensual penetrative sex, we asked who orgasmed (from any type of stimulation) during the first sexual encounter that involved intercourse:

- In 14.2% of couples, both partners climaxed.
- In 11.6% of couples, neither partner orgasmed.
- In 1.2% of couples, only the wife orgasmed.
- In 73.0% of couples, only the husband orgasmed.[27]

Break that down and 87.3% of men but only 15.4% of women reached orgasm (from any stimulation) during the first encounter involving intercourse.

With a few simple tweaks on what we expect from the wedding night and honeymoon, we can change people's stories. Instead of thinking, *Don't have sex until you're married and then it will be great*, think instead, *Once I'm married, we get to start the journey to great sex.*

That journey should be a three-step process:

1. Get comfortable being naked together and talking about what you want to do.
2. Figure out how to help her feel aroused, and even bring her to orgasm (you can also bring him to orgasm at this stage, but focus on her first).
3. Have intercourse when you're both ready for it.

Some couples can experience all three in one night, and some may take a few weeks (or even months). It doesn't matter how long it takes because if you do things in the right order, you'll save yourself years of having to undo bad patterns. Do things in this order, and you'll set yourself up for a much better sexual future!

Figure 4.8

At what age did respondents learn that women can orgasm?

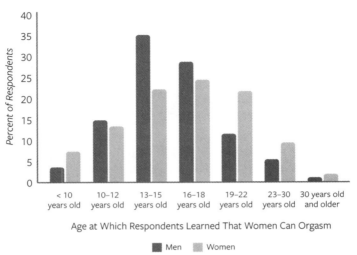

Age at Which Respondents Learned That Women Can Orgasm

■ Men ▨ Women

> **KEY TAKEAWAY:** Female sexual pleasure is often an afterthought. Many people, but especially women, didn't know about female orgasms until adulthood.[28]

deserves to be made to feel that their pain is an acceptable price for someone else's pleasure.[29] If you're experiencing pain with intercourse that doesn't clear up in a few days or doesn't ease even when you're aroused, please see a pelvic floor physiotherapist, and read *The Great Sex Rescue*.

Sex Is Mutual

If sex is supposed to be an intimate expression of your relationship, it means you both have to show up and you both have to matter. Sadly, though, when conducting research for *The Great Sex Rescue*, we found this teaching was replaced in our evangelical resources by what we call the "obligation-sex message." Fused with the gender stereotype of men having higher sex drives than women, it is usually phrased like this: "A wife is obligated to give her husband sex when he wants it." The verses that are usually quoted in support are 1 Corinthians 7:3–5:

> The husband should fulfill his marital duty to his wife, and likewise the wife to her husband. The wife does not have authority over her own body but yields it to her husband. In the same way, the husband does not have authority over his own body but yields it to his wife. Do not deprive each other except perhaps by mutual consent and for a time, so that you may devote yourselves to prayer. Then come together again so that Satan will not tempt you because of your lack of self-control.

Too often, these verses have been weaponized against lower-drive wives (but almost never against lower-drive husbands), telling them that "do not deprive" means they ought never to say no to their husband's sexual desires. But if sex is an obligation and you don't have a choice, then sex isn't a knowing; it's an owing. And if one person's needs and preferences don't matter because of the other's entitlement or rights, then sex won't feel like an intimate experience. It will feel like an erasure of you as a person. Is that really God's plan for sex in marriage? Christian teachers don't help when they say things like "God gave men the need for sex and women the gift of sex."[30] Telling low-drive wives who don't enjoy unorgasmic or dehumanizing sex that they should just like it anyway because it is a gift from God is phenomenally unhelpful.

A more accurate reading of 1 Corinthians 7:3–5 shows that this passage teems with mutuality. It doesn't describe one spouse unilaterally giving to the other but both experiencing the exact same gift from each other. It is not saying not to deprive each other of one-sided intercourse. It is saying *do not deprive each other of the fullness of what God intended sex to be in marriage*. In these verses, everything he gets she gets too. True mutuality is God's plan, not one-sided obligation. Plus, the fruit of mutuality is that

What Does Consent Look Like in Marriage?

If you can't freely say no, then you can't truly say yes either.

If someone can't say, "Not tonight, honey," without experiencing consequences, then they can't freely say, "Yes, tonight sounds great!"

People often misunderstand sexual coercion, because they assume it means being physically forced to have intercourse or perform different sex acts. But if you have to have sex to prevent something bad from happening, then you are being coerced. Coercion can look like having sex so that (and this is not an exhaustive list):

- your spouse won't yell at you, belittle you, give you the silent treatment, or withdraw emotionally from you
- your spouse won't yell at the children or treat the children badly
- your spouse won't embarrass you in front of friends, acquaintances, and family
- your spouse will give you access to money
- your spouse won't threaten to watch porn, have an affair, masturbate, or lust after someone else

It can also look like a spouse having sex with you while you're asleep or using a sex toy on you or performing a sex act that you asked them not to do, even if you orgasm from the experience. If you recognize these dynamics in your marriage, please call a domestic violence hotline or talk to a licensed counselor about how to set boundaries and maintain safety. See the appendix for more help.

desire builds, so frequency is not really a problem. In our study of 20,000 women, we found that when:

- women frequently reach orgasm
- women feel emotionally connected during sex
- women report high marital satisfaction
- there's no sexual dysfunction
- there's no porn use—

then frequency pretty much takes care of itself! When sex is not pleasurable, when sex hurts, when sex is coerced, when sex leaves you feeling used, then having sex detracts from intimacy rather than contributing to it. Until these basic foundational components of good sex are met, having sex more frequently can actually make your marriage worse. Seeking sex instead of seeking health will result in short-term gain for long-term pain. Now, if you are struggling, can you still be having sex in this interim period for the purpose of figuring out how to make sex pleasurable? Sure! But the goal should be making sex great for both of you, not "doing your duty."

Sex Is the Physical Expression of Your Relationship

Sex is also mutual because it is the embodiment of who you are together. It is natural and appropriate that what is happening in your relationship is reflected in your sex life. Sex does not have to look the same at all times. The evangelical church, however, has often taught women the "seventy-two-hour rule": that you have to give your husband sexual release every seventy-two hours, regardless of what is going on in your relationship, in order for him to resist temptation and feel close to you. Author Kevin Leman pushes this narrative in his book *Sheet Music*:

> If you're not willing to commit yourself to having sex with this person two to three times a week for the rest of your life, don't get married. . . .
>
> This means that there may be times when you have sex out of mercy, obligation, or commitment and without any real desire. Yes, it may feel forced. It might feel planned, and you may fight to stop yourself from just shoving your partner away and saying, "Enough already!" But the root issue is this: You're acting out of love. You're honoring your commitment. And that's a wonderful thing to do.[31]

Leman's message is clear: No matter what is happening in your relationship, no matter how you are feeling, you should have intercourse, even if you want to push your partner off you, even if it feels forced. How is this intimate, mutual, and pleasurable for both?

Leman opens his book with the story of Mark and Brenda. Brenda's super busy with the children and always exhausted, so Mark turns to porn and masturbation several times a week. The solution? It's not that Mark needs to realize how overwhelmed Brenda is feeling and help; it's not that Mark needs to understand that his selfishness is turning her off and making her feel like she doesn't have a partner; it's not that Mark needs to realize that by turning to porn he is training himself to see Brenda as an object rather than a person and he is betraying her. No, it's that Brenda needs to have more intercourse. Sex, in this all-too-common mindset, is separate from whatever else is happening in their marriage.

Leman is not alone in teaching this mindset. We once heard a big-name pastor answering a question on a panel about whether it was okay for a wife who discovered her husband's porn use to take a break from sex for a period of time while her husband worked on his issues and rebuilt trust. The pastor was adamant: You cannot deprive your spouse, regardless of what else is happening. This contrasts starkly with the common clinical counseling practice of suggesting a period of sexual abstinence for the exact reasons the woman mentioned. But this pastor couldn't fathom that possibility. He couldn't see sex as an organic part of the relationship but only saw it as a transaction that was owed.

Sex and desire thrive in relationships where sex is intimate. One of the best predictors of sexual satisfaction and marital satisfaction that we found in our surveys of both men and women is emotional closeness during sex. When sex is an expression of how we feel, then sex thrives—and so does desire. So we face a choice: We can keep stressing frequency and the seventy-two-hour rule and telling people they must have sex even if it feels forced, or we can give up our feelings of entitlement around sex and simply love each other and allow sex to naturally blossom.

In an integrated view of sex, what is happening in the relationship and to each of you individually will affect your sex life, and that's okay. If she suffers from postpartum depression and a traumatic birth, then naturally she may not want sex for a while, because it's too vulnerable and she's not in the headspace to "play."

If his mom just died, he may not want sex for weeks or even months because he's grieving, and that's okay (conversely, one or both of you may want comfort, and that's okay too).

If you're overwhelmed with small kids, you may not have sex as often as you wish you could, and that's okay because you're parenting together. And as you embrace this role together, you give desire a chance to return in later life stages because you're building it by parenting as a team. Couples who are equally involved as parents, who are equally likely to google "how to get a three-year-old to eat vegetables" or "how to help a five-year-old stop wetting the bed" tend to be much happier with their sex lives. Sex likely doesn't happen as often as it did before they had kids, but they both are okay with it because they both are mentally and emotionally focused on parenting.

But what happens when we tell women who are postpartum or on their periods that they have to service their husbands or else their husbands will be tempted? We should not be surprised to find that for women sex becomes something fundamentally threatening, dehumanizing, and even traumatizing. When she is physically unable to have sex, when she is exhausted, torn, and bleeding, and we prioritize making sure he has as many orgasms as he is accustomed to? This fundamentally tells her, *In your marriage, you are unimportant. His sexual release matters more than your healing.*

How Do You Handle Libido Differences?

All of this adds up to this central truth: *Your sex life grows out of how you treat each other and how you approach sex.* If your sex life isn't at the tier you want it to be at, the answer is not to push your spouse down to an even lower tier so you can experience some frills. Instead, if sex isn't great, recognize that it's likely not because your spouse is deliberately trying to deprive you (and themselves!) of amazing sex, and be curious about what is actually preventing you from experiencing awesome sex. Perhaps it's the ongoing influence of past trauma, how you handled roadblocks that came up in your marriage, or how much you focused (or failed to focus) on making sure sex felt great for your partner. Work on those foundational issues first. Once the foundation is good, libido usually grows, and you're both more likely to want sex.

What if the foundation is good and sex feels great, but one (or both!) of you still doesn't seem to want sex? We wonder if part of this is due to a misunderstanding about how libido actually works. After all, TV shows and movies always seem to show the same plot when it comes to sex: The couple is together, and they're panting. So they start to kiss, take off their clothes, and end up in bed. That's the order: pant, kiss, clothes, bed. That ends up being our definition of libido because that's pretty much the only narrative we ever see.[32]

There you are at home, then, waiting to pant. If nothing much happens, you figure, *I guess I'm not in the mood*, and you go back to prepping for a presentation tomorrow or dreaming about redecorating the throw cushions on your couch. Maybe you even think, *I guess I'm just not a sexual person*. But here's the thing: If sex feels good when you have it, and if you can get aroused and reach orgasm, *then you are a sexual person*. You just may not tend to spontaneously feel a desire for sex. You may have what Emily Nagoski calls in her book *Come as You Are* a "responsive libido."[33] Although it may be harder for you to get into a sexy frame of mind, just remember you can get there. Many people don't feel in the mood before they start kissing and touching but know they'll get there if they start. In our surveys, those people enjoyed sex just as much as those who had a more spontaneous libido. Sometimes the answer is telling yourself, *Hey, I may not feel much right now, but if I jump in, I know I'm going to have a good time and we'll feel great together*.

It can feel pretty lonely if your spouse with a more responsive libido assumes they are just not in the mood and repeatedly turns you down. So if you're the responsive spouse, remember that you don't need to be panting first to have a good time. Remind yourself how great you feel after sex. Remind yourself how much you enjoy being together. And then make it happen!

One interesting group we found in our surveys was the 22% of couples who seem to have equal libidos. But what does an "equal libido" mean?[34] Is it really that they desire sex the same? Or is it that when the foundation of the sex life is so strong, libido differences don't register as much? That's what we think is going on, and we explain it this way in *The Great Sex Rescue*:

> So, what characterizes couples who have figured out the libido piece? They are mutually satisfied during sex and treat each other well outside the bedroom too. That's why it's not a surprise that couples who have the same level of libido are overrepresented in the happiest marriage group—not because having the same libido makes people happier, but because the way happy couples negotiate frequency of sex minimizes the issues found in libido difference conflicts.
>
> After all, what does it actually mean if you have the same libido? Is it that both of you need sex every 87 hours, and you just managed to find your perfect sexual match? We think a better explanation is that for these couples, sex isn't a source of contention, so any libido differences that exist just don't register. If the Netflix movie ends and the couple starts kissing and that leads to sex, who initiated it? In marriages in which sex is a natural result of the closeness they share, it can be hard to quantify who asks for it more when both of you are eager and willing.
>
> This dynamic explains successful marriages with significant libido differences as well. If mutual serving is the norm, then libido differences do not pose the same threat they do in marriages with less sacrificial giving. In marriages marked by mutual serving, each spouse can delight in meeting the other's needs knowing that their needs will also be met because they can trust each other's goodwill. The lower-drive spouse doesn't feel that more sex is an inconvenience because caring for your spouse is not seen as a hassle. Likewise, the higher-drive spouse doesn't feel resentment when practicing self-control because it's a way to serve and honor the other.[35]

Don't wait for a great sex life to happen. Work on whatever parts of the "intimate, mutual, and pleasurable for both" foundation are missing for you. And then once that is rock solid, celebrate your sexuality, even if you have to remind yourself to start panting.

Investing in your relationship and making sex something that flows naturally from that relationship will allow sex to be what it was meant to be: the physical outflowing of an emotional and even spiritual connection between you and your spouse.

That's the kind of sex we should be prioritizing.

Responsibility

Functioning as a Team as You Bear Each Other's
Burdens, Each Carrying Your Own Load

CHAPTER FIVE

The Partnership You Want

One of the fun—and scary—things about running a survey is that you don't actually know what you're going to find. We have theories, but until we actually run the numbers, we don't know if we're right. A large part of what we were attempting to measure in our matched-pair survey was teamwork. We were pretty sure it mattered—but we were not prepared for *how much* it mattered.

It may not surprise you that your marital flourishing is highest when your spouse does half of the housework and lowest when they do virtually none. What we found shocking, though, was the magnitude of the difference—a 31% drop! To put this in perspective, let's consider the other things we're typically told are vital to a happy marriage. Having sex a few times a week versus once a month? That's a 10.6% change. Having money stress in your marriage? That's a 5% change. Going to church weekly instead of once a month? Five percent change too. So when we see a 31% change? Wow!

Given the magnitude of its effect, we simply must address the division of household labor if we want to see marriages flourish. We're quite aware we may step on some toes here because, while the negative effects of having one spouse carry significantly more weight around the house are the same for both men and

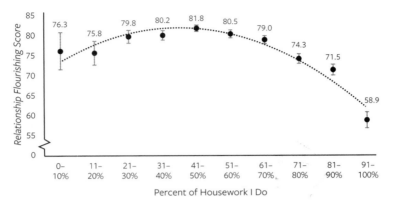

Figure 5.1

How does housework distribution affect marital flourishing?[1]

Percent of Housework I Do

KEY TAKEAWAY: Doing the vast majority of the housework is associated with less marital flourishing.

women, this is largely a one-gendered problem. Overall, women are 4.2 times more likely than men to say their spouse does not do their fair share of housework.[2] When both spouses work full-time, women are 3.9 times more likely to say that men don't do their fair share than men were to say that women don't.[3] Even when only one spouse works, carrying the full responsibility for the housework drives down marital satisfaction. In this chapter, we'd like to show you why.

Lack of teamwork is a primary reason why people's marital satisfaction goes down over time—and particularly women's marital satisfaction. A 2024 study in the *Psychological Science* journal found that women find it easier to love their partners wholeheartedly at the beginning of a relationship, but they also find those feelings deteriorating over time more than men do. "Whereas men showed a 9.2% reduction in their romantic feelings toward their spouses, women underwent a 55.2% drop. A similar effect is seen in the realm of passion, where marriage leads to a 55.3%

decrease in women's desire for their partners, and a much smaller deterioration in ardour from men."[4] Why is this? The author hypothesizes that one primary reason is that often women don't feel like they have reliable partners because responsibility for the household isn't shared. This particular study found that over the course of a long relationship, women spent increasing time on cooking and cleaning. Men, on the other hand, spent increasing time resting and napping.[5] A 2023 Australian study found that women's sexual desire plummeted in relationships when there was an uneven division of household labor.[6] Around the same time, another groundbreaking study found that when men and women don't share responsibilities at home, the dynamic between the wife and husband becomes that of caregiver and dependent—and a woman's sex drive naturally heads south.[7]

Are we saying that men are inherently lazy? Nope. What we are saying is that the data overwhelmingly show that when one person in a relationship doesn't carry their fair share of the load, it can eventually destroy the relationship. And on the whole, while women have historically not been allowed to get away with that, *men have.* We're not trying to pick on men, but if we want this book to actually help people, then we need to tell the truth about what the data reveal. According to a Pew 2023 research study, employed men enjoy more leisure time than employed women across the board, with the greatest difference being among those with children under the age of five. Men with small kids have 4.5 more hours per week of leisure time than their wives do. When there is at least one child under the age of eighteen at home, men have around 3 more hours of leisure time per week than their wives do.[8] Remember, that's average, so it's worse in some marriages and better in others. Now, if you're in a marriage where things are divided in a way you both feel is fair and this isn't a factor, then pat yourselves on the back! But keep reading so you can encourage the couples around you to emulate you and never fall into these dynamics. And if you experience these dynamics but the genders are reversed—then the same solutions we're going to present in this chapter hold for you too.

Figure 5.2

How do respondents rate the fairness of the amount of housework their spouse does depending on how much housework the spouse actually does?[9]

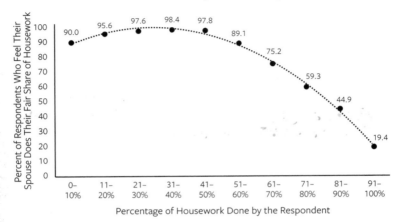

KEY TAKEAWAY: The farther things get from a 50-50 split, the more likely one spouse is to feel the amount of housework they do is unfair.

Why Is Teamwork Often Difficult?

One of the biggest ways balance can be thrown off in a marriage is by divvying up responsibilities based on gender rather than circumstances, giftings, and preferences. A roles-based marriage will tend to be inflexible, while a team approach allows flexibility when circumstances change. And let's be real: Can anyone point us to the biblical passage that decrees it's a man's role to take out the trash and a woman's to sort through the never-ending rotation of kids' clothes every season? Of course not. The idea of "biblical roles" has become loaded down with purely cultural constructs and then regurgitated as if it's straight from Jesus himself.

A teamwork approach says, "Our marriage has certain things that need to get done to keep it healthy. How can we distribute them the best?" rather than simplistic reductions like "she ought to look after the kids while he works" or "lawn care is a man's job." Instead, a teamwork approach asks questions like, does a husband who did most of the childcare while he finished up his MDiv keep doing that when he gets a full-time job as a pastor? Or do they reshuffle the responsibilities? When a woman who was working full-time now stays home to care for their new twins, does the husband stop all the housework because now she's a stay-at-home wife? Or do they find a new balance?

Here's what teamwork boils down to: When you marry, you will both work toward the well-being of your family, even if you do not work in the exact same way. One may earn more income while the other does more housework or childcare, for instance. But you both should work, and you both should enjoy roughly equal rest and downtime.[10] Responsibility in marriage means that each of us needs to carry our own load, as Paul says in Galatians 6:5. It's okay to expect your spouse to be your partner—and marriages flourish best the more you see household responsibilities as shared responsibilities.[11]

I (Sheila) did all the housework when Keith was working those long hours during his pediatric residency. When he finally stumbled home, even if he was exhausted, he took over with the kids because it was our priority that our kids spent time with both parents. A few years later, as he was launching his medical practice, I continued to do most of the housework since I was home with the girls all day. Initially, I also had the job of balancing the finances, but over the years as my work grew and Keith's hours slacked off a little, we swapped roles with the bills and investments. Now that I work more hours than he does, he's also taken on most of the housework, but I still do the cooking. One of the great things about being married is that you get the chance to specialize! I love cooking, but I'm rather challenged when it comes to remembering what to clean on a schedule. Keith loves listening to podcasts while he works at his very strict cleaning routine every Saturday morning, but he would have no idea how to make pesto chicken risotto. Over the years, then, what we do has changed with the ebb and flow of our lives, but the foundation has always been that we will work as partners: We each contribute fairly, and we each get roughly equal leisure time.

If you're partners in life, you should each be putting in the same effort, even if you're not doing the same things. If one of you is able to sit down when you'd like while the other rarely gets a break, or if one of you is always exhausted while the other is fairly well rested, then (barring some truly exceptional circumstance) that's almost certainly a sign that you're not acting as partners.

Negotiating Work In and Outside the Home

There is no one-size-fits-all when it comes to balancing who works outside the home and who does what housework. The stereotypical "ideal" of a husband as breadwinner and a wife as homemaker certainly does work for many families (as it did, for a time, with ours). There's nothing wrong with falling into traditional gender roles, provided you make that choice as a couple because it's what works for you, not because you feel that's what you *should* do. When couples believe that these gender roles are prescribed by God and that this is the way it must be, we found that marital flourishing suffers.[12] Women report feeling more heard and seen in their marriages when they don't believe that they have to act out gender roles. Even when women do live out stereotypical roles, if they do so by choice, they're more likely to report feeling heard and seen by their spouse.

The default dynamic of the wife being primarily responsible for the kids and the home becomes particularly problematic when both spouses work outside the home. Many couples allow responsibility for housework to default to the wife without either spouse realizing that's what they are doing. But when both partners are already busy with work outside the home, for everything to fall on her shoulders is a recipe for entitlement for him and bitterness and exhaustion for her.

Time Spent at Paid Work Is Not a "Get Out of All Housework" Card

From our research, the biggest mistake couples make when figuring out how to split up paid work versus housework is that they think in terms of "areas of responsibility" rather than work hours. For instance, a social media post recently came across our feed in which a young woman announced, "I expect to be the one fully taking care of our baby girl. My husband will not have to change one diaper. He works so I can be a stay-at-home mom and give our daughter the proper attention she needs. The least I can do is fully take care of her while keeping our house clean and serving him."[13]

Let's unpack what she's saying: Because her husband works outside the home 40 hours a week, she will be on call 24/7, working 168 hours a week, so that her husband doesn't have to nurture a relationship with his daughter. Children are not a task to divvy up; children are people who desperately need a healthy relationship with both parents.

So, how about this instead? He works eight to nine hours a day, and she looks after the house and the baby for eight to nine hours a day while he's gone, and then, while he's home, they *both* look after the house and the baby. That's what a partnership is. Instead of saying, "I am responsible for the paid work, and you're responsible for the kids and housework," simply acknowledge that you each have work hours when you care for your primary area of responsibility, and then in the other hours, you're both on duty, except when you cover each other so you can have breaks. If one of you has more breaks during the day, then you can certainly take on more of the responsibility in the evening. But one spouse's time is not more valuable than the other's, and no one is completely excused from being "on" at home because they also work outside the home.

Mental Load Is the Real Energy Zapper

It's not just the seemingly never-ending work that goes into running a house that is the problem; it's also the mental energy that

119

goes into keeping track of everything that needs to get done, planning how to make sure it happens, and assuming responsibility for the outcome. This is called "mental load." In our book *The Good Guy's Guide to Great Sex*, we demonstrate this concept with this story of Sandra and Mark:

It's a beautiful Saturday morning, and Mark has blessed Sandra with a morning all to herself while he takes the kids. Sandra's up early, excited about her outing. As she leaves the house, she says to Mark, "Remember to get the clothes out of the dryer when the load is done."

While she's gone, Mark feeds the kids a fun pancake breakfast, and then they head out on a bike ride. When Sandra gets home, the kids are energetic and happy, and Mark is beaming.

Sandra smiles, relaxed from her morning, and starts to make lunch when she notices that the birthday present for her son Brian's friend is still sitting on the kitchen counter, unwrapped. And they have to leave in two hours. "That's okay," Sandra thinks, sighing. "I'll just do it."

As she fetches the wrapping paper, she sees Brian's science fair project on the dining room table, untouched. "Didn't Mark get Brian to work on the science fair project? We won't have time to work on it tomorrow, and it's due Monday!" Then another thought occurs: "What about Janie practicing piano?"

Now they're under the gun because Sandra was planning on staying with Brian at the party this afternoon. So, in the next two hours, Brian needs to make headway on the project and Janie needs to practice piano. Sandra starts ordering the kids around, and they get grumpy. Mark tells her to calm down, but Sandra feels the clock ticking.

After much protest, the kids comply, begrudgingly, as Mark heads outside on the riding lawn mower, listening to podcasts. Sandra goes to grab a new shirt and realizes nothing's folded on the bed. Are they still in the dryer? Uh-oh! All of Mark's work shirts were in the dryer. If he didn't pull them out when the dryer was done, then she'll need to do extra ironing. She checks the dryer. Yep. The laundry is still there.

Mark's done mowing the lawn, and he calls out, "Oh, hon, I forgot to tell you. My sister called this morning. She wants to know what venue we should book for Mom and Dad's fortieth anniversary party."

"What did you tell her?" Sandra asks.

"I told her you'd call her back."

But they're your parents, Sandra thinks. Anger starts showing on her face. Mark can't figure out what's going on but then says, "Oh, is this about the laundry? Look, I'm sorry. I just forgot."

And then Sandra bursts. It wasn't just the laundry. It was the unwrapped birthday present and the homework and the piano. It was everything.

"But if you needed me to do all that," Mark says, "you should have given me a list."

Sandra feels the frustration rise, even as she tries to stuff it down. *Is it so bad to wish that I didn't have to write him a list? Is it wrong to want him to know some of this stuff without having to be told?* The present was right in the middle of the kitchen where he had made pancakes. They had talked about the science fair project last night at dinner—it was all over the dining room table. Janie had been practicing for weeks, and the Tuesday recital was circled with stars on the calendar. Was it so unreasonable that she wanted Mark to think of some of these things too, without being reminded?

Mark tries to calm her down. "Honey, you're overreacting. We can get all of this done later. You don't have to go crazy now."

But when is this magical "later" when everything is supposed to get done? Why didn't Mark realize that their schedule was tight this weekend? Why did she always carry the mental calendar?[14]

That's mental load—always feeling like you have to carry everyone's calendar and the family to-do list in your head, always remembering what everyone else needs to get done. The spouse who is not bearing the mental load may wonder why their spouse can't be more spontaneous, oblivious to what their spouse is doing in the background. The spouse who is bearing the mental load might similarly be confused as to why nobody else in the house seems to know how to do anything.

Let's take Sandra and Mark again and put them in a new scenario. This time we'll fast-forward to summer, when one Friday night, Mark, in a fit of familial joy, announces, "Let's go to the beach tomorrow!" The kids are ecstatic, and Sandra wants to be, too, for everyone else's sake. But inside, the wheels start turning frantically as she tries to figure out all the things that she needs to do to make this happen. For the rest of the evening, she's pulling things out of drawers, rummaging in the fridge, and snapping at everybody. Mark fetches the bathing suits and towels and stuffs them into a backpack and is bothered that Sandra is so grumpy.

"Hon," Mark says, "I just want to have fun with the family, and you're turning this into a big production. You're overthinking things. Calm down. It doesn't need to be a huge deal. Just relax with us. Come and watch a movie instead."

Sandra says, "I'm not making it into a big production, Mark! But we can't just 'go to the beach.' It's not that easy. If you want to go to the beach, then why aren't you helping?"

"I'd be glad to help! Tell me what to do," Mark says.

Sandra breaks down in tears. "That's the problem! You make all these plans, and you never think about how it's going to affect me because you never consider how much work goes into this. You just sit back and let me figure it all out!"

What is going on in Sandra's head? Well, let's think about it:

- She has to pack snacks and lunches for everybody to eat.
- She has to pack diapers and changes of clothes for the baby.
- She has to find all the sand pails, shovels, and flotation devices. She thinks they're in the bottom of the basement closet in a storage container, but she's not sure, and she has to move the Christmas decorations to find them.
- Janie, their middle child, burns easily and needs SPF 60 for her body and SPF 100 for her face. She also needs a rash shirt and pants. Sandra isn't sure they have enough sunscreen, and she may have to run to the drugstore to get it.

- The baby will need to nap in the early afternoon and will have to be kept shaded. They have a little baby beach tent, but Sandra lent it to her friend Emily two weeks ago. She has to phone Emily to see if she can pick it up.
- The picnic, water toys, and everything will take up a lot of space in the trunk, but right now, the trunk is filled with donations for the thrift store. Sandra has spent this week cleaning out the kids' closets and weeding out their toys, figuring out which ones she wants to keep for the baby, and before they can fit everything in the trunk for tomorrow, they have to go drop off the donations. She's trying to figure out if the place is open in the evening and whether they can go drop them off tonight.
- Sandra's period started today, which means tomorrow will be her heaviest day. She's wondering if there are good bathrooms to change tampons in. She's also wondering if she still has a bathing suit wrap she can wear so she doesn't have to be so self-conscious.
- Her maternity bathing suit won't fit anymore, but she's worried about fitting into her pre-pregnancy bathing suits. Does she have to run out to get another one? And will breastfeeding work at the beach? She really wants to find a beach wrap she can use just in case.
- She would absolutely LOVE to read a book on the beach and just relax. She's hoping she may have time. She wants to pick out a novel for her Kindle and take it with her.

In many families it becomes a running joke how much of a buzzkill Mom is because she's always worried about everything like this. But are *all* of these things superfluous? Maybe they could make do without the noodles or the pails and shovels, but the kids wouldn't have as much fun. And they could just move the donations into the garage to free up the trunk space if they can't make it to the thrift store now, but someone still has to figure that out. Regardless, shouldn't all these arrangements that need to be made (snacks for the kids, sunscreen, what beach toys to take, etc.) be a shared task, not something that automatically devolves onto Sandra?

When we shared this scenario on the blog, several readers suggested Sandra should just take a step back, not do all those things, and let Mark learn from his mistakes. This sounds good in theory (if a little passive-aggressive), but who actually bears the consequences if things go badly? If the kids have a terrible time and whine and cry and are hungry, then Sandra is going to have a terrible time too. If the baby misses her nap and her schedule is thrown off, who is going to be up at night with her or when she misses those naps over the next few days? Likely Sandra. If the kids get sunburned and don't sleep well for the next little while, who is going to be dealing with cranky kids during the day?

That is the burden of mental load, a burden that should be shared if we are truly to be a team. Frankly, a lot of husbands have marriages in which they have the privilege of not having to worry about what the kids are going to eat on the beach trip tomorrow, of not having to think ahead and anticipate the family's needs. If the wife is always the one having to anticipate the family's needs, that means she is carrying the load of caring for everyone, while no one is really carrying the load of caring for her. It's intrinsically unfair and incredibly exhausting.

What often frustrates women, too, is that they carry the mental load out of necessity, not because they're naturally better at it. How often have you heard "women are better at multitasking"? It turns out that's a myth. Studies have shown that women are not naturally better at multitasking than men—they just have more practice! A study from the University of Norway, published in the *Harvard Business Review*, details an experiment in which people were supposed to set up a room for a meeting while simultaneously dealing with multiple distractions. Women were just as bad at it as men![15] To put it more positively, men are just as capable of learning how to manage mental load as women are—provided they devote time and energy to learning the skill set. Wise men will do that.

Entitlement Sneaks In When There's Uneven Mental Load

In 2016, Matthew Fray wrote an article that took the internet by storm: "She Divorced Me Because I Left Dishes by the Sink." The issue wasn't the dishes as much as what the dishes represented. He explains, "I understand that when I leave that glass there, it hurts her—literally causes her pain—because it feels to her like I just said: 'Hey. I don't respect you or value your thoughts and opinions. Not taking four seconds to put my glass in the dishwasher is more important to me than you are.'"[16] When a spouse doesn't do basic chores but waits to be reminded (or ignores the reminder anyway), it's communicating, "I have the privilege of ignoring this because I know that you won't ignore it." The spouse who is always tidying the house, taking care of the chores, or making meals is constantly thinking and planning for the good of the family. But if the other spouse can't remember the basic tasks they've agreed to do or, even worse, refuses to do them when asked? They're communicating, "You're not worth thinking about." It's not about the dishes by the sink. It's not about the trash needing to be taken out. It's about communicating, "I want you to think about me, but I can't be bothered to think about you."

How many times have you heard advice, often aimed at women, to stop nagging? But what if nagging isn't the real issue? What if the real issue is that one spouse isn't doing what they've promised to do, or isn't helping at all, and the other spouse has no recourse except to keep reminding them? In that case, is the problem nagging, or is the problem that the chore isn't getting done, putting the mental load to monitor that task back onto the spouse who isn't even supposed to do it? In our survey for this book, we found that 51.8% of women and 24.4% of men have to remind their spouse to complete recurring tasks. Think about it—that's more than half of women and almost one-quarter of men who are left frustrated because their spouse isn't following through. That's going to hurt your marriage—and even your sex life! When women had to remind their spouse to do recurring tasks, they were 2.2 times less likely to be sexually satisfied.[17] Not good. Rather than villainizing nagging, then, let's address the problem at its root and create the expectation that people will follow through on the tasks they've promised to do.

Mental load, though, isn't just about keeping track of tasks. Here's how Melissa, one of our blog commenters, explains mental load:

> I finally found a mental load analogy to describe a dynamic that has always left me feeling vaguely used/devalued in a way I couldn't pin down. In addition to the chronic, "Hey, where's the [household item that's been kept on the same shelf for years]?" questions, my husband will also call me from work at random times to ask questions he has more business knowing than I do, like his own shirt size or the name of the restaurant one of his acquaintances used to own.
>
> Then it struck me that if we were computer equipment, I would expect us both to be like laptops connected on a private network. Complete, autonomous units that can do what they need to do individually, but can also communicate with each other in order to collaborate on other tasks like parenting and finances.
>
> But too often he treats me, a metaphorical fully functioning laptop, like an external hard drive. A peripheral device. An extension of himself, storing and retrieving data at his convenience as if I don't have 20 other programs running at once (and on a very low battery most of the time). He may not be using or devaluing me in an overtly egregious way, but in a way that nevertheless makes me want to reconfigure those network settings.

We know you don't want that for your marriage, so let's get practical about how to fix this imbalance.

How Do You Create a Mental Load Partnership?

No More "Give Me a List"!

It seems the go-to response for husbands who have some understanding of distributing work fairly but who haven't learned about the concept of mental load is "Just give me a list, and I'll get it done." As Joe Pinsker writes in *The Atlantic*, "In many house-holds, men think like helpers and women think like managers."[18] Many men will jump in and do things when they are told what to do, but it is women who tend to carry the details of everything that has to be remembered in their heads. When someone has to make a list, though, they are still carrying the mental load. They're putting themselves in the managerial position, while the other is the subordinate. And that's not partnership.

As Matthew Fray explains about his own marital breakdown,

> I remember my wife often saying how exhausting it was for her to have to tell me what to do all the time. It's why the sexiest thing a man can say to his partner is "I got this," and then take care of whatever needs taken care of.
>
> I always reasoned: "If you just tell me what you want me to do, I'll gladly do it."
>
> But she didn't want to be my mother.
>
> She wanted to be my partner, and she wanted me to apply all of my intelligence and learning capabilities to the logistics of manag-ing our lives and household.[19]

A spouse who is truly acting as a partner doesn't need to ask for a list *because they already know what needs to be on it.*

Own the Whole Task

Eve Rodsky made a big splash with her book *Fair Play*, outlining the problems with uneven mental load in a marriage—and how to solve them. And her big solution to this "give me a list" problem is simple and effective: Rodsky argues that instead of one person being responsible for planning and keeping track of the task while the other person executes it, you divide up tasks so that you each "own" the whole thing, from conception to planning to execution. To use our commenter Melissa's computer analogy, when you have decided as a couple that a task belongs to you, then you need to be a "fully functioning, autonomous laptop" without relying on your spouse to be your "external hard drive."

Too often we give credit to the person who executes the task and ignore the other two steps, which can be more onerous. We say that the person who got in the car, went to the grocery store, and came home with food did the grocery shopping, not the person who kept track of which grocery staples were running low, planned the meals for the coming week and figured out what extra ingredients were needed, checked the grocery store apps to see what was on sale, and made the list. Owning the task doesn't just mean completing it but keeping track of everything that goes into that task.

When you own the laundry, for instance, it doesn't just mean you put clothing into machines and fold it afterward. It means you keep track of when you need more supplies, like laundry detergent or fabric softener, and add them to the grocery list. You learn what clothes need to be washed on the delicate cycle and notice when there's a tricky stain that needs dry cleaning. You're responsible for taking things to the dry cleaner's and picking them up too. You're responsible for seeing if the supply of one of the kids' underwear is running out and matching up all the stray socks. You're responsible for noticing if a zipper isn't working and needs to be replaced.

Now, zippers and dry cleaning and stains all logically fall under the umbrella of "clothing care." Some tasks, however, have far more extraneous responsibilities attached to them. Let's revisit Mark and Sandra to see how this can play out. Sandra usually drives their son, Brian, to hockey practice, but this week she can't, so Mark says he will take him. What does Mark believe is being asked of him at that moment? He might think that he has to get Brian in the car, get him to practice on time, and get him home again. That's the execution phase of the task.

But there's the planning phase, too, and here's where things get complicated. Sandra knows that last week, Brian borrowed one of Jared's jerseys and needs to return it. *But where is the jersey? Has it been washed yet?* Plus, this week, all the fundraising money from selling chocolate bars is due. Plus, two weeks ago, Sandra brought in cupcakes to celebrate Brian's birthday, and she has forgotten to bring home that big Tupperware container for two weeks straight now. And it's an expensive one. She doesn't want to lose it.

Sandra starts to bark out all these extra orders, and it sounds to Mark like she's become a drill sergeant as she yells at everyone to find Jared's jersey. Is it still in the dryer? And where is Grandpa's check for all the chocolate bars? She thinks it was on the side table and was never put into the fundraising envelope. Like always, Sandra is fussing about everything and can never calm down, and now everyone is stressed.

What went wrong?

Extracurricular activities, like sports, lessons, or clubs, often add stress when you try to share them because they encompass so many moving pieces:

- keeping track of schedules and making plans to ensure transportation, snacks, or anything else
- caring for equipment and making sure it's ready
- paying all dues and tending to fundraisers (that never seem to end!)
- carrying the emotional labor of navigating relationships with peers and teachers/coaches
- overseeing individual practicing, if necessary

If one person can fully take all this load off their spouse's shoulders—from conception to planning to execution—imagine the breathing room that spouse now has!

Take the Initiative to Learn the Whole Task

Once you've decided what your tasks are going to be, take the initiative to truly learn all aspects of that task—which may involve understanding *why* the task was being done in a certain way beforehand. You can certainly put your stamp on it and change the way it's done, but sometimes there is a reason your spouse did the task a certain way.

If you put the bowls in the top of the dishwasher and your husband suggests you rearrange them, he's not necessarily micromanaging. Maybe the dishwasher doesn't clean dishes well on the top rack, so the bowls need to go on the bottom even if they fit better on the top. Similarly, laundry may need to be folded in a certain way to fit neatly into a linen closet or drawers. It may not be that your wife is nitpicking when she insists that things be folded one way; if she's been completing the task for a while, she may have discovered a method that works best. Once you understand what the reason is, you may have your own ideas and decide to change things. But to assume that your spouse is being unreasonable isn't the best course of action.

Other times, when attempting to redistribute household tasks, people throw up their hands and say, "Well, you'll never be happy," and give up without putting real effort into learning. Academics have called this dynamic "weaponized incompetence," or "strategic incompetence." One recent study published in the British Sociological Association's *Sociology* journal looked at how couples negotiated division of labor after men were laid off from work. Now that men had more time at home, it would make sense to move toward a more equitable division of household labor. But instead, researchers found that men often employed "strategic incompetence," claiming, "I just can't meet her standards" or "I'm just not as good at cleaning the bathroom as she is," as a way to get out of having to do chores.[20]

Everyone Needs Grace

When you're dividing up tasks, decide what counts as "good enough." Things need to be done to an acceptable standard, but they don't need to be perfect. In fact, even expecting your spouse to do something as well as you did may not be fair. If you prefer twelve throw cushions on the bed, but your spouse (who now makes the bed) doesn't like putting them all on every morning just to throw them on the floor every night, then maybe you compromise at three. If your spouse is making dinner three nights a week, you can agree that it needs all four food groups and it can't break the bank—but other than that, if it's edible, don't make a fuss.

Weaponized Incompetence

Weaponized incompetence can look like expecting your spouse to teach you how to do basic things—which can take so long, it ends up being easier for your spouse to just do it. Our daughter Rebecca came up with four rules about executing the task. You don't get to ask your spouse how to do it until you have worked through these four steps:

1. Have you googled it?

   When Keith cut back his work hours just as Sheila was increasing hers and he took over a lot of the housecleaning chores, he learned how to get mold off shower caulking and how to wash delicates in our new washing machine by googling them—not by asking Sheila.

2. Is this something a fourteen-year-old babysitter would reasonably be expected to know how to do?

   If your fourteen-year-old babysitter can do it, then you can too.

3. Is this something you would be expected to figure out if you were in the workplace?

   If your boss would expect you to figure it out at work, you can figure it out at home.

4. Have you used your eyes?

   Don't ask, "Where are the scissors?" until you've looked where they're supposed to be.

Everybody Needs to Do Some "Daily Grind" Tasks

When you're figuring out how to be partners, remember that some tasks are inherently more draining than others. Eve Rodsky in *Fair Play* separates tasks into "daily grind" tasks, which have to be completed repeatedly at certain times with little wiggle room, and tasks that can be done on your own schedule. Kids need breakfast at roughly the same time every day. Kids' homework needs to be completed (for the most part) every day. But mowing the grass or balancing the bank accounts can often be done on one's own time.

Each of you should have some daily grind tasks in addition to tasks you can do at a time of your choosing. And a tip from a pediatrician: If one of you generally does less day-to-day childcare than the other, take on daily grind tasks that involve the kids as much as possible (e.g., bath time, homework, etc.). It's a great way to spend time with your kids that they will remember long after.

Downtime Should Be Equal

The Baroness von Sketch Canadian comedy troupe has a must-see skit on the Salem witch trials (which, we realize, were not at all funny in real life). The skit opens in a supposed seventeenth-century courtroom as a woman testifies against a friend, who is locked in stocks next to the witness box. The witness explains how she woke up at night to do the "night work," like "night milking" and "night sewing," and noticed that her friend was sitting outside, doing (gasp!) nothing.

Her testimony causes great consternation to the other women listening to the court hearing, all of whom are simultaneously knitting, peeling potatoes, or spinning yarn. Finally, the witness admits that she was envious of her friend who had nothing to do. The judge then sentences her to the stocks, too, for the sin of envy. As she is locked into the stocks, her friend comforts her and tells her it is actually quite relaxing. You don't have to knit or sew or cook or anything! Suddenly the whole courtroom erupts with women yelling, "I'm envious! I'm envious too! Sentence me to the stocks!"[21]

Having no time to oneself can certainly leave one almost panicky. I (Sheila) knew I had to slow down and rethink things about a year ago when I had an MRI and had to lie still for twenty minutes—and realized how much I enjoyed it. We all need time to do nothing. And "nothing" can't be like Sandra going out on Saturday morning and then having to rush around on Saturday afternoon to make up for what she missed. It has to mean that you truly have that time off.

Unequal free time is simply hard on marriages. Women were 3.0 times more likely to have below average Relationship Flourishing scores[22] and 2.5 times more likely to have below average Trust in Close Relationships scores[23] when they had less free time than their spouse. Similarly, men were 1.7 times more likely to have below average Relationship Flourishing scores[24] and 1.8 times more likely to have below average Trust in Close Relationships scores[25] if they had less free time than their wives. If you're able to sit down and do nothing but your spouse isn't, then it's time to reshuffle responsibilities so resentment doesn't build!

Beware the Unfairness Threshold

This has been a heavy chapter, but we can't stress enough how much teamwork matters, especially if you look at the long-term effects of unfair distribution of housework. In our survey, respondents who did more than 75% of the housework were more likely to report that their spouse did *not* do their fair share of household management tasks if they'd been married for at least a decade (see figure 5.3). The same thing that didn't seem unfair to them in the first year of marriage seemed very unfair the longer it lasted. Over time, even if the unfairness doesn't get objectively worse, a person's willingness to put up with it steadily diminishes. They cross that unfairness threshold, and resentment builds.

We would say to that Instagram user who never wants her husband to change a diaper: That may be sustainable for a few months or even years. But decades into the marriage, it's unlikely to be. We would tell that guy who won't put the dish in the dishwasher: It's four seconds of your life. Show her you care. We would tell Mark: If you want to give Sandra a morning off, then anticipate what your family needs to get done that morning and do it. Don't make more work for her when she gets back.

Some of you might have found the material in this chapter challenging, especially if you have a history of benefiting from a spouse who has borne most of the household labor and/or mental load. Owning your share can seem overwhelming. But if you don't make the right choice, your marriage—and your sex life—will suffer tremendously. When resentment grows in one area of the relationship, it spills over into all the others, leading to a lack of connection, less affection, and even less sex. You can't enjoy a great marriage if you're taking advantage of your spouse by making them do more work. All of us have a choice between personal privilege or thriving as a couple. Make the right choice!

Figure 5.3

How do respondents who do the lion's share (at least 75%) of the housework rate whether or not their spouse does their fair share of housework, depending on how long they've been married?[26]

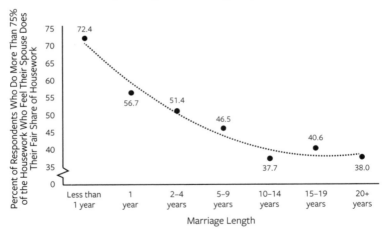

KEY TAKEAWAY: Unequal household labor distribution may feel okay in the honeymoon phase, but it gets old quickly.

Figure 5.4

How does feeling that your spouse does their fair share of housework affect how you describe your marriage?

To interpret these data, use the following: If [I / my spouse] believe(s) that the other does their fair share of housework, [I am / my spouse is] [#] times more likely to describe our marriage as [descriptor].

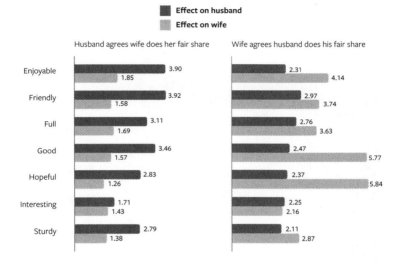

■ Effect on husband

▨ Effect on wife

Husband agrees wife does her fair share | Wife agrees husband does his fair share

	Effect on husband	Effect on wife
Enjoyable	3.90 / 2.31	1.85 / 4.14
Friendly	3.92 / 2.97	1.58 / 3.74
Full	3.11 / 2.76	1.69 / 3.63
Good	3.46 / 2.47	1.57 / 5.77
Hopeful	2.83 / 2.37	1.26 / 5.84
Interesting	1.71 / 2.25	1.43 / 2.16
Sturdy	2.79 / 2.11	1.38 / 2.87

KEY TAKEAWAY: If you feel the division of household labor in your marriage is fair, you are more likely to use positive words to describe your marriage.

Figure 5.5

How does feeling your spouse does their fair share of housework affect your marriage and sex life?

To interpret these data, use the following: If [I / my spouse] believe(s) that the other does their fair share of housework, [I am / my spouse is] [#] times more likely to say that _____.

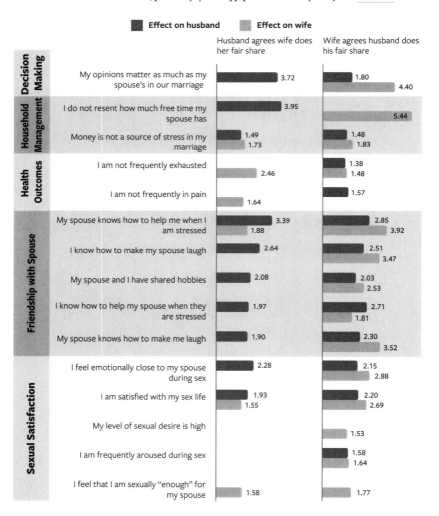

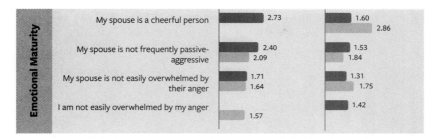

Emotional Maturity	My spouse is a cheerful person	2.73	1.60 / 2.86
	My spouse is not frequently passive-aggressive	2.40 / 2.09	1.53 / 1.84
	My spouse is not easily overwhelmed by their anger	1.71 / 1.64	1.31 / 1.75
	I am not easily overwhelmed by my anger	1.57	1.42

KEY TAKEAWAY: Feeling that your spouse does their fair share of housework is correlated with higher marital satisfaction, sexual satisfaction, emotional maturity, and other positive outcomes.

Figure 5.6

How many people have low to no libido depending on how much housework they do?[27]

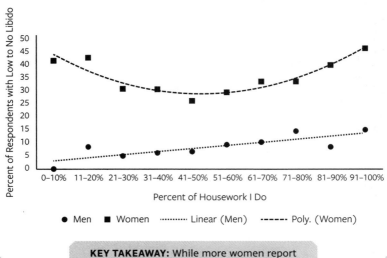

KEY TAKEAWAY: While more women report having a low to nonexistent libido, there was an increase in low sexual desire in both genders if they did the vast majority of the housework.

Figure 5.7

How does feeling that their spouse does their fair share of housework affect sex frequency in men and women?

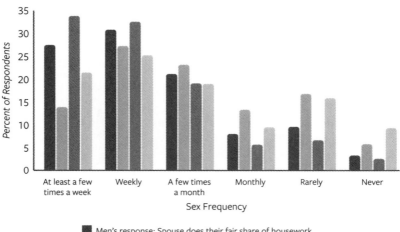

KEY TAKEAWAY: Ensuring that you both feel that the management of household labor is fair is associated with more frequent sex.

How Do Couples in Our Survey Split Household Tasks?

When we look at twelve basic household responsibilities and ask couples who does what, we see some interesting trends. For these charts, we looked only at couples in which both members were employed full-time. Household task splitting can be impacted by a variety of life circumstances, and we wanted to control for as many of these factors as we could.

Men and women agree that women do the majority of

- laundry
- grocery shopping
- cooking
- reorganizing and decorating
- cleaning bathrooms
- tidying
- organizing medical and dental appointments

They agree that men are more likely to do the bulk of

- dishes
- yard work
- garbage

And they agreed that these tasks tended to be split evenly:

- paying bills
- vacuuming

Figure 5.8

Housework Distribution Heat Maps

We were really curious when we finished the collection of responses on the survey to see how couples each rated who does more of each chore. We asked couples to rank . . .

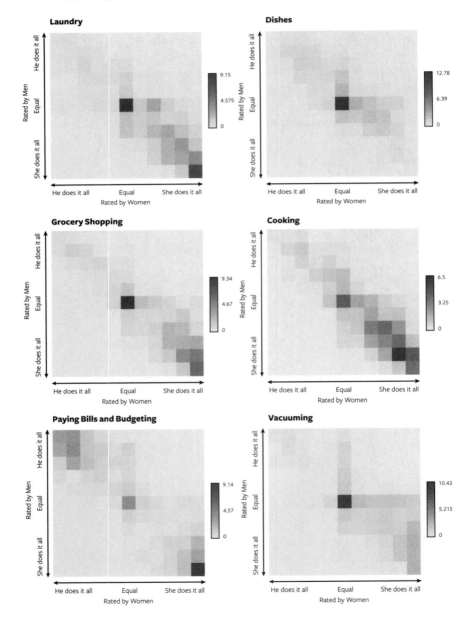

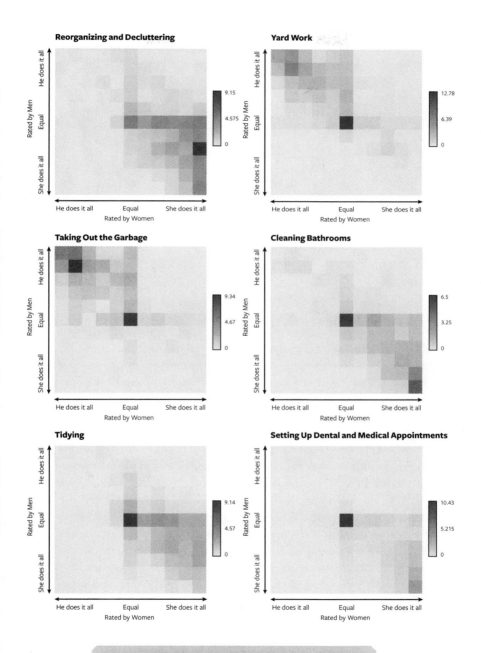

KEY TAKEAWAY: Many couples split household tasks evenly. However, when one spouse does the lion's share of a task, it is most likely to be the woman.

CHAPTER SIX

The Dependability You Want

We were married for twenty-three years before Sheila discovered that I (Keith) like mustard on my sandwiches. She hates the stuff, and so she never bought it. And since I gravitate to the path of least resistance, I'll just make a sandwich with whatever is in the fridge. Then one day while out for lunch at a sandwich shop, I ordered mustard on my sandwich, and she almost fell over. We both laughed about it because it was such an aberration. We usually know everything about each other. I know that she'll smile politely at flowers but she'll devour chocolate truffles, that if she's wandering around the house aimlessly in the middle of the workday it's because she has an email she doesn't want to open and is waiting for me to offer to read it for her, that we have to keep the heating vents closed in our bedroom or she overheats at night (thanks, hot flashes!). She knows that I need her to be the navigator while I'm driving or I'll forget to turn. She saves the ends of the bread for me because she knows I'm one of those weird people who actually prefers them. And when I'm unusually quiet after work, she knows I need to be reminded of what a difference I've made as a doctor because a patient likely had an outcome that was difficult to handle. We know these things because we've paid attention.

Paying attention communicates, "You're important to me, so I will spend mental energy making sure I'm up-to-date on what's going on in your life and figuring out how I can make it easier for you." When you deliberately notice what's going on in your spouse's life, you're saying, "I'm not going to drift through this marriage expecting you to do the heavy lifting; I'm all in, right here beside you."

One word that describes this mindset is *initiative*, and it's part of what responsibility in marriage looks like. It's the key to being a dependable partner in marriage, one who your spouse knows will show up and make the health of the marriage the priority. Let's look at what that entails.

You Need to Be Each Other's Understudy

As we were writing this book, I (Sheila) developed one of the worst cases of bronchitis I've ever experienced. For six weeks my chest was so congested I could barely stop coughing. But as bad as I had it, our oldest daughter had it even worse. All the doctors at our local after-hours clinic knew her by name without needing to check the chart. She was seriously ill for almost two months, but during that time, her household did not fall apart. Her husband, Connor, who worked from home, still managed to get most of his work done, and so did she. The children both ate. They showed up at playgroup and preschool. The bathrooms got cleaned, and the bedding got washed. The secret? Connor was able to "power up" for a while and take some stress away so that Rebecca could rest and recuperate and eventually get back to normal.

Ecclesiastes 4:9–10 says, "Two are better than one, because they have a good return for their labor: If either of them falls down, one can help the other up. But pity anyone who falls and has no one to help them up." This is one of the best things about marriage: If something goes wrong for one of you, the other can step in to help. It's just like in a theatrical production, where every actor has an understudy for their role, somebody who learns their lines just in case they're not able to perform at some point. Marriage allows each of you to have an understudy as you go through life. What a blessing—and a relief!

Specialization is a great benefit of marriage; you each get to do what makes the best sense given your talents, interests, and time. But that doesn't mean that you should absolve yourself of knowing what goes into doing the other tasks; you still have to be able to do the other person's job in a pinch. Do you know where your investments are or who provides your home insurance? Do you have access to all the bank accounts, investments, and bills? If you have to cook for your kids, do you know all their allergies? Do you know that Rosie will eat her vegetables but only if they're not touching anything else? Do you know that if you let Ezra eat too much cheese, he gets constipated?

Be your spouse's understudy! Maybe that means that once in a while you take on the other person's tasks so that you each know how to operate the lawn mower, what to buy for school lunches, what to say to the vet when you take the Yorkie in for his shots. Or perhaps it just requires regularly checking in and talking about it. Remember that Australian study we talked about in the last chapter, which showed that women lost libido when they felt like their husbands were dependents? That tends to happen when the other person has no clue how to take over a task. In contrast, showing your spouse that "I value what you do, and I understand how hard this is, but I can take over if necessary" is sexy. It's teamwork. And it makes you grateful all over again that you're married to someone who pays attention!

Some of us may need to understudy for a paycheck too. We all need to be able to earn some money in a pinch. Even if your spouse is the main breadwinner, you don't know when health concerns may mean they have to take a back seat. Perhaps the economy could change and their job could be unstable, or they may need to go back to school to retrain. To be a team, you need to be able to step in for each other as your family works out your next steps. If you're a stay-at-home spouse, make sure you keep any qualifications you have up-to-date (if it's financially feasible) or get some qualifications that are easy to renew. Research jobs that

The Power of Understudies

Respondents who were confident their spouse could take care of the house if the respondent had a minor surgery were

- 7.6 times more likely to have above average Relationship Flourishing scores[1]
- 16.7 times more likely to agree their spouse does their fair share of housework[2]

Additionally, women who were confident their spouse could take care of the house if they had a minor surgery were 76% more likely to orgasm every time they have sex[3] and 4.9 times more likely to be sexually satisfied.[4] Men who were confident their spouse could take care of the house were 2.2 times more likely to be sexually satisfied.[5]

you'd be able to step into. See if you can turn some of your hobbies or skills into income, like housecleaning, lawncare, childcare, or party planning. It makes you and your family feel less vulnerable and takes stress off your spouse as you look toward the future.

Take Initiative to Deal with the Things Holding You Back

In chapter 1, we told you about that marriage triangle. It illustrated that we're either going to be moving away from each other or moving toward each other; moving away from God or moving toward God. Movement is a given; direction is not. But direction is actually more important than position. A tortoise pointed in the right direction will eventually get to the finish line, but a hare that is miles ahead will lose the race if it stops moving and goes to sleep under a tree. If we don't take the initiative to grow and change, we will settle into stagnation, unfairly forcing our spouse to bear the brunt of our failure to grow.

I (Sheila) was forty-two the first time my back started to spasm. You know that twinge you get when you turn wrong, and you know that if you do it again, your whole back will seize up and you won't be able to move? I've had that too; the spasms I'm talking about are worse. One particular muscle spasms rhythmically, every thirty seconds or so. It's agony. It doesn't happen often, but a few times a year—often when I'm standing on my feet all day getting a big holiday meal together—I will set it off. I've missed several important family events because I'd get everything ready and then be in too much pain to enjoy it.

I didn't want that to be my future. So I started taking exercise classes to strengthen my core. I changed my sleeping position and bought new pillows. I developed the habit of spending my workdays switching between a standing desk and a chair. I haven't yet completely cracked the code of what ails my back, but I'm slowly improving, and the spasming is becoming less frequent because of all the work I put in.

Now, I could have just expected Keith to fill in for me whenever I started feeling a back twinge. But I didn't marry Keith to allow me to get lazy about my health and well-being. I married to enjoy life to the fullest, and I owe Keith—and my kids and grandkids—my effort at being the best I can be. I owe him my initiative to get better. When Rebecca couldn't do anything but cough, Connor needed to step in. But there is a difference between being your spouse's understudy when a problem crops up and relying on your spouse so that you don't have to do the work of making yourself better. As Paul tells us in Galatians 6, we bear each other's burdens, but we still have to work on our capacity to carry our own loads (vv. 2, 5).

Part of carrying your own load is taking initiative for the stuff that should naturally come under your purview. Some of those things are pretty basic, like taking care of your own personal hygiene or making your own medical appointments. Others are more difficult, such as getting ourselves on a positive health trajectory. In our survey, 45.5% of women and 37.8% of men said that they were concerned for their spouse if they continued on their current health trajectory. And that impacts marital and sexual satisfaction too. When people reported being concerned about their spouse's health trajectory:

Who Makes the Healthcare Appointments?

All of us need to visit the dentist and the doctor. But instead of taking care of this individually, in most marriages one spouse bears the burden for both of you. That arrangement isn't healthy, likely because it's signaling a broader dynamic in which one person is doing things for another that they really should do for themselves. Men reported that 6.2% of them do the majority of medical and dental appointment booking for the two of them, compared with a whopping 66.4% of women.

Compared to couples who split medical and dental appointment booking evenly, a husband who does the lion's share of appointment booking is 1.9 times more likely to have a below average Relationship Flourishing score,[6] while wives are 1.7 times more likely to have a below average Relationship Flourishing score.[7] When spouses share scheduling the medical and dental appointments, though, the marriage flourishes!

- Respondents were 83% more likely to have a below average Relationship Flourishing score.[8]
- Women were 76% more likely to be dissatisfied with their sex life.[9]
- Men were 68% more likely to be dissatisfied with their sex life.[10]

The moral of the story: Caring for ourselves as best as we can also helps our marriage!

Nathan married Emma because he was over the moon in love with her. She understood him so deeply. She was compassionate to all, ready with a listening ear. Emma also suffered from anxiety and depression. While she had been working on these things prior to meeting Nathan, once their relationship got serious, she began to rely on him more and more to regulate her moods for her instead of doing the self-care exercises her therapist had been prescribing. Now, when Nathan arrives home from work, he frequently

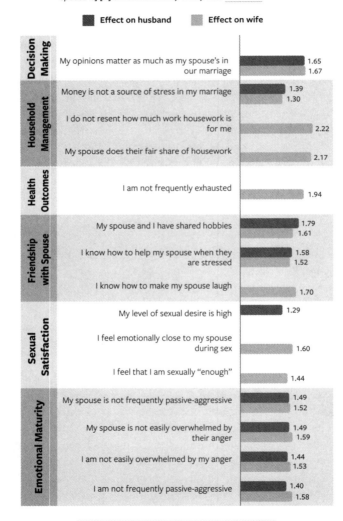

Figure 6.1

How does each spouse making medical and dental appointments for themselves affect marriages?

To interpret these data, use the following: If [I / my spouse] book(s) [my/their] own medical and dental appointments, then [I am / my spouse is] [#] times more likely to say that _____.

■ Effect on husband   ▨ Effect on wife

Decision Making

My opinions matter as much as my spouse's in our marriage — 1.65 / 1.67

Household Management

Money is not a source of stress in my marriage — 1.39 / 1.30

I do not resent how much work housework is for me — 2.22

My spouse does their fair share of housework — 2.17

Health Outcomes

I am not frequently exhausted — 1.94

Friendship with Spouse

My spouse and I have shared hobbies — 1.79 / 1.61

I know how to help my spouse when they are stressed — 1.58 / 1.52

I know how to make my spouse laugh — 1.70

Sexual Satisfaction

My level of sexual desire is high — 1.29

I feel emotionally close to my spouse during sex — 1.60

I feel that I am sexually "enough" — 1.44

Emotional Maturity

My spouse is not frequently passive-aggressive — 1.49 / 1.52

My spouse is not easily overwhelmed by their anger — 1.49 / 1.59

I am not easily overwhelmed by my anger — 1.44 / 1.53

I am not frequently passive-aggressive — 1.40 / 1.58

KEY TAKEAWAY: Dealing with your own appointment booking is associated with better marital flourishing finds her curled up in the bedroom, watching Netflix, having not yet showered. He understands Emma can't change how she feels, but he wishes she would change what she does. And he wonders how they can ever have children together if Emma won't put in the effort to do the things that she knows promote good mental health, like going outside once a day for a walk, eating well, or seeing her therapist.

We've talked to couples in which one spouse has trauma or some other issue in their background that is triggering anger issues, anxiety episodes, and more. We've talked to couples in which one has been dealing with sexual dysfunction disorders that make intercourse impossible (such as sexual pain or erectile dysfunction). And in too many cases, the spouse with the problem refuses to seek help and, when pushed to do so, pushes back, saying their spouse should "accept them just as they are." Now, it's true that we need to accept one another, especially when we promise "in sickness and in health." But that doesn't mean we no longer have to strive to be better. Wanting to avoid the uncomfortable, scary, and vulnerable work of getting better may be understandable, but it is deeply unfair to your spouse and certainly won't help your marriage to thrive.

Accommodation, Yes. Free Pass, No.

Many of us deal with conditions that make life harder for us than for other people. Some of us may have ADHD, OCD, or other neurodiversity. Accomplishing basic tasks or staying up-to-date on finances, errands, or housework can seem beyond our capacity. Sometimes the one who is living with one of these conditions can honestly be doing their best, but their effort is not recognized by their spouse, who doesn't understand the challenges their spouse faces. Educating ourselves about conditions (like ADHD or PTSD or anxiety) not only shows we truly want to know our spouse but also helps us not make things worse by unintentionally responding in ways our spouse will find hurtful. A spouse who doesn't understand how anxiety actually works might ask,

"Why do you always blow things out of proportion?" rather than helping their spouse use the strategies that have been proven to work. Grasping how much of an issue impulse control is for people with ADHD might help us show more grace toward our partner when they are trying to apologize for leaving something out on the counter overnight. If the unaffected partner doesn't keep an open, compassionate mindset or take time to educate themselves, they may be overly quick to feel their spouse is using this as a crutch.

At the same time, even if something is harder for you than it is for your spouse, that does not mean that your spouse should have to take it all on. Unsurprisingly, we found that ADHD did impact couples: Our respondents were 2.8 times more likely to report that they had to give their spouse reminders to do recurring tasks if their spouse had ADHD.[11] We want to say this as gently as possible because we know the shame that can come with neurodiversity. But we also found that among respondents with a spouse with ADHD, respondents were more likely to have to remind their spouse to do recurring tasks if the husband had ADHD (67.7%) than if the wife had ADHD (45.5%). ADHD, then, is not the only issue at play, and people can't use the diagnosis as a reason not to have to fully show up in their marriage.

One thought experiment is the "singleness test." If you would have to find a way to be able to do a certain task if you were single, or if you *did* do it before you got married, then as much as possible try to find a way to be able to do it now. That doesn't mean it's easy. And if something simply isn't possible—if you would also need to get outside help to do it as a single person—then obviously this is just something outside of your capacity. If there are accommodations that would make it easier, work together to find them. Maybe you move to a no-fold laundry system, where everything stays in baskets, or you just make the same seven meals every week. I (Keith) spend much of my in-office consultation time helping families make accommodations for those with ADHD, autism, or other neurodiverse conditions, and finding ways to make everyday tasks simpler and more routine can go a long way.

Please remember, though, that saying, "Because I have this condition, I cannot be expected to try," turns your spouse into your caregiver rather than your teammate. Your spouse may be able to do most things easier than you can, but if they start doing most things, they're going to become exhausted and burnt out. That's unsustainable in the long run. Commit to doing what you are capable of handling while being wise about not exhausting or overwhelming yourself. And, of course, talk to a licensed professional who can help you figure out how to manage daily living tasks in an accessible, practical way.

Our Capacity Can Expand or Shrink

I (Sheila) grew up in the middle of Toronto and attended a downtown school that didn't even offer driver's ed. Most of the families in my neighborhood didn't have cars; everyone took the subway. Like most of my peers, I didn't get my driver's license until I was in my twenties, and for the next few years, I still rarely got behind the wheel. When we left Toronto to live in a small town, suddenly I faced a terrifying dilemma. My preference was to keep taking buses, but public transit in our small town was nowhere near as efficient as in Toronto. The kids and I just couldn't get around when Keith was at work. I realized that my family would be better off if I took the plunge, despite my fear, and started driving regularly.

Becoming comfortable driving later in life was a challenge, but my young daughters were great encouragers. For years, they would cheer and say, "Good job, Mommy! We're proud of you!" every time I parked between two cars instead of at the far end of the parking lot where it was much roomier. But facing my fears meant I could do the grocery shopping; I could get the kids to playgroup and the library and doctor's appointments. And most of all, my husband, with his really busy schedule, didn't have to worry about us being alone at home. Pushing through enlarged my capacity for what I can do, to the point that now, decades later, I regularly drive downtown in strange cities without it bothering me at all (though I still hate parking garages).

Earlier in our marriage, when we were still in Toronto, I had to grow my capacity in another way. Keith's training program meant he rarely slept, constantly had to study, and was always dealing with stress, both from the emotional toll of caring for sick children and from the incessant demands of the crazy life of a medical resident. That left my life largely untenable too. During his four-year residency, I gave birth three times. In the middle was our son, Christopher, who lived only twenty-nine days. While Keith was away from home so much, I was often left alone raising two babies while grieving another.

Keith didn't want that for me, but there was absolutely nothing he could do about it. He had to get through training (and we knew that once he did, our lives would be much better). So I faced a choice: I could grow resentful, or I could grow my capacity so that I could handle this. I chose the latter route. I sought out counseling to deal with my grief. I developed a routine to deal with the fact that I was alone with my girls so much. I made sure that we ate healthy meals and that Keith had food to take with him so that we weren't spending our whole paycheck eating out. But I had no idea how to do these things at first. I knew very little about cooking or cleaning or developing routines. But I read and experimented and put things into practice. And with each little success, I felt a greater sense of competence, which gave me more mental energy to help with the next task. I joined several playgroups so that I had other adults to talk to on a daily basis, and I had friends to help if ever I was sick and couldn't manage the kids. I went to a gym that had babysitting so I would have time off. We made it work because I took initiative to do what I could and grow my capacity.

Our son-in-law Connor recently decided that he wanted to learn how to computer code. He had been running the technical side of our blog and online world, but he wanted to learn how to do more so that he could save us even more time—and develop his skills so that he could start his own business. And he loved it! Despite never having taken computer classes while in university, soon he was learning how to analyze computer architecture and create data structures. To make time for this, he had to stop watching Netflix and other streaming services at night after the kids went to bed.

Once he cut back on those time wasters, though, he found he had even more time than he expected. He began to add going to the gym to his nighttime routine, and now he's meeting one of his other longtime goals: growing muscle. He does it all in the first two hours after the kids are in bed, so he and Rebecca still have some time together before they turn in. What he laughs about, though, is that he couldn't even imagine having the time or energy to do this before he had kids. Before the children came, he had thought he was busy. But once you have two toddlers, you realize your time is never your own. Having to be on for the kids and grab time off when he could essentially forced him to be much more efficient and intentional with his schedule. So now, with two kids, he's getting more done than he did before the children. Plus, he's increasing his skills and income potential while helping his long-term health trajectory. Taking initiative to set you and your family up to thrive in the future is a powerful way of loving and caring for your spouse.

Taking Initiative to Get Your Life on a Good Trajectory

Amanda's parents didn't have a lot of money when she was growing up, and credit card debt was always an issue. In fact, Amanda didn't know anybody in her family who didn't carry a credit card balance. When she got her first credit card at seventeen, she went on a shopping spree, running up a couple hundred dollars on her balance because she thought that was normal. She later took out tens of thousands in student loans, and by the time she graduated, she was heavily in debt. She had little money to buy a car or for repairs, so she decided that leasing was the best option.

A few years later, she met Derrick. Derrick had similarly graduated with student loan debt but had done everything he could to bring down the balance in the five years since graduation. He was now well on his way to saving for a down payment on a house. When Derrick and Amanda married, Derrick sat down with a

> ## Survey Said: Money and Finances
>
> Overall, we found that 54.3% of respondents feel that money is a source of stress in their marriage. And money stress affects other areas of your life too. Women were 78% more likely, and men 52% more likely, to be dissatisfied with their sex life if they also found money to be a source of stress.
>
> However, the more money couples earned, the less stressful money was. Compared to those who made more than $100,000 per year, those making less than $40,000 were 2.78 times more likely to report that money is a source of stress in their marriage. Higher incomes do make life easier.

spreadsheet and showed Amanda what would happen if they kept carrying credit card debt—how much longer it would take to buy a house and how much longer it would take to pay off that student loan debt. But he also showed her where they would be at thirty-five if they lived in a small apartment, got rid of the car lease, and cut down their expenses. It was a stark difference.

Amanda wasn't used to budgeting. She was used to relying on a credit card to tide her over between paychecks. But she decided that it was time to get responsible. Derrick had taken the initiative to think about their financial future, and Amanda did something that perhaps is even harder: She took the initiative to change her financial habits so that they as a couple would be better off and able to thrive (and even able to be more generous with others who needed help).

Few of us have life totally figured out when we walk down the aisle. Maybe we're super good with money, like Derrick, but we can't cook. Or we don't know how to entertain and have people over for dinner. Or we don't know anything about looking after babies, keeping our cholesterol low, or managing insurance plans. It's okay not to know these things! But it makes a tremendous difference when we take the initiative to learn. And if it's our spouse who does the learning, then if we jump on board with them, it also enhances teamwork.

If your spouse is learning about something that will ultimately help your family, recognize that they are saving you some work while making your life better. Support them on this journey. If you can't jump on board with their solutions, figure out one for yourself. If your spouse wants to go vegan to lose weight and you just can't manage it, then do some research and figure out an alternative plan so that you are also caring for your health. If your spouse is massively into certain investments you think are a bad idea, then do your own research and find an alternative (and it is okay to say no to unsafe investments!). But honor your spouse for the time that they are putting into trying to grow your family, and join them in a way you can authentically embrace.

Taking Initiative for Your Family of Origin

Keith is one of four brothers who are all married, but I (Sheila) have been around for about fifteen years longer than the next daughter-in-law in the family. I've become the default person to host family events and organize things with the extended clan. But recently, when it came time to think about retirement homes for Keith's parents, I texted one sister-in-law to ask what she thought—and she shot me down pretty quickly. "The guys can figure it out. They're the kids, not us." I was actually quite glad to be let off the hook, and the brothers certainly did figure it out together.

Your parents are still your parents when you marry. And keeping up with extended family does take work. Birthdays, anniversaries, and graduations need to be marked. Holiday gatherings need to be coordinated across many different family schedules. Parties need to be hosted, gifts need to be bought, and phone calls need to be made. What can happen in marriage, though, is that this work—often known as "kinkeeping"—is taken on by women. Among our respondents, kinkeeping was either split evenly by family of origin (49.7% of couples) or the entire task was owned by the wife (46.8% of couples).[12] Very few men took on the kinkeeping for both families of origin. And what happens when wives take on the task of caring for his family as well as her own? They are

- 94% more likely to have a below average Trust in Close Relationships score[13]
- 36% more likely to have a below average Relationship Flourishing score[14]
- 39% more likely to be dissatisfied with their sex life[15]
- 28% more likely not to orgasm every time they have sex[16]

When kinkeeping is split between both spouses, marriages do much better.

Figure 6.2

How does splitting kinkeeping between both spouses affect how men and women describe their marriages?

To interpret these data, use the following: If [I do / my spouse does] kinkeeping for [my/ their] own family of origin, then [I am / my spouse is] [#] times more likely to describe our marriage as [descriptor].

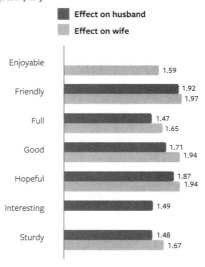

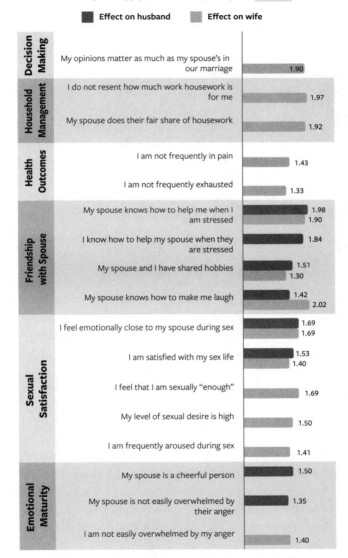

Figure 6.3

How does splitting kinkeeping between both spouses (instead of having women do all of it) affect marriages?

To interpret these data, use the following: If [I do / my spouse does] kinkeeping for [my/their] own family of origin, then [I am / my spouse is] [#] times more likely to say that _____.

Effect on husband   **Effect on wife**

Decision Making

My opinions matter as much as my spouse's in our marriage — 1.90

Household Management

I do not resent how much work housework is for me — 1.97

My spouse does their fair share of housework — 1.92

Health Outcomes

I am not frequently in pain — 1.43

I am not frequently exhausted — 1.33

Friendship with Spouse

My spouse knows how to help me when I am stressed — 1.98 / 1.90

I know how to help my spouse when they are stressed — 1.84

My spouse and I have shared hobbies — 1.51 / 1.30

My spouse knows how to make me laugh — 1.42 / 2.02

Sexual Satisfaction

I feel emotionally close to my spouse during sex — 1.69 / 1.69

I am satisfied with my sex life — 1.53 / 1.40

I feel that I am sexually "enough" — 1.69

My level of sexual desire is high — 1.50

I am frequently aroused during sex — 1.41

Emotional Maturity

My spouse is a cheerful person — 1.50

My spouse is not easily overwhelmed by their anger — 1.35

I am not easily overwhelmed by my anger — 1.40

KEY TAKEAWAY: Calling your mom yourself leads to better marital and sexual satisfaction outcomes.

Even if your spouse has a good relationship with your parents, your family of origin is still *your* family. Honor your parents by caring about their birthdays and anniversaries yourself rather than expecting your spouse to do so.

Kinkeeping, though, goes beyond trips to the drugstore for birthday cards. How you navigate extended family relationships is also important. Your spouse shouldn't have to take on the emotional labor of managing the relationship with your parents. Having in-laws who criticize, belittle, or make snide remarks is so demoralizing. If your parents are treating your spouse that way, don't let your spouse bear that burden alone. Take the initiative to care for your spouse and set proper boundaries with your family of origin. On the other hand, if one spouse has a relationship with their own parents that is fraught with tension, and the other one is more emotionally removed from the situation, sometimes a way for that spouse to show love is to run interference where they can.

Being on the same page regarding in-laws is actually more important than whether or not the relationships with those in-laws are good. One 2021 study using longitudinal data from the first sixteen years of 373 couples' marriages found that "even after controlling for husband and wife reports of connections with in-laws, discordance on closeness with the wife's family predicted divorce."[17] When husband and wife disagreed with how close they were to the wife's family, that's when problems came. The researchers go on to say, "Perhaps the most compelling evidence in support of the importance of consensus is that couples even benefit from agreeing about problematic in-law relationships. . . . Couples who agreed about conflict with the husband's mother (e.g., mother-in-law's motives for hurtful comments) were more satisfied than couples in which spouses differed in their attributions of hurtful behavior." Seeing yourselves as a team and listening to each other's perspectives on interactions with your parents and in-laws, then, is the key to making sure that in-law relationships don't disrupt your marriage—even more than those relationships actually being good.

Emotional Labor in Your Marriage Needs Your Initiative Too

Emotional labor is the work that goes into maintaining smooth relationships and managing people's emotions in the family with the goal of creating positive emotional connection. People who are skilled at emotional labor will actively notice their spouse's emotional state and try to help navigate it. If they see that their spouse is down, they may suggest something that tends to make them feel better. They are more likely to notice when one of the children is upset and try to figure out why while looking for solutions. *Should we take him out of soccer? Should we try to get her a different piano teacher?* They're also the ones managing the relationships within the family. They're trying to deal with sibling conflicts and teaching the kids to be kind to one another. They're likely the ones trying to figure out, *How can I make my marriage better?* They're reading marriage books. They're listening to relationship podcasts. They're trying different communication techniques.

When one person shoulders most of the emotional labor in the marriage, it can feel as if the other person isn't really invested, even if they swear up and down that they are. Both of us need to be bearing the work of emotional labor if a relationship is to thrive. Other responsibilities in a marriage can be divided out, but emotional labor can't because emotional labor is what creates feelings of connection. Strong marriages require that we're both dedicated to maintaining that relationship; we cannot abdicate our role and put it all on someone else. It's this emotional work that ends up mattering most in marriage because it's most correlated with how we feel about each other. If we want a marriage in which we're fully seen and still fully accepted, then we have to pay attention to this emotional side of our relationship. So let's turn to the final element of our BARE marriage acronym—*E*—and look at emotional connection.

Emotional Connection

Being Truly Seen—and Feeling Like You're Home

CHAPTER SEVEN

The Understanding You Want

Richard Carlson's book *Don't Sweat the Small Stuff . . . And It's All Small Stuff* spent two years at the top of *The New York Times* bestseller list after its release in 1997. "Don't sweat the small stuff" became the mantra of self-help gurus everywhere. Just let it go, *hakuna matata*, or even my (Sheila's) least favorite song—Bobby McFerrin's "Don't Worry, Be Happy." Around the time that song hit the airwaves, my mother took me to an all-inclusive resort in the Dominican Republic to celebrate my high school graduation. Above our bedroom was the resort's second floor disco, which seemed to have only this one song—"Don't Worry, Be Happy"— and played it repeatedly over the loudspeakers until two in the morning, making me increasingly more worried and increasingly less happy.

This idea that *you're miserable because you're worrying about things instead of letting them just slide off you* is prevalent in marriage advice. It's not your spouse's behavior that is the problem; it's what you're *telling yourself* about your spouse that's the problem! Just change how you think about it, then it won't bother you and you'll be happier.

But is this true?

A 2008 longitudinal study of 250 newlywed couples, following them for the first four years, concluded: "It depends."[1] They found that believing the best and not letting negative experiences define your relationship did end up making people feel happier in the short-term, even in marriages with frequent negative behaviors and severe problems. In the long-term, though, the outlook was rather bleak. The strategy created increasingly "steeper declines in satisfaction among spouses in more troubled marriages by allowing marital problems to worsen over time."[2] Overlooking small things in an otherwise healthy relationship can be a good strategy, but telling yourself, "Don't sweat the small stuff" or "Believe the best about your spouse" in order to paper over real issues in your marriage only makes things worse in the long run.

At its most basic, we want to feel like our spouse cares about us, that when something is bothering us, it will matter to our spouse too. If our emotional state has no effect on our spouse, then we have no connection. And if we fail to deal with issues that are bothering us, we grow an emotional chasm between us. As we tackle this last element that contributes to the marriage

When Should You Speak Up?

Some people gravitate toward saying nothing when things are bothering them, and in the long run, that doesn't always serve their marriage. Others treat small issues like big ones and blow up trust unnecessarily. So, ask yourself:

- Is this part of a wider problem that shows disrespect / hurtful behavior in the relationship?
- Is this something I can live with happily for the rest of my life, or will this cross the unfairness threshold (see chapter 4)?
- Is this something that is due to temporary stress and not indicative of bigger issues in our marriage? Is this something I can let go in order to bless my spouse now? Or is this something that will continue to cause stress long-term?

you want, let's find a way to turn the tensions we're all going to face in marriage into things that grow our emotional connection rather than creating disconnection.

Iron Sharpens Iron

Whenever we go to weddings, we like to silently pray two blessing prayers over the couple: "As iron sharpens iron, so one person sharpens another" (Prov. 27:17) and "Let us consider how we may spur one another on toward love and good deeds" (Heb. 10:24). God's heart is for marriages to make us better people, to sharpen us, to spur us on to greater Christlike character development. But marriage does not automatically do that. In some marriages, people disconnect and grow more and more selfish and even potentially emotionally abusive. Even good people can develop bad habits and treat each other badly because of these two truths of the human condition:

- Actions that are encouraged tend to be repeated.
- People tend to travel in the direction of least resistance—so the direction they are going will continue, and even accelerate, unless something stops them or causes them to change course.

As I (Sheila) was writing this, an Instagram post came across my feed in which a woman said that whenever she felt angry at her husband for leaving his stuff everywhere, she reminded herself that she'd rather pick up his stuff every day for the rest of her life than to never see him come home again. But are these truly the only two options? Pick up his things every day forever or see him walk out the door (or die)? By not saying anything, she makes it easy for him to keep leaving his stuff around. And why assume he is not open to change? He may not even notice he's doing it and might be happy to fix the problem! But if this becomes a habit for him, it's going to build and accelerate—unless you step in to address it.

Sometimes when a marriage goes south, it's truly because of a character issue in one or both spouses. But many times it can be because marriage dynamics that fostered unhelpful behaviors weren't dealt with early. If we welcome this "spur one another on toward love and good deeds" mindset, though, we create a marriage in which we are both constantly growing and becoming more Christlike. Our daughter Rebecca, who coauthored *The Great Sex Rescue* and *She Deserves Better* with me (Sheila), has shared on our *Bare Marriage* blog about how she and her husband Connor "sharpened each other" in the first few months of marriage by bringing up things that, if left unaddressed, may have spiraled into really negative patterns. Rebecca explains:

> Connor had been living with four other amazing guys who were still rooming together after our wedding. When Connor had lived in that house, they would all often stay up until 2 or 3 in the morning gaming together. Shortly after we were married, Connor went over to his old house for the first time and didn't tell me when he'd be home. Now his staying out until 2 in the morning was affecting more than just him.
>
> In the morning I told him I had no problem with him going out with the guys periodically, but he couldn't impact my night like that by doing something that would make me worry. So he always had to tell me when he'd be home (or update me if the plan changed) and then either had to be home by midnight or he could just crash at their place—either was totally fine. He agreed, and we didn't have any other issues.
>
> Similarly, I got frustrated when he'd start online games he couldn't pause in the evening. It was cutting into our time after school/work together and it meant he was completely unavailable for a minimum of 45 minutes at a time. So I told him I wanted to make sure gaming wasn't getting in the way of us and we agreed that he wouldn't start a game he couldn't pause after 9:30 PM.
>
> But Connor got frustrated with me, too. About a year into our marriage, Connor started working more and I was working from home. As a result, it was a lot easier to talk to my mom about things than to talk to Connor, who wouldn't be home for a few hours. Connor realized after a few weeks that my mom was becoming the

person I told everything to first, not him. And so he sat me down and said, "I need you to tell me about important things first before you tell your mom so that it truly is OUR life and we don't start living lives parallel to each other." It was exactly what I needed, and he was entirely right, and I made a concerted effort from that point on to make Connor my primary emotional support.

What if we hadn't said anything? What if I hadn't said I wasn't comfortable with him walking home so late, or if I hadn't spoken up about the bad gaming habits? What if he hadn't confronted me about how I wasn't turning to him for emotional support and thereby creating distance in our marriage? I'd be experiencing a lot more resentment and irritation towards Connor's friends and towards him. Connor would not be as considerate about how much time he's spent away from home or understand the impact that it has on me. Connor would not be as emotionally available if he were addicted to video games and our marriage would not have gotten such a great start if we didn't have our evenings together. I would not feel as secure and safe with my husband because I would not have given him the opportunities to be my emotional support if I were still turning to family instead of to him. By speaking up, both of us were able to put each other back on a path that was healthy and beneficial for both of us.[3]

They didn't blame or name-call. They just addressed stuff that they didn't want to see continue. And now they're on a much better trajectory!

What "Ezer Kenegdo" Tells Us about Iron Sharpening Iron

God created Eve as Adam's "ezer kenegdo," or "helper suitable for him." It's easy to assume *helper* is a subordinate term, a meaning that isn't implied in the original text. This can lead us into a distorted understanding that a wife's role is to be a subordinate rather than a partner. Theologian Carolyn Custis James took a deep dive into what *ezer kenegdo* means, looking up all twenty-one instances that *ezer* appears in the Old Testament, sixteen of which are in reference to God being Israel's helper in military terms (Defender,

Shield, Protector). This insight changed how James saw her own role in marriage. She said, "The kind of help the man needs demands full deployment of her strength, her gifts, and the best she has to offer. His life will change for the better because of what she contributes to his life. Together they will daily prove in countless and surprising ways that two are always better than one."[4]

Unfortunately, this isn't widely understood in evangelical circles, and a distorted view of womanhood teaches women that communicating directly with their husband is bad. One teacher put it like this: "A woman's . . . influence may be personal and non-directive, or directive and non-personal."[5] So, she can't ever be direct about what she feels he should change. In this worldview, the logical conclusion is that in the most personal of relationships (i.e., with her husband), a woman should be the most indirect in her communication. A woman who has bought into this teaching may silence herself and deprioritize her perspectives and desires even without realizing it. Meanwhile, her husband may have no idea this is happening. A small issue arises in the marriage and the wife dutifully tries to suppress it for years until she finally can't take it anymore and then blows up at her husband, who wonders where this all came from. Even if he is 100% on board with changing, the marriage has years of habits to undo, which wouldn't have been the case if she had just told him up front that this was an important issue to her.

One woman told us:

> I was "submissive" (aka "a doormat") for a long time and it built resentment which really hurt our relationship. Once I finally started telling my husband how much certain things bothered me—and how much resentment I had actually built up over the years—he was shocked. It taught us both a valuable lesson: someone can't fix a problem that they don't know is a problem. Now I'm far more open and honest and our relationship is so much healthier. There are healthy ways to handle conflict and being silent and suffering is not one of them. I often think back to the time that I heard that a wife's submission was "getting out of the way so God could smack your husband." I lived by that philosophy for a long

time only to find that when you're "one flesh" God smacking your husband hurts you too. But iron sharpening iron? That's a LOT less painful and a lot more fulfilling and healthy. I no longer try to be that "perfect, non-argumentative, submissive wife" and we are so much better off for it.

How to Speak Up for What You Want

A 2017 study out of New Zealand gives some clues about how we should approach problems in our marriage. Treating small problems aggressively didn't work and often created distance. However, the same was not true when big issues arose. In such cases direct, oppositional communication was best.[6] Let's turn to small problems first, and then later in the chapter we'll address how to handle bigger issues.

Imagine your spouse repeatedly leaves half-empty glasses and coffee mugs all over the house, and you find this creates stress every time you walk in the room. The first step is deciding, *How big a deal to me is this really?* If it's a small issue, that doesn't mean you don't address it. You just do it in a way that's appropriate for a small issue!

You might:

- Preface a discussion with how much you appreciate your spouse, or say something you love about them, and then state your request clearly. "I love you, babe, and love sharing a home with you. But I would appreciate it if you would stop leaving your empty glasses everywhere."
- Frame it as "I'm having this issue that you can help me with." For instance, "When you leave half-drunk glasses of water around the house, I find myself annoyed when I have to clean them up, and I don't want to be annoyed at you. I'd appreciate it if you would put them in the dishwasher or the sink."
- If nothing happens, you can revisit it: "Hey, remember when I said I'd appreciate dishes in the sink? I notice it's not being done. Do you have any other solutions?"

- If a small issue seems to be "blowing up," acknowledge that you should probably talk about it at a time when you are both in a better place to see it in perspective. But book a time to talk about it so it doesn't go unresolved and actually become a big issue.

This sounds easy enough, but what if you struggle with asking for something directly? One woman told me about a conversation between her husband and his mother that she witnessed. She and her husband were cleaning up after Thanksgiving dinner when his mom came into the kitchen and started talking about Aunt Betty and how lonely she was in the nursing home and how few people she had to talk to since so many of the other residents had dementia. When her mother-in-law left the kitchen, the wife turned to her husband and said, "Your mom wants you to visit Aunt Betty." Her husband looked flabbergasted and said, "If Mom wanted that, she would have asked me!" He called his mom back into the kitchen and said, "Are you trying to get me to visit Aunt Betty?" His mom, relieved, replied, "Well, of course! I've been waiting for you to finally get it!"

Why didn't his mom just ask? Sometimes it's the way we've been conditioned: Asking directly seems proud, selfish, or forceful (or like a sin, if you're a woman). But there's another element that's often at play, especially in marriage. Sometimes our main goal is to keep the relationship on an even keel. Asking directly for something means someone can refuse you outright. Asking indirectly allows that person to refuse without it being acknowledged openly so that you can keep up a facade that everything is fine.

Jesus told us that he is the way, the truth, and the life (John 14:6). Jesus didn't shy away from uncomfortable truths. He said them out loud. And those around him still felt incredibly loved, even though he sometimes upset the applecart. He was our great example of what "speaking the truth in love" (Eph. 4:15) means. Certainly, we need to be kind, and we always need to consider how the other person will perceive what we are saying, but if we want to have truly intimate relationships, we need to be able to share what we're thinking and feeling.

You're a Team Even When You're in Conflict

Speaking directly means owning your own thoughts and feelings, explaining what the problem is, and putting it out there so you can come up with a solution together that helps you both feel cared for. Often, by the time we're ready to share, though, it's because resentment has built up. Instead of saying, "Here's my issue; let's solve it," we frame it as, "You're the issue; here's how I'm going to solve you!" But when someone feels attacked, the ability to think rationally often disappears as the fight-flight-freeze-or-fawn response is triggered. We feel threatened, so we turn to a response that minimizes the perceived threat. That may look like fighting (being defensive, lobbing your own accusations). It may look like flight (refusing to engage, stonewalling). It may look like collapsing in a pile of tears, saying, "I'm such an awful person; why do you even want to be with me?" as a diversionary tactic to try to get the other person to stop talking about this. We'll look at these counterproductive ways of handling hard emotions later, but for now let's simply acknowledge that resolving issues is just plain difficult when someone feels under attack. That's why framing issues in marriage as a problem that we can both solve together can be so helpful.

When we frame conflicts only as a matter of who is right and who is wrong, we're saying that one person must win and one person must lose. And then, even if you win, you're going to be married to a loser! When we see the problem as separate from us, though, we overcome this dynamic. Sometimes it even helps to write the issue down on a piece of paper and then sit on the same side of the table (or sofa), looking at that issue in front of you. This short-circuits the cycle of feeling attacked because you've become teammates working toward the same goal rather than opponents attacking each other. Fixing things starts with correctly identifying the issue—so you can find the win-win.

171

How Do You Identify the Real Issues?

Imagine a conflict in which you can't come to an agreement—say she wants to move closer to her mom, and he wants to stay where they are. It seems like one has to win, and one will inevitably lose. There's no real way to get them both what they want. But let's take a step back and identify the real underlying issues.

Why does she want to move? Perhaps because she's overwhelmed with the kids and rarely gets a break, she hasn't been able to make a lot of friends where they live, and she doesn't like

---

The Rules of Engagement for Arguing from . . . High School Debate?

Did any of you do high school debate? If so, you likely remember putting in hours assembling arguments for and against each side of an issue, using mountains of note cards, and learning a good filing system in the process.

It turns out that those skills are also important in marriage!

The Kansas Marital Conflict Survey asks couples how well they can identify what *specifically* they are disagreeing about and what they are agreeing about. It also asks if you can both express how the other feels about the issue and if you can both express the other's viewpoint nearly as well as you can your own.[7]

Compared with women who were confident that both spouses could express the other's viewpoint *every time* they had conflict, women who said both spouses did this

- *frequently* (but not every time) were 1.6 times more likely to be dissatisfied sexually;[8]
- *sometimes* were 3.2 times more likely to be dissatisfied sexually;[9]
- *rarely* were 6.0 times more likely to be dissatisfied sexually;[10] and
- *never* were 14.2 times more likely to be dissatisfied sexually.[11]

Being able to articulate each of your points of view is associated with higher Relationship Flourishing scores too.

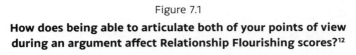

Figure 7.1

How does being able to articulate both of your points of view during an argument affect Relationship Flourishing scores?[12]

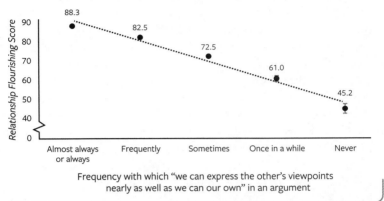

Frequency with which "we can express the other's viewpoints nearly as well as we can our own" in an argument

their apartment. She misses her old friends. Why does he *not* want to move? Perhaps he likes the job that he has right now and feels like there may be room for promotion.

The issues, then, are not really about whether they should move or not; they're about her feeling overwhelmed, unsupported, and lonely, and him wanting a job with a promising future. When you identify those as the issues, you can start asking different questions, like, *How can we help her feel less overwhelmed? Are there other ways for us to make friends with other couples? Does she need more support with managing the kids' behavior? Can we pay for a gym membership to help her make friends and utilize the babysitting to get some time off? Do we need to join a new church with more people our age who are more welcoming? Can we move to a better neighborhood?* Or you could ask, *Are there promising job prospects for him closer to her parents?* When you're asking questions that get at what you both emotionally need, you're better able to come up with solutions you may not have thought of. And that brainstorming can actually grow you closer as a couple. Conflict can actually bring connection.

Asking Why

Asking questions can help unpack what is really going on in your emotional world and in your spouse's emotional world and can help spur brainstorming. Sakichi Toyoda, the founder of Toyota car company, noticed that when a problem popped up, the solution to the problem ultimately lay in addressing a root cause. But finding that root cause isn't always as easy as you might think. It usually requires some digging, so he began asking, "Why?" But he didn't just ask it once. He found you typically have to ask five times before you identify what the real core issue is. His "five whys" method has been widely adopted in the corporate world, but it can work well for resolving marriage conflicts too.

Let's say you find that the most difficult part of your day is the morning, when you are often testy with each other then leave the house grumpy, which taints your whole day. And you and your spouse want to solve this problem. Let's ask the five whys!

Why do we always fight so much in the mornings and start our days off grumpy? Because our mornings are chaos.

Why are our mornings chaos? Because the children don't get up on time and can't find their homework, and the laundry isn't done, and nobody has clean underwear, and there's nothing to make for lunches.

Why does this all happen? Because there's no routine the night before to get things ready.

Why is there no routine? Because we're spending our nights on Netflix and time wasters.

Why are we spending time on time wasters? At this point there may be a whole number of reasons:

- Because we've never talked about how to have a good routine to get things ready.
- Because we're so emotionally exhausted from our jobs that we feel we need to do absolutely nothing.
- Because the kids are so rowdy at night and so badly behaved that we're depressed.

And so on. Each stage of questioning can lead to insight into where we are emotionally, which can then lead to very different solutions. As we ask the *why* questions, we get a window into our own emotional world and into our spouse's emotional world. And we may even come up with practical solutions to problems that have been bothering us!

What If the Problem Doesn't Get Resolved?

What if, after all the discussion and brainstorming, you still don't see eye to eye? If the issue is a small one, you can agree to disagree. If it is something you would have preferred but could live without, then sometimes for the good of the relationship you can choose to just let it slide. But that is not the only option available, and it is likely not the best option in cases where you feel your spouse is doing something that is harming rather than building your marriage.

That New Zealand study, for instance, found that for big issues that were harming your marriage, favoring "direct and firm" (though not unkind!) communication over "affectionate and minimizing" is key.[13] Your message to your spouse should be crystal clear: "This is an important issue to me, and something needs to change. I am open to discussing how things might change, but it is not healthy for our marriage to leave the issue unaddressed."

Some spouses, though, just don't get with the program, and they refuse to talk about it. They try to shut down the conversation by stonewalling, crying, or getting defensive. When you start asking for things to change and holding people accountable, you're often framed as the problem. But if there is something your spouse is doing that is increasing distance in your marriage and decreasing emotional connection, you should not be painted as the problem for bringing it up. If your spouse needs some time to get their bearings, then yes, respect that. But it is unacceptable to use this as an excuse to permanently avoid engaging with the issue. If this happens, it is perfectly reasonable to say to your spouse, "You may not want to talk about this, but this is not going away.

This is important because our marriage is important. And if you can't talk about this now, we will still have to talk about it later. So, we'll revisit this on Tuesday night."

Refusing to engage with your spouse's emotions is a form of emotional immaturity, which can grow into abuse all too easily. Despite what you may have been taught, you are not being disrespectful if you want to address issues in your marriage. In fact, it is an attempt to build intimacy, not to destroy it. It can be difficult to be assertive and stand up for yourself when you've been told your whole life that to do so is selfish or disrespectful, or when others have punished you in various ways when you've asserted your opinion. But what is it that God ultimately wants? He wants us all to be "conformed to the image of his Son" (Rom. 8:29). And in the same way that loving ourselves means doing what is for our best rather than merely whatever feels good, when our spouse is acting in a way that is making them less Christlike, loving them means not accepting that. God can use marriage to help us grow emotionally if we are willing to let him.

But that can't happen if we allow stonewalling or defensiveness or accusations like "it takes two to tango" to be the last word. Of course, it is always vital to practice humility and ask, "Am I contributing to the problem?" and if so (even partly), take ownership of your part. But remember: Your spouse doesn't have the right to reap the benefits of having you emotionally engaged with them if they sow disconnection by refusing to emotionally engage with you.

This is where the concept of boundaries comes in. When talking about issues hasn't resolved something that is putting distance between you, it may be time to change how you act. In their book *Boundaries*, Dr. Henry Cloud and Dr. John Townsend speak of the "law of sowing and reaping" that God baked into the world.[14] What we sow, we are supposed to reap. But often people interrupt the law of sowing and reaping in the interest of keeping the peace. One spouse sows discord by speaking harshly and refusing to engage emotionally, and the other walks on eggshells to avoid setting off the spouse while simultaneously running interference with the children so they don't feel neglected. One spouse is sowing something ugly, but the other spouse is reaping the discomfort by turning themselves inside out to minimize the negativity in the marriage or the family. The wrong spouse is bearing the burden for the bad behavior.

It is a much healthier response to set an appropriate boundary so that the law of sowing and reaping is not interrupted. A boundary isn't about controlling the other person; it is merely stating what you are and are not willing to do. Here are just a few examples:

- "I am not willing to be in a room with you when you yell and criticize me. From now on, when you do this, I will go to another room and take the kids with me too. I'm happy to discuss things calmly when you're ready."
- "The kids and I want to be at church on time so that we don't miss Sunday school, seeing friends, and the start of the service. It's very difficult when you're consistently fifteen or twenty minutes late. From now on, we will be leaving the house at the right time to get to church, and we hope that you will be there with us."
- "I've noticed that you are often exhausted and unable to be present with me and the kids on the weekends, but at the same time you're staying up until two in the morning on your phone. I am not willing to keep the kids quiet or take them out of the house so that you can nap in the afternoon on the weekends."
- "I am happy to do the laundry, but I am not willing to pick up clothes that are strewn around the floor. From now on, I will only be washing clothes that are in the hamper."

We might feel like we are being mean saying things like this and following through on them. (If your spouse is acting from a place of emotional immaturity, they may say that to your face!)

177

But setting a boundary simply allows the person to reap the consequences of what they have sown while simultaneously allowing us to function with less stress, making life more manageable.

What if you are worried that doing this will trigger rage or even violence? Then please call a domestic abuse hotline, because your marriage is not safe (more on this in the appendix). We wish we could tell you that when you ask clearly for what you want and maintain healthy boundaries, your spouse will get on board and things will improve. But sometimes abusive spouses can manipulate you into thinking you are the cause of their bad behavior or that you are hurting them because you're not being forgiving or gracious enough.[15] They paint you as the problem for bringing up the issue because they don't want to change, and they want to maintain the status quo. If you think that dynamic is occurring, seek out a licensed counselor to talk to (as an individual, not as a couple, since marriage counseling is contraindicated when abuse may be occurring). And if you do not feel safe bringing up issues in your marriage or if your spouse intimidates, threatens, or otherwise makes it feel dangerous when you do, that is abusive behavior, and you need to protect yourself.

Who Initiates Repair?

Inevitably, even in healthy marriages, we are going to say or do things that hurt our spouse. That's the nature of being two imperfect people in such a close relationship. That's why learning how to repair is a crucial skill in building emotional connection. Taking the initiative to repair a rift, even a small one, can be a healing gift. After days of feeling tension and distance, when one person chooses to bridge that gap by taking a risk and being vulnerable, it's like rain during a drought.

We asked couples, "Who takes the initiative to repair when there's a breach in your relationship?" In our survey, 24.7% of men and 33.2% of women reported that they did an outsized portion of relationship repair in their marriage. And when one spouse tended to do most of the repair work, the relationship suffered.

Figure 7.2

How does doing the lion's share of repair in marriage affect your marriage and sex life?

To interpret these data, use the following: If [I do / my spouse does] the vast majority of relational repair work in our marriage, then [I am / my spouse is] [#] times more likely to say that _____.

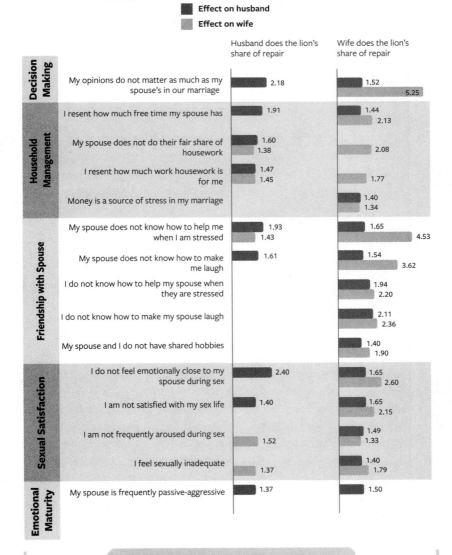

■ **Effect on husband**
■ **Effect on wife**

	Husband does the lion's share of repair		Wife does the lion's share of repair	
Decision Making				
My opinions do not matter as much as my spouse's in our marriage	2.18		1.52	5.25
Household Management				
I resent how much free time my spouse has	1.91		1.44	2.13
My spouse does not do their fair share of housework	1.60 / 1.38		2.08	
I resent how much work housework is for me	1.47 / 1.45		1.77	
Money is a source of stress in my marriage			1.40 / 1.34	
Friendship with Spouse				
My spouse does not know how to help me when I am stressed	1.93 / 1.43		1.65	4.53
My spouse does not know how to make me laugh	1.61		1.54	3.62
I do not know how to help my spouse when they are stressed			1.94 / 2.20	
I do not know how to make my spouse laugh			2.11 / 2.36	
My spouse and I do not have shared hobbies			1.40 / 1.90	
Sexual Satisfaction				
I do not feel emotionally close to my spouse during sex	2.40		1.65	2.60
I am not satisfied with my sex life	1.40		1.65	2.15
I am not frequently aroused during sex	1.52		1.49 / 1.33	
I feel sexually inadequate	1.37		1.40 / 1.79	
Emotional Maturity				
My spouse is frequently passive-aggressive	1.37		1.50	

KEY TAKEAWAY: Being alone in initiating repair in your marriage is an intimacy killer.

Figure 7.3

How does length of marriage affect Relationship Flourishing scores in women who do more than their fair share of relational repair?[16]

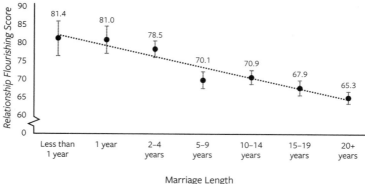

- Men and women who did an outsized portion of repair in their marriages were 2.0 and 3.3 times more likely to have below average Trust in Close Relationships scores, respectively.[17]
- Men and women who did an outsized portion of repair in their marriages were 1.4 and 2.1 times more likely to be dissatisfied with their sex lives, respectively.[18]

While the marriage suffers when initiating repair is one-sided, the effects are more profound when women are the initiators. When we looked at the relationship between initiating repair work and length of marriage, once again we found that carrying the burden of repair hurts women's marital flourishing over time. The same relationship wasn't found with men.

How Do You Initiate Repair?

When mistakes are minor, repair often just takes a hug, an "I'm sorry," and a few deep breaths. Your spouse needs to have their feelings acknowledged, heard, and understood, but often that's enough. Other times, though, we have trouble admitting our fault until after an argument (or two or three!), and in the interim, we may have said some hurtful things. Repair then requires a more thorough acknowledgment of the hurt caused while expressing how you're going to do things better from now on.

Some conflicts, though, attack the very core of the marriage—an emotional or physical affair, porn use, lying, or an addiction. To think these should be dealt with in the same way as the more minor or momentary infractions is utter foolishness. Repair in these major cases involves calling the betrayal exactly what it is. Something can't be fully dealt with or fully forgiven if it can't even be fully named. Until the initial offense is properly addressed, no restoration or rebuilding is possible.

Ruth Bell Graham famously said that a good marriage is the union of two good forgivers. Fair enough, provided it is also accompanied by the idea that we should get good at repenting too. Emphasizing the importance of forgiveness is helpful in many circumstances, but it can cause tremendous problems in others. Quoting the verse "Be kind to one another, tenderhearted, forgiving one another, as God in Christ has forgiven you" (Eph. 4:32 NRSVue) is one thing if you are trying to help two reasonable people have a bit more empathy for each other's quirks, but it is an entirely different thing when it is used to fast-track forgiveness after a serious breach of the marriage covenant.

Repair needs two things: The offender needs to repent, and the offended party needs to forgive. But these two things are not equal, and for repair and reconciliation to happen, one is contingent on the other. The offender must admit what they have done—admit the depth of the hurt they have caused—make plans to heal that rift, and then follow through before trust can properly be rebuilt. Yet some Christian teachings explicitly say that forgiving and rebuilding trust can be simultaneous—or even that it will be easier for the offender to do the right thing if they are forgiven first![19] That's backward and is a distortion of the scriptural view of repentance in human relationships (see Matt. 5:23–24).

It is "cheap grace" that requires the person who did the wrong to merely say they are sorry and receive instant absolution. In circles where this view of forgiveness holds sway, the goal is the preservation of the marriage, so the advice tends to be aimed at the offended spouse, who is often the most invested in fixing the marriage. The offender says they're sorry (which might just mean they are sorry they got caught), and now the offended spouse is told to forgive and restore the relationship. And if they aren't willing or able to do that, the wronged spouse is shamed for their lack of forgiveness or for their lack of ability to trust again. Yet in Scripture, repentance is not simply saying you're sorry; it is living a changed life. When trust is broken, trust needs to be rebuilt. And if you're the one who broke it, you must take the responsibility to do the rebuilding. The bigger the issue, the longer the repair has to be. It is not wrong for the offended spouse to want to see "fruit in keeping with repentance" (Matt. 3:8) before they put themselves in the vulnerable position of trusting again.

For instance, when someone who has been watching porn for years expects the betrayed spouse to jump right back into sex just because the porn user apologized, that isn't fair, nor is it wise. Taking a sexual fast while the offender works on feeling intimacy outside of sex, on dealing with counterproductive coping mechanisms, and on learning to be truly emotionally vulnerable is the better course of action. If someone has racked up credit card debt and kept it secret, a period of time where they can only carry cash and don't have access to the credit cards may be needed to get the family financially back on an even keel until they show their spouse they're safe again. And in cases of abuse, separation (and even divorce) is usually warranted, with the offended spouse encouraged to go on and build a life for themselves while the offender gets help individually. If the abuser ever does fully repent and heal, and the offended partner is willing to reconcile, that may be an option. But the focus needs to be on healing and repentance, not on reconciliation. And trust, in the case of abuse, needs years to safely earn back. Licensed clinicians working with abusers say this rarely happens.

What If Trust Remains Broken?

If someone has violated the marriage covenant, through infidelity, through abuse, through chronic dangerous issues that they will not address (by getting help for substance abuse issues or mental health issues that pose a danger to you and/or your children), then they are the ones who have abandoned the marriage, not you. In such cases, you are not bound to them. Seeking separation or divorce is not you ending the marriage; it is merely making official and visible what they have already done. God cares more about the people in the marriage than the marriage itself, and he does not expect you to sacrifice your well-being and safety in order to cover or enable someone else's sin. Longitudinal studies have shown that children do better after divorce than they do if parents remain in a high-conflict, abusive, or destructive marriage.[20] Please seek out a trauma-informed, licensed therapist and any legal help you need to get counsel and navigate next steps.

God does not ask the betrayed spouse to do more than he asks of himself. In Scripture, God compares his relationship with his people to a marriage, so how he treats his covenant with Israel gives us some insight into how marriage should work. Jeremiah 3 tells the story of how God gave Israel "a certificate of divorce" (v. 8) because of her unfaithfulness in chasing after other gods. God had kept his part of the covenant, but Israel had not. By giving the certificate of divorce, God made plain and visible the fact that Israel had already ended the covenant through her own actions. The covenant was over, not because of what God had done but because of what Israel had done. One person's sin *can break a covenant all on its own.* And when a covenant has been broken, keeping up a facade that nothing is wrong is just plain offensive (see Isa. 1:12–14).

An Ounce of Prevention Is Worth a Pound of Cure

If we learn to deal with rifts early in the marriage, before they become serious problems, then many couples can avoid some of these heartbreaking episodes. Bring up issues when they're still small issues. When you make a mistake and hurt your spouse, repent and make it right before it becomes a big deal. And remember that you are "iron sharpening iron," engaging with issues as they arise, confident that as a team you can solve them. By "speaking the truth in love," communicating directly with each other while always seeking what's best for your marriage, you will help each other become more Christlike. In becoming more like Christ, though, we don't become less of ourselves; we become who we were truly made to be. So, let's talk next about how you can enter into each other's deep inner lives and grow the intimacy you long for.

CHAPTER EIGHT

The Closeness You Want

In November 2023, the longest marriage of a United States president ended when Rosalynn Carter passed away at age ninety-six. Her husband Jimmy, in a wheelchair and unable to talk, insisted on attending the funeral. Hunched in his chair in the front row, flanked by his daughter and his son, he paid tribute to the woman he had loved for eight decades. Their daughter, Amy Lynn, read a letter that Jimmy had written to his bride seventy-five years earlier, while he was serving in the navy. "My darling, every time I have ever been away from you, I have been thrilled when I return to discover just how wonderful you are. While I am away, I try to convince myself that you really are not, could not be as sweet and beautiful as I remember. But when I see you, I fall in love with you all over again. Does that seem strange to you? It doesn't to me."[1]

Isn't that what we want—to feel that joy of discovery when we see our spouse, that spark of deep knowing, deep longing, deep loving? Intimacy means that you see all of someone. You know what makes them tick. You know what they're scared of and what they dream of. It's the difference between knowing about someone and knowing someone, between understanding someone's emotional state and actually entering into it with them. True intimacy requires vulnerability. We must have courage to share what's on our hearts, and we must provide safety so that our spouse can do the same.

Do You Open Up to Your Spouse?

The impact on Relationship Flourishing scores of being confident your spouse will share things with you is shown in figures 8.1 and 8.2. Opening up emotionally helps your marriage. And one spouse agreeing that their spouse could open up to them was associated with 3.12 times higher odds of the other spouse also agreeing.[2] And it affects other areas of marriage too!

- Women who agreed that their husbands would share things with them were 1.52 times more likely to orgasm every time they have sex.[3]
- Women who strongly agreed that their husbands would share their hearts were 5.03 times more likely to be satisfied with their sex life than those who disagreed.[4]
- Men who believed that their wives would share things with them were 4.59 times more likely to be satisfied with their sex life than those who disagreed.[5]

Understanding Different Levels of Communication

In his book *Why Am I Afraid to Tell You Who I Am?* John Powell identifies five levels of communication—cliché/surface talk, facts, opinions, feelings, and vulnerability—with the most surface level of communication being the most common and fewer and fewer people having access to the deeper levels as you progress toward higher levels of intimacy.[6] Here are some examples of these levels:

Cliché/surface talk: "What a long day!"

Facts: "I'm going to be late tomorrow because of a meeting at work."

Opinions: "My boss calls too many meetings."

Feelings: "I'm starting to dread going to work on days my boss is there because she always asks things at the last minute when it's impossible to get done in time."

Figure 8.1

How does men feeling confident their wife will share things with them affect both partners' Relationship Flourishing scores?[7]

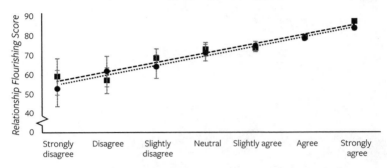

Men's Agreement That Their Wife Will Share Things with Them

■ Men's Relationship Flourishing scores

● Women's Relationship Flourishing scores

Figure 8.2

How does women feeling confident that their husband will share things with them affect both partners' Relationship Flourishing scores?[8]

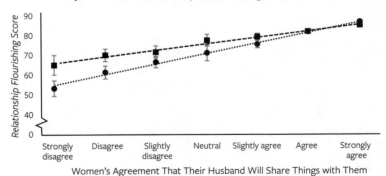

Women's Agreement That Their Husband Will Share Things with Them

■ Men's Relationship Flourishing scores

● Women's Relationship Flourishing scores

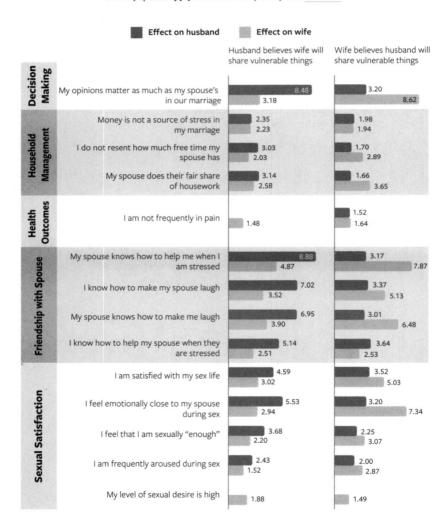

Figure 8.3

How does being confident your spouse will share vulnerable things with you affect your marital and sexual satisfaction?

To interpret these data, use the following: If [I / my spouse] believe(s) the other will share vulnerable things with [me/them], then [I am / my spouse is] [#] times more likely to say that _____.

Effect on husband   Effect on wife

	Husband believes wife will share vulnerable things	Wife believes husband will share vulnerable things
Decision Making		
My opinions matter as much as my spouse's in our marriage	8.48 / 3.18	3.20 / 8.62
Household Management		
Money is not a source of stress in my marriage	2.35 / 2.23	1.98 / 1.94
I do not resent how much free time my spouse has	3.03 / 2.03	1.70 / 2.89
My spouse does their fair share of housework	3.14 / 2.58	1.66 / 3.65
Health Outcomes		
I am not frequently in pain	1.48	1.52 / 1.64
Friendship with Spouse		
My spouse knows how to help me when I am stressed	8.88 / 4.87	3.17 / 7.87
I know how to make my spouse laugh	7.02 / 3.52	3.37 / 5.13
My spouse knows how to make me laugh	6.95 / 3.90	3.01 / 6.48
I know how to help my spouse when they are stressed	5.14 / 2.51	3.64 / 2.53
Sexual Satisfaction		
I am satisfied with my sex life	4.59 / 3.02	3.52 / 5.03
I feel emotionally close to my spouse during sex	5.53 / 2.94	3.20 / 7.34
I feel that I am sexually "enough"	3.68 / 2.20	2.25 / 3.07
I am frequently aroused during sex	2.43 / 1.52	2.00 / 2.87
My level of sexual desire is high	1.88	1.49

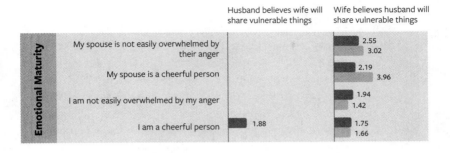

KEY TAKEAWAY: Emotional intimacy and vulnerability are a key part of building a flourishing marriage.

Vulnerability (fears and dreams): "I worry that technology is moving so fast that I'm not going to be able to do this job well for very much longer. I might become obsolete. I wish I had chosen a different path a decade ago. This seems like a dead end."

The depth to which you can share with someone reflects the intimacy of your relationship. You share surface talk about the weather at the local grocery store and with people in the elevator at your building, you share opinions about the new schedule with fellow parents warming the benches as you watch hockey practice, but you share your deepest fears with your sister. And hopefully with your spouse!

Many marriages, though, stall on levels 2 and 3, sharing details about what groceries need to be picked up and whose birthday party they're going to this weekend. The couple talks about budgeting and what they think about the sermon this week. They may go on date nights. They may even laugh at the same Netflix shows. But if they don't actually communicate at the "feelings" level and beyond, the marriage is always going to feel like there's something not quite *there*. Sure, you may think, *But I provide for my family and we spend time together*, or *We've created a good life together*.

But consider that there are only a few people you could ever get to levels 4 and 5 with because that level of vulnerability needs a level of trust you won't experience in most relationships. Do you want your spouse to be able to be more intimate with other people—say, a best friend or a sibling—than they are with you? Don't you want to be in that most intimate and vulnerable circle? One study of 239 couples looked at "dispositional authenticity," or the ability of people to share authentically about their inner lives. When both could share, researchers labeled that quality "mutuality," concluding, "Mutuality, the sense of oneness with a partner in a romantic relationship, has been found to promote the greatest level of satisfaction and authentic behaviour in romantic relationships. Individual and relationship outcomes were maximized for both partners in relationships with higher mutuality."[9] In other words, if you want to have the best marriage you can, you have to open up and share!

Why is this so hard? Well, a marriage that stagnates at levels 2 and 3 may actually feel safe since opening up to your spouse can require you to confront things about yourself that you don't want to face. But avoiding vulnerability does not lead to a fulfilling or rich life. There's a special kind of loneliness when you hide your emotional life from your spouse. While a level 3 relationship with a coworker may feel warm and close and fun, a level 3 relationship with a spouse may feel lonely, disjointed, and alienating. When your level of closeness doesn't match what your relationship should enjoy, it can even feel like a rejection.

Researchers at Harvard launched their "Study of Adult Development" in 1938, not knowing at the time the reach this incredible study would have. Early on, it followed 724 men, some from the Harvard community and some from a more impoverished community nearby. Over the decades they added participants' spouses and kids, and even grandkids, to the study, which has now been running for over eighty years. No other longitudinal study has ever lasted this long, and it's given us a wealth of information, specifically about what enhances people's longevity and well-being. And overwhelmingly it's one thing: connection. People with meaningful relationships do better, experience more joy, and live longer. In fact, those relationships

190

are more important to those outcomes than exercise, income, or career success.[10] Part of living a good, fulfilled life is being able to be vulnerable and intimate with other people.

Mourn with Those Who Mourn

When we asked survey respondents how many people they could mourn with, the differences were stark between those who said they could mourn with their spouse and those who said they could not, whether or not there were other people they could also mourn with. Not being able to mourn with your spouse was associated with 90 times greater odds of having a below average Relationship Flourishing score[11]—even including those who had no one else to mourn with.

Figure 8.4

How does having people to mourn with affect Relationship Flourishing scores?

We asked respondents how many people they have to mourn with when they are going through a hard time. We then looked at how having (or not having) community affected Relationship Flourishing scores.

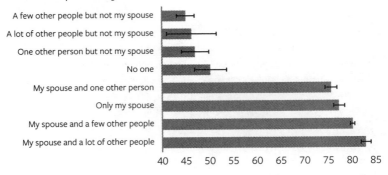

Being able to rely on your spouse when you have things to mourn is key to a flourishing marriage. But having a lot of other people (and your spouse) is better for your marital flourishing than only being able to rely on your spouse.

> **KEY TAKEAWAY:** It takes two partners, and a village, to build a marriage.

Getting Comfortable with Emotional Language

Connection has two ingredients: vulnerability and trust. It requires the risk of opening up and being vulnerable, combined with the responsibility of providing a safety net so your spouse can trust you and risk in return. Vulnerability often feels scary for those who didn't grow up experiencing safe intimate relationships, which can cause them to miss out on important ones later. One *Bare Marriage* blog reader shared this story about her frustration with how her husband acted when their adult children visited:

> When your adult child who lives out of state drives 10 straight hours to come home for Christmas . . . and his dad spends almost the entire evening after his arrival on his phone, ignoring everyone, except maybe a brief half hour break when I asked him to get off his phone. When we went to bed I was triggered by that very familiar old feeling of "this behavior doesn't make any sense." I asked why he did this. I thought he was past the emotional withdrawal, distancing behavior. I reminded him (again) that his kids also need him to be emotionally available, not detached and disconnected, not just me.
>
> He said he was looking online for a folding bed we can keep on hand for his visits. I pointed out that he certainly wasn't searching for it for the entire evening. So then he said he wasn't feeling that good. I pointed out that nobody was asking him to do any physical exertion, just engage in some of the conversation and hang out with his family, and that he certainly hadn't had any difficulty engaging with what he was doing on his phone (games and social media). He pushed back a little more with the same excuses that I wouldn't accept. So he got mad and went to sleep on the couch. Arrgghh.

For decades, she hadn't been able to fully connect with her husband because he fled any time anything emotional was required from him—and now he was repeating the pattern with his adult children. This obviously was not what any dad would want from his relationship with his kids, but many people would rather work a double shift, bungee jump, or clean out a barn than actually have to speak emotional language. They want desperately to connect, but connection feels scary, so they turn to things like their phones instead. In this dad's mind, he may even have been trying to grow the relationship in the only way he felt comfortable—by looking at how to practically facilitate an easier visit. But in the process, he was hiding from real connection. This self-isolation can go beyond our human relationships. Another commenter, echoing 1 John 4:20, asked, "If a person struggles with the basic principles of relationship with human beings whom he can see and touch, how is he supposed to have a deep meaningful relationship with Yeshua, our Savior?" We need connection, with ourselves and with others. And connection is something that, at heart, is emotional. So, let's get down to the basics and look at what emotions really are.

What Are Emotions?

In church, we're often taught that we aren't to trust our feelings. "The heart is wicked and deceitful above all things!" (see Jer. 17:9) is quoted ad nauseam. We're supposed to live on faith and fact, not feelings! But what, exactly, are these feelings that we're supposed to flee from? Becky Castle Miller is pursuing her PhD at Wheaton College, studying emotional growth as a form of discipleship. She explained to us,

> Emotions are actually cognitive (formed in our brain). In the church, we often think of emotions as separate from thought, separate from logic. But that's not how emotion works in human brains.[12] Emotion is the meaning that our minds make based on our body's sensations, our circumstances, and the predictive function of what's going to happen next. So the idea that emotions aren't true doesn't make any sense because emotions are constructs of true things that are happening.
>
> Now, there's a narrative component to an emotional experience, and there are times that we are telling ourselves a story that might not be based on facts. The emotions are still true to the story we're telling, but we might have some of our facts wrong. If my husband doesn't return a text and I start panicking because I'm afraid he's

been in a horrible car accident, and then I'm feeling scared for the future and lost and grieving, my emotions are telling me true things about my care for my husband and my fear of losing him and my concern for him. But then he texts me back, "Sorry. My phone died." All of those emotions were based on incorrect information and a story I was telling myself. But my emotions were still telling me true things about what I value and what I see in the world.[13]

Let's go over that again: Emotions are how the brain makes sense of what you are experiencing, including your body's physical reactions to your environment (heart racing, stomach churning, excited butterflies, etc.), your circumstances, and what you anticipate is coming next. Can you see how emotions are actually the most personal part of you, the core of who you are? You can't have intimacy with others, or with God, if you can't share that emotional life. That's why emotions are the main building block to intimacy.

It's tragic that some schools of Christianity paint emotions as somehow bad. It's not a far leap, then, to think that being angry or disappointed at God or scared of the future is sinful (in which case, most of the Psalms are David sinning!) or that being sad or anxious means you don't trust God enough. Then, when we have emotions that are a logical response to our situation, we feel ashamed, as if God is disappointed in us. That leads to trying to stifle those emotions so they don't cause this discomfort. Do this enough times and it will be hard to be open with your spouse too.

But as Marc Alan Schelske explains in his book *The Wisdom of Your Heart*, "Your emotions are made in God's image."[14] In Scripture, God shows joy, tenderness, compassion, grief, jealousy, anger. Jesus laughs with tax collectors and sinners; he becomes overwhelmed and has to withdraw from crowds; he's in anguish in the garden of Gethsemane. God has a rich emotional life—and you can too!

Trauma is also stored in our bodies. Trauma is the lasting emotional response that is stored in the body after experiencing a distressing event. When something bad happens to us, our bodies can go into fight-flight-freeze-or-fawn mode. When that trauma isn't properly resolved, our brains can remain stuck in that place. A person who can't sleep without a night-light or who flinches when someone touches them from behind isn't crazy, isn't weak, isn't too emotional. They actually are likely quite strong because they've managed to function despite what they've been through. But they may need help processing the trauma that is still stored in the body and in the brain, and a licensed counselor trained in evidence-based trauma therapies can help them move through that trauma so it doesn't keep them stuck.

A large part of how we construct that inner emotional life is based on our stories. Marc Alan Schelske explains, "Our stories are the narratives we hold about our own lives. Our stories are the history of the experiences, but they're more than that. They're the web of meaning, explanation, and even justification that we've woven around our memories and history. Much of the time, without even knowing it, we choose to live out of these stories."[15] And, he explains, if we don't process these stories, then they will keep shaping our choices, even if subconsciously. Part of becoming emotionally healthy, then, is examining our own stories. In their book *The Deep-Rooted Marriage*, licensed therapists Dan Allender and Steve Call talk about how, when we don't process our stories, they keep being reenacted in our marriages. "When our bodies feel a familiar old pain, our default response will be to live out the past in the present, to do what we've always done to self-protect. But, instead, we can learn how to consciously disrupt the pattern and create a new story in the present."[16]

Many of us ignore those stories, though. Due to attachment issues, childhood trauma, abuse, or even just normal hurts and rejections, we've been left feeling like there's something deeply and fundamentally wrong with us. We battle feelings of shame, and it's easier to try to stuff that emotion down than to face it in the open. When we don't examine and process our stories, though, they will show up in how we respond to our spouse—becoming sullen, defensive, or aggressive—as we try to hide from what our emotions may be telling us about ourselves.

We can also turn to other methods to silence the shame. Julie was in an impossible situation. Her daughter was in an abusive relationship with a boyfriend, and her grandchildren were paying the price. But her daughter didn't want Julie's help, and Julie's husband kept pressuring Julie to cut her daughter off—something Julie couldn't do for the sake of the grandkids. Julie felt like a horrible mom. She found herself downing an entire bottle of wine every night. The bottle helped her deal with her husband's criticism and her own fears about her parenting.

Questions to Help Examine Your Emotions[17]

What is my body feeling right now?

For example: racing heartbeat, stomach churning, tightened chest, butterflies in your stomach, sweating, blood rising to your face. What are these feelings telling me?

What am I preoccupied with right now?

For example: something at work, wondering how a family member is doing, rehearsing a fight with my spouse. What are these thoughts telling me about how I am feeling? Why am I feeling drawn to or pulled away from this person right now?

How am I painting myself right now?

Do I hear a narrative in my head, like, *You never get anything done on time; you're so lazy,* or *It's no wonder you're lonely; who would want to spend time with you?* What are these accusations telling me about my story?

What story am I narrating to myself right now?

Am I worried about something happening tomorrow? Do I think I've been treated unfairly in a situation? Am I thinking, *My spouse doesn't really love me,* or *My spouse will never want me sexually the way I want them to?* How is the story I'm telling myself right now tied into bigger stories I tell myself about my life?

When negative emotions crop up, often when something triggers feelings of shame, inadequacy, or fear we had during formative years, many of us try to soothe and numb ourselves in very counterproductive and hurtful ways: pornography, substance use, gambling, shopping. Speaking specifically about unwanted sexual behaviors, licensed counselor Jay Stringer writes in his book *Unwanted*, "Your life story set you up to experience the bondage of unwanted sexual behavior, and owning that story with a heart of curiosity and agency will provide a way out."[18] Whatever kind of counterproductive reaction we have to our emotions, whether it's blowing up at our spouse, withdrawing, or numbing ourselves, the path forward is the same: curiosity about how our story is affecting us, compassion for ourselves and our stories, and then reclaiming our agency as we confront and heal our stories and choose how to act now.

Facing our emotions and our emotional stories—but not being ruled by them—is the mark of emotional maturity. An emotionally mature person is able to completely feel their emotion but also put a buffer between that emotion and deciding how to react to it. None of us have the ability to decide how we are going to feel about something, but when we create a buffer between that feeling and our response, we can give ourselves the ability to decide how we want to respond. This is part of what is meant by taking every thought captive to Christ (see 2 Cor. 10:5).

Emotional Maturity Is Not a Feminine Trait

Before we move on to practical steps to becoming emotionally aware individually and emotionally connected as a couple, we have to address one big misconception when it comes to emotional health: that emotions are somehow a feminine thing and not a masculine thing. In most marriages, when it comes to handling emotions, because of the way men and women are socialized, the unfortunate reality is that the wife starts off with a larger skill set than the husband. But there is nothing about being a man that means he can't be emotionally healthy and nothing about being a woman that means she automatically will be.

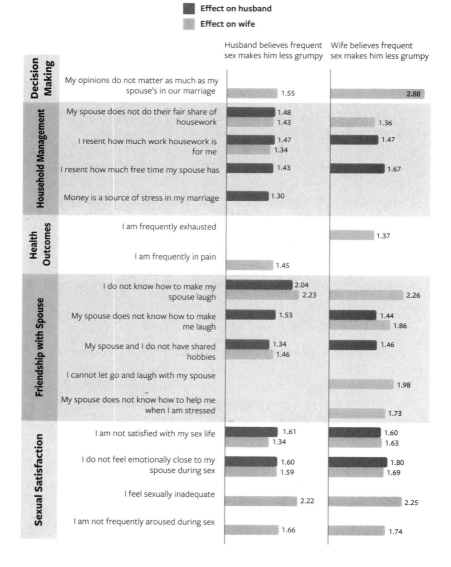

Figure 8.5

What happens if you believe when you get married that "it is important for wives to have frequent sex with their husbands so their husbands won't get grumpy"?

To interpret these data, use the following: If [I / my spouse] believed when we got married that "it is important for wives to have frequent sex with their husbands so their husbands won't get grumpy," then today [I am / my spouse is] [#] times more likely to say that _____.

Effect on husband
Effect on wife

	Husband believes frequent sex makes him less grumpy	Wife believes frequent sex makes him less grumpy
Decision Making		
My opinions do not matter as much as my spouse's in our marriage	1.55	2.88
Household Management		
My spouse does not do their fair share of housework	1.48 / 1.43	1.36
I resent how much work housework is for me	1.47 / 1.34	1.47
I resent how much free time my spouse has	1.43	1.67
Money is a source of stress in my marriage	1.30	
Health Outcomes		
I am frequently exhausted		1.37
I am frequently in pain	1.45	
Friendship with Spouse		
I do not know how to make my spouse laugh	2.04 / 2.23	2.26
My spouse does not know how to make me laugh	1.53	1.44 / 1.86
My spouse and I do not have shared hobbies	1.34 / 1.46	1.46
I cannot let go and laugh with my spouse		1.98
My spouse does not know how to help me when I am stressed		1.73
Sexual Satisfaction		
I am not satisfied with my sex life	1.61 / 1.34	1.60 / 1.63
I do not feel emotionally close to my spouse during sex	1.60 / 1.59	1.80 / 1.69
I feel sexually inadequate	2.22	2.25
I am not frequently aroused during sex	1.66	1.74

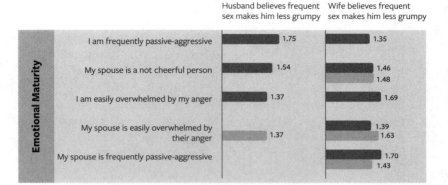

	Husband believes frequent sex makes him less grumpy	Wife believes frequent sex makes him less grumpy
I am frequently passive-aggressive	1.75	1.35
My spouse is a not cheerful person	1.54	1.46 / 1.48
I am easily overwhelmed by my anger	1.37	1.69
My spouse is easily overwhelmed by their anger	1.37	1.39 / 1.63
My spouse is frequently passive-aggressive		1.70 / 1.43

Emotional Maturity

KEY TAKEAWAY: Seeing sex as an obligation to regulate a husband's emotions signals that your marriage isn't as intimate as it could be.[19]

Both men and women can struggle with emotional language and emotional vulnerability, but in our society, men do struggle more. It's not biology, though, that makes women better at emotional connection; it's practice.[20] From a young age, girls are praised and rewarded for recognizing and processing their emotions, whereas boys are praised and rewarded for denying and repressing theirs. And this double standard continues through into adult life, where the stereotypical man is supposed to be "tough as nails" and can expect to be ridiculed if he shows weakness (that is, emotion).

This macho image is such an anemic view of what it means to be a man, and we desperately need to let it go. Despite the church's penchant for teaching about a stoic version of manhood, Scripture is full of counterexamples of strong men who felt deeply, from David pouring his heart out in the Psalms to our Savior weeping over Lazarus. We have so much evidence that feeling deeply does not make you any less of a man in God's eyes, but too often we fail to challenge the idea that being able to speak emotional language is somehow unmanly. When we assume that men aren't emotional beings at heart, though, we discourage them from learning how to communicate and emotionally connect, which tragically creates a self-fulfilling prophecy.

One of the common ways that emotional immaturity shows up especially, but not exclusively, among men is channeling all one's needs for connection and intimacy into sex. In our marriage survey, 43% of men said their love language was physical touch. Since men often think physical touch equals sex, many men channel their needs for connection into sex or into touch rather than into sharing feelings or experiences. As therapist Michael John Cusick taught me, they are trying to feel connected without having to do the vulnerable work of connection. And ultimately it can backfire.

One woman wrote to the Bare Marriage team, saying,

> We have been married for almost a decade with several children. I just feel like I'm at the end of my rope and I want to give up, but I

How Did Men and Women Rank Physical Touch among the Five Love Languages?

As part of the survey for this book, we asked people to rank the five love languages (physical touch, words of affirmation, quality time, acts of service, and gifts) in order of how important they are to them. We looked at how men and women ranked physical touch—how many put it as their top love language, how many second, etc.

Men who ranked physical touch as their highest love language were . . .

- 1.8 times more likely than other men to be dissatisfied with their sex life[21]
- 1.6 times more likely to be dissatisfied with the amount of closeness they share with their wives during sex[22]
- 2.1 times more likely to feel their wife is not sexually enough for them[23]

Obviously not all men who report having a high felt need for physical touch have channeled their emotional needs into sex. But choosing physical touch instead of other ways to connect may be a sign that deeper emotional work feels too vulnerable.

Figure 8.6

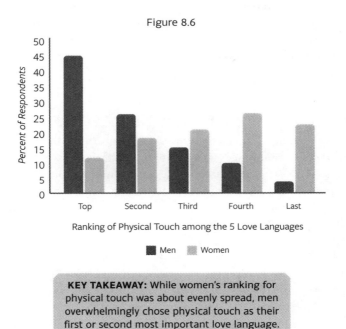

Ranking of Physical Touch among the 5 Love Languages

■ Men ■ Women

KEY TAKEAWAY: While women's ranking for physical touch was about evenly spread, men overwhelmingly chose physical touch as their first or second most important love language.

know there's no option of divorce. We don't talk. Yes, he's a quiet guy but I feel like we never have a conversation, like I usually feel like I'm talking to a wall. I am so lonely. I don't know how many times I have cried and pleaded to just talk to me. And nothing ever changes, it's like he just doesn't care. He's nice and attentive when he wants to have sex and then the next day he's right back to being uncaring and rude. Communication is basically nonexistent because he doesn't talk to me. How can I have sex when there is zero emotional connection? How do I want to have sex with someone who doesn't take my feelings into consideration?

When we (men or women) channel emotional needs into sex, sex bears a weight it was not meant to support, and it collapses, often pulling the marriage down with it. If we look to great sex for our emotional connection, we will ultimately get neither, but if we work to create a strong emotional connection, it will make us healthier as individuals and as a couple—with better sex as an added bonus. So, let's turn to how to express agency and curiosity about our emotions—something both men and women can do!

Widening Your Window of Tolerance

Allowing ourselves to face our stories and experience our emotions can be overwhelming. We can feel flooded, with so much coming at us all at once that we act without thinking, often to other people's detriment. That's part of the reason why emotions get a bad name in some circles. But it's still not the emotions that are the problem; it's our inability to use our agency and hit the pause button so we can choose how to react.

The "window of tolerance" is a counseling term that describes what this type of agency should look like. It represents that environment in which we feel flexible, at peace, and able to show up as our best self in our everyday life. For many of us, our window of tolerance is very small. It doesn't take much to flood us, causing us to feel panicky, as our heart races and anger often erupts. In desperation, we try counterproductive techniques to calm ourselves down, such as blaming those around us, demanding sex, or abusing substances. The mirror image of this *hyper*arousal is *hypo*arousal, where we shut down, become passive, and almost feel nothing at all. But if we grow our window of tolerance by learning how to express emotions and regulate those emotions, we're able to show up authentically in more situations in our everyday life. We don't get triggered as easily or withdraw as much. We're able to be present, and we're able to connect with our spouse, even in stressful situations. And it all starts with learning to exercise agency over our emotions.

Learning to Regulate Your Own Emotions

Our oldest daughter, Rebecca, used to have terrible temper tantrums when she was two years old. In the nineties, we were taught that this behavior in toddlers was a result of defiance, and it was imperative that we show her that she was not going to control the family with her outbursts. We did the time-outs just as we were taught, and her tantrums grew worse. She would scream for half an hour in the stroller all the way home. She would scream for hours in her room. Over time, she eventually grew out of this, but those years were tough!

Just over two decades later, Rebecca gave birth to a little boy who emotionally was the very image of his mom. Yet when Alex started to show signs of temper tantrum tendencies, Rebecca handled it completely differently. Today, we have new and better information about toddlers. When two-year-olds have tantrums, they're not being intentionally defiant; they're just unable to regulate their emotions. They're feeling deeply and they can't figure out what to do. Emotional regulation is a skill (just like walking or talking) that needs to be learned over time. The role of a parent is to help the child learn emotional regulation. And that's what Rebecca and her husband did with their son.

One of our favorite pictures of Alex is him at three, sitting at the dinner table with his eyes closed and his dad's hands cupping his head, as they touch foreheads. Alex had become overwhelmed when what was on the menu for dinner was not to his liking, and his parents had told him to take deep breaths, and he had. His tantrums never accelerated the way his mom's did. He learned to calm himself down. And now, at four, when he's angry or upset, rather than throwing a tantrum, he can say, "Mimi, I feel frustrated. I need to jump right now!" or whatever other coping strategy he wants to try. And he does. And it works.

Alex has a leg up because he's learning this as a preschooler. But what if you never learned how to handle big feelings? Most of us didn't, after all. What if you were chastised for showing emotions rather than taught how to label and process them? The best thing you can do for your marriage, and for your own mental health, is to start learning to emotionally regulate yourself today—and that's something that we, as spouses, can often help with. Much of emotional regulation is actually calming down our nervous

Figure 8.7

How does agreeing that your spouse is easily overwhelmed by their anger affect couples?

To interpret these data, use the following: If [I / my spouse] believe(s) that the other is easily overwhelmed by their anger, then [I am / my spouse is] [#] times more likely to say that _____.

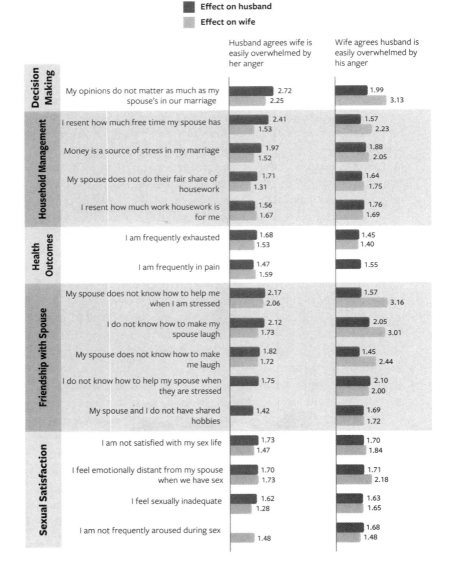

■ Effect on husband
▨ Effect on wife

Husband agrees wife is easily overwhelmed by her anger

Wife agrees husband is easily overwhelmed by his anger

Decision Making

My opinions do not matter as much as my spouse's in our marriage — 2.72 / 2.25 — 1.99 / 3.13

Household Management

I resent how much free time my spouse has — 2.41 / 1.53 — 1.57 / 2.23

Money is a source of stress in my marriage — 1.97 / 1.52 — 1.88 / 2.05

My spouse does not do their fair share of housework — 1.71 / 1.31 — 1.64 / 1.75

I resent how much work housework is for me — 1.56 / 1.67 — 1.76 / 1.69

Health Outcomes

I am frequently exhausted — 1.68 / 1.53 — 1.45 / 1.40

I am frequently in pain — 1.47 / 1.59 — 1.55

Friendship with Spouse

My spouse does not know how to help me when I am stressed — 2.17 / 2.06 — 1.57 / 3.16

I do not know how to make my spouse laugh — 2.12 / 1.73 — 2.05 / 3.01

My spouse does not know how to make me laugh — 1.82 / 1.72 — 1.45 / 2.44

I do not know how to help my spouse when they are stressed — 1.75 — 2.10 / 2.00

My spouse and I do not have shared hobbies — 1.42 — 1.69 / 1.72

Sexual Satisfaction

I am not satisfied with my sex life — 1.73 / 1.47 — 1.70 / 1.84

I feel emotionally distant from my spouse when we have sex — 1.70 / 1.73 — 1.71 / 2.18

I feel sexually inadequate — 1.62 / 1.28 — 1.63 / 1.65

I am not frequently aroused during sex — 1.48 — 1.68 / 1.48

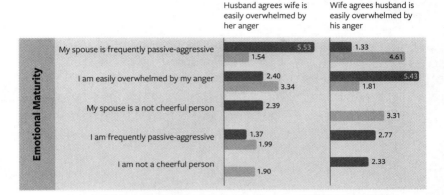

KEY TAKEAWAY: Emotional regulation is part of being a mature adult and a key part of building a marriage based on trust.

system, which is going out of control. When you feel flooded, these things can help:

1. Take deep breaths.
2. Move: Go for a run, skip rope, do a few yoga poses, even jump up and down like Alex did. Allow some of the stress to move through your body.
3. Listen to calming music that can help you regulate your breathing.
4. Touch: Hug your spouse, dance to some music, or even just hold hands.

That last one is such a beautiful picture of how we can help each other through these emotional roller coasters—and it's a gift that God designed for us. In fact, even a simple hug can reduce our cortisol levels and get our heart rate down. One 2021 study reports that "receiving hugs [is a] simple and yet potentially powerful means for buffering individuals' resilience against stress."[24] Sometimes you just need someone to hold you.

205

Showing Curiosity about Emotions

Marriage guru John Gottman has said, "It has become clear to me that happy couples live by the credo 'When you are in pain, the world stops and I listen.'"[25] Throughout this book we've been stressing that marriages work best when we're a team. We can approach emotional connection with a teamwork mindset, too, especially when it comes to understanding and processing emotions. This is such a precious way that we can care for our spouse because emotional support is often in short supply. Emotional support means helping your spouse work through what they are experiencing and feeling, something that has tremendous health benefits. Showing curiosity about your spouse's emotional life and helping them identify emotions can help them move through difficult emotions, like depression, anxiety, and anger, faster.[26] In fact, the act of rating anger (or even just admitting you feel anger) reduces heart rate and other autonomic physical signs of anger. When we can talk about difficult emotions, or even just admit that they're difficult, they don't have the same long-term negative emotional weight when the incident is brought up again later.

How do you show curiosity to aid with this emotion labeling? Producing "intimacy on demand" doesn't work that well. But there are some rituals that we can add to our days that make it more natural and give low-stress opportunities to be curious about emotions and help each other identify them.

The Emotional Recap Ritual

Have you ever ended the day and felt icky but haven't been able to put a finger on why? Or maybe something great happened to you, but you never had a chance to celebrate it. A few years ago, when Keith was working in a different city, we found ourselves losing connection and not knowing what was going on in each other's lives. So we started a ritual that helped us build connection while also helping us process our own emotions.

We call it the "success/defeat ritual." Here's how it works: You take a few minutes to recap the two most important emotional

Are You in Tune with Your Spouse?

Respondents who knew how to help their spouse when they were stressed, or who were confident they knew how to make their spouse laugh, were more likely to use positive words to describe their marriage. And interestingly—it seems like a husband knowing how to help his wife with stress does more than a wife helping a husband, while a wife knowing how to make her husband laugh does more than the other.

Figure 8.8

How does knowing how to help your spouse when they are stressed impact how you describe your marriage?

To interpret these data, use the following: If [I am / my spouse is] confident that [I/they] know(s) how to help the other when they are stressed, then [I am / my spouse is] [#] times more likely to describe our marriage as [descriptor].

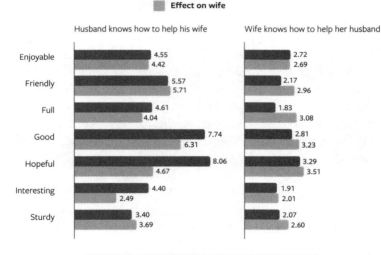

KEY TAKEAWAY: Knowing how to connect in joy and sorrow is part of what makes marriage so worthwhile. Laughter is good medicine, and so is a foot rub after a hard day!

moments in your day. You share the moment you felt the most "in the groove," when you felt joy, like you were doing what God put you on earth to do, and then you share the time during the day when you felt the most defeated. As you share these emotional moments, you enter into each other's emotional world, which promotes intimacy. But you also learn to identify and name your emotions. When you have to think back and share the moment that you felt the most defeated, and then you have to describe that feeling, it all clicks into place.

What if a spouse is having trouble fully expressing why something bothered them? You can show curiosity, asking questions like

- What happened next?
- What was your body feeling?
- Do you remember feeling that way with anyone else or in any other situation? What about this situation reminds you of that?
- What do you wish you could have said?

If they still have trouble, you can volunteer some insights: "I might have felt very nervous about my job security or very ashamed that the presentation didn't go well. Do either of those things sound like what you felt?" You can even keep an emotions list handy on your phone to identify two or three emotion words that most resonate. We found that people who felt they could admit their weaknesses to their spouses were much happier in their marriages (see figure 8.9). When we hold space for our spouse to share difficult things, we don't just build their emotional resilience and emotional knowledge. We also build our marriage.

Uncovering Your Spouse's Story

Understanding your spouse's emotional backstory can also grow your intimacy as a couple and help your spouse process difficult emotions. You likely know the facts of your spouse's

Can You Share Your Weaknesses?

We asked respondents to rate how much they agree with the statement "I can rely on my spouse to react in a positive way when I expose my weaknesses to them" and then looked at how that agreement correlated with marital descriptions, marital satisfaction, and sexual satisfaction.

Figure 8.9

How does being able to safely share your weaknesses with your spouse affect how you describe your marriage?

To interpret these data, use the following: If [I / my spouse] believe(s) that the other will react positively if [I/they] expose personal weaknesses, then [I am / my spouse is] [#] times more likely to describe our marriage as [descriptor].

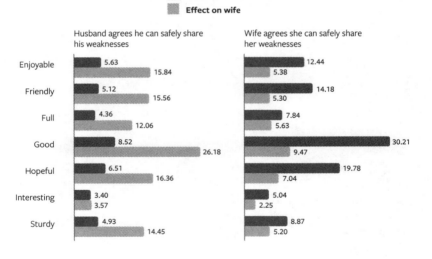

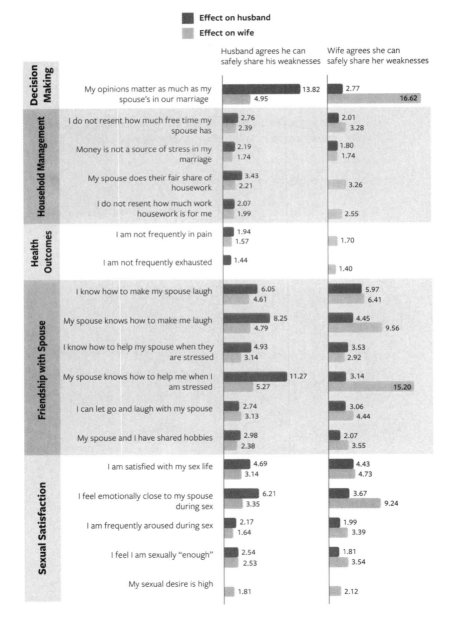

Figure 8.10

How does being able to safely share your weaknesses with your spouse affect your marriage and sex life?

To interpret these data, use the following: If [I / my spouse] believe(s) that the other will react positively if [I/they] expose personal weaknesses, then [I am / my spouse is] [#] times more likely to say that _____.

■ Effect on husband
░ Effect on wife

Husband agrees he can safely share his weaknesses / Wife agrees she can safely share her weaknesses

Decision Making

My opinions matter as much as my spouse's in our marriage — 13.82 / 4.95 | 2.77 / 16.62

Household Management

I do not resent how much free time my spouse has — 2.76 / 2.39 | 2.01 / 3.28

Money is not a source of stress in my marriage — 2.19 / 1.74 | 1.80 / 1.74

My spouse does their fair share of housework — 3.43 / 2.21 | 3.26

I do not resent how much work housework is for me — 2.07 / 1.99 | 2.55

Health Outcomes

I am not frequently in pain — 1.94 / 1.57 | 1.70

I am not frequently exhausted — 1.44 | 1.40

Friendship with Spouse

I know how to make my spouse laugh — 6.05 / 4.61 | 5.97 / 6.41

My spouse knows how to make me laugh — 8.25 / 4.79 | 4.45 / 9.56

I know how to help my spouse when they are stressed — 4.93 / 3.14 | 3.53 / 2.92

My spouse knows how to help me when I am stressed — 11.27 / 5.27 | 3.14 / 15.20

I can let go and laugh with my spouse — 2.74 / 3.13 | 3.06 / 4.44

My spouse and I have shared hobbies — 2.98 / 2.38 | 2.07 / 3.55

Sexual Satisfaction

I am satisfied with my sex life — 4.69 / 3.14 | 4.43 / 4.73

I feel emotionally close to my spouse during sex — 6.21 / 3.35 | 3.67 / 9.24

I am frequently aroused during sex — 2.17 / 1.64 | 1.99 / 3.39

I feel I am sexually "enough" — 2.54 / 2.53 | 1.81 / 3.54

My sexual desire is high — 1.81 | 2.12

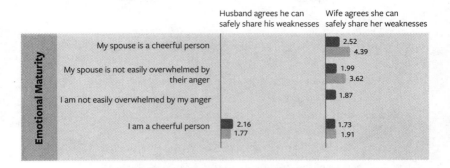

KEY TAKEAWAY: Being confident that you can share your vulnerabilities safely with your spouse is a major predictor of marital and sexual satisfaction.

story—the number of siblings, where and what kind of house they grew up in, what extracurricular activities they were involved in as kids, who they dated in high school—but do you know what they were scared of when they were eight? Do you know why certain relatives cause their hair to stand on end? Do you know the first time your spouse really experienced grief, rejection, or inadequacy? Knowing the answers to these kinds of questions helps us understand their emotional reactions today much more easily. And as we open up to our spouse, then often these stories lose some of their power over our emotional lives today.

How can you show curiosity about your spouse's story? Here's one idea: Choose a low-key time of day, like when you go for a walk after dinner or as you're lying in bed at the end of the day, and start asking some questions, like these:

- What is a good and a bad memory from when you were nine?
- When's the first time you remember crying?
- What was your biggest fear when you were in junior high?

- When did you feel most lonely in high school?
- What secrets did you feel you had to keep from your parents?

Start the process, and you'll think of more questions! Even if this feels uncomfortable, challenge yourself to give an answer— and a few sentences is fine. Let your spouse in on your inner life, and they'll know you better. And when they know you and they still stick around? That's the true acceptance we all long for. When we can each see what is going on with our spouse and compassionately enter in, when we can hold space to allow them to experience those emotions and work through them, when we can see and praise the things God is doing in their life (even if it is helping them work through something difficult), we can be such an incredible source of healing and emotional growth.

And that's ultimately what we think marriage is supposed to be.

We Need a Witness to Our Lives

There's a beautiful monologue about marriage in the movie *Shall We Dance?* Susan Sarandon's character hires a private investigator because she is afraid that her husband is having an affair. (Spoiler alert: It turns out he's not.) She and the investigator debate the reason people get married, and the investigator declares confidently that it's love. Sarandon's character disagrees, saying,

> We need a witness to our lives. There are eight billion people on the planet . . . I mean, what does any one life really mean? But in a marriage, you're promising to care about everything—the good things, the bad things, the terrible things, the mundane things . . . all of it, all the time, every day. You're saying, "Your life will not go unnoticed because I will notice it. Your life will not go unwitnessed because I will be your witness."[27]

Over the course of more than thirty years of marriage, we have been each other's witnesses. We have shown up. We have been

212

curious. We have not always been emotionally healthy. We have not always had the right words or said the right words. But there is no one else on earth who understands our emotional life as well as we each do. There is no one else who quite knows what September 4 means to us, as each year we're reminded of the death of our tiny son. There is no one else who walked with us in those moments in the same way, who with us experienced the joy of other babies being born yet had the same realization that a grandson's smile looks an awful lot like the baby we didn't get to hold for nearly long enough. Witnessing a life is a gift we give—the gift of being present and caring about all of it.

And, dear readers, that is the marriage we want for you.

Conclusion

Creating the Marriage You Love

Usually books end right about here with a "Rah rah, you can do it!" send-off. And, yes, we're going to do that, but first we have one more question we'd like to ask you:

Is marriage hard?

The evangelical circles we've inhabited have tended to treat this question like the answer is obvious: Of course marriage is hard! But honestly, if someone asked us today if our marriage was hard, we'd both likely laugh and say, "Not really!" Yes, we have had our share of difficulties, but we can talk about anything. We're good friends. We've supported and encouraged each other for over three decades. Overall, marriage makes our lives easier, not harder.

Now, admittedly, this wasn't automatic. When we were first married, the adjustment was challenging. But please hear us because we really want you to know: Marriage doesn't need to be a huge slog you endure until one of you dies. If you put in the work and build on solid relationship principles, like the ones we've shared here, marriage can and should be what makes life *easier* to handle because there are two of you sharing the load. Instead of saying, "Marriage is hard," we'd phrase it as "*Life* is hard. But marriage is meant to make it easier!"

Life brings job losses and financial insecurities, illnesses, interpersonal conflicts, and more. When you're married, you have an additional set of relatives who could get sick, who may need

215

extra care, whom you have to navigate relationships with. That's complicated. On top of that, marriage often brings children, who add huge layers of additional responsibilities and complexities (as well as much love and laughter and hugs). Even the struggle to have children can add stress and heartache. So, yes, being married can make life more complicated. But marriage also gives you a safe place to land and can be a source of great strength to face the storms life brings. The good should outweigh those complications!

For some of you, that definitively is not the case. We hope that in this book we've helped you identify the red flags that show when your relationship is unhealthy and when you need help, because *hard* should not be the word we use to define the state of our marriage.

And now, as we end this book, we want to encourage you to approach any issues in your marriage with curiosity rather than resignation. Is your marriage hard? The answer isn't to shrug your shoulders and say, "Oh well. I guess that's how it is." Instead, copy the wisdom of Sakichi Toyoda and ask why!

Is the problem related to balance? Is one of you letting a rigid view of gender roles impede intimacy? Is one of you disappearing into the other? Or is one of you struggling at tier 1 on the marriage hierarchy of needs, just trying to survive through each day, while the other enjoys much more rest and fulfillment?

Or perhaps you're feeling like affection and passion have dried up, and you can't figure out the reason. Are you making a habit of spending time together? Are there things in your daily life you can do differently to build connection? Or, if libido has disappeared, ask why. Are you feeling connected in other ways? Is sex, when you have it, leaving you feeling better or worse? Why?

One of the biggest culprits we found that can make marriage hard is when responsibility isn't shared. If one of you is carrying too much mental load, then marriage will certainly feel hard. Does one of you take most of the initiative to repair conflicts or make life better? Has one of you turned into a caregiver, while the other feels like a dependent? Nothing kills passion quicker than that!

And finally, are you able to open up emotionally to each other? Do you feel safe sharing what you're feeling? Are you even able to figure out what you're feeling? If not, why not? Keep asking until you get to the root of the problem—and then tackle it with your spouse.

It's going to take curiosity to discern the root of the issues. It's going to take humility to address the things that may fall into your blind spots. It's going to take boldness to bring up the things that you may be upset about. It will take compassion to listen to and understand your spouse's story and triggers so that you can be part of their healing journey. And it will take courage to address your own story. But when you put all those things together, isn't that a lovely picture of growth in Christ?

Yes, life is hard. Yes, marriage takes a set of skills that takes time to master. But when you approach your spouse and your marriage with curiosity, and when your spouse does the same, then marriage doesn't have to be some heavy weight you carry your whole life. Instead, marriage can be the relationship that helps you bear life's burdens as you run up the hill together. What the data in this book has consistently shown is that when you follow the teamwork approach we've shared, marriage becomes something that makes your burdens feel a little lighter, makes your footsteps land a little easier, and makes your smile shine a little brighter.

So often the message we've heard in church circles about marriage is that it's hard, but God wants you to just stick with it regardless. But we want more for you. We don't want you to just stay in a marriage you hate; we want you to create a marriage you love. And given that Jesus said he came that we might have life to the full, we think he agrees!

He invites you on this wonderful, adventurous journey when you marry: the journey to know yourself better as you join with someone else. The journey to live not just for yourself but also for someone else. The journey to show up, fully yourself, and not hold anything back. The journey to become more responsible, more compassionate, more emotionally aware.

Take that journey. It may require using some muscles you're not used to using, and it may stretch you in new ways. But it's what we wish for all of you, because that's the way to grow the marriage you want.

Appendix

Reading this book may have alerted many of you that you need more help. Here are some other resources that we recommend:

If You Need Counseling

Please seek out a licensed counselor who is trained in marriage issues and trauma. Even if you're not specifically dealing with trauma, most who are trained in it are actually better able to identify unhealthy marriage dynamics when they pop up. Licensed counselors include licensed marriage and family therapists, licensed social workers, clinical psychologists, or others who have licensure and official accreditation. This licensure means that they have been trained in evidence-based practices and they have professional ethics and standards they must adhere to in order to maintain their licensing. They must maintain your privacy and won't divulge what is said in counseling to a pastor or your spouse without your permission.

On the other hand, many church counselors or biblical counselors don't necessarily have training in evidence-based therapies and do not guarantee privacy. Biblical counseling is a specific type of counseling that believes the Bible is sufficient for counseling. Many licensed counselors are Christians and believe the Bible but also use evidence-based therapies and what we have learned about psychology to counsel clients. While some biblical counselors are wonderful, we strongly recommend licensed counselors for best practices and for protection.

To find one in your area, google "licensed counselors," your area, and words like "trauma therapy," "EMDR," "Christian," etc. Most counselors will give a free fifteen-minute consultation by phone, and that will help you see if they are a good fit for you.

Please remember that if there are abusive dynamics in your marriage, individual counseling is best, not marriage counseling. Marriage counseling can actually exacerbate abuse, and it is better to get help yourself on next steps.

Resources for Those in Destructive or Abusive Marriages

Books

Bancroft, Lundy. *Why Does He Do That? Inside the Minds of Angry and Controlling Men.* New York: Berkley, 2003.

Baskerville, Gretchen. *The Life-Saving Divorce: Hope for People Leaving Destructive Relationships.* Torrence, CA: Life Saving Press, 2020.

Hoffman, Natalie. *Is It Me? Making Sense of Your Confusing Marriage.* Rosemount, MN: Flying Free Media, 2018. You can also find Natalie at FlyingFreeSisterhood.com.

Paynter, Helen. *The Bible Doesn't Tell Me So: Why You Don't Have to Submit to Domestic Violence and Coercive Control.* Abingdon, UK: BRF, 2020.

Vernick, Leslie. *The Emotionally Destructive Marriage: How to Find Your Voice and Reclaim Your Hope.* New York: Waterbrook, 2013. You can also find Leslie at Leslie Vernick.com.

Other Online Resources

Called to Peace Ministries, CalledToPeace.org.

Leslie Vernick, LeslieVernick.com.

Sarah McDugal, WildernessToWild.com.

Please be wary of Christian counseling hotlines, such as the one operated by Focus on the Family. While Focus does allow separation if you believe you are at risk of harm, they do not condone divorce for abuse, and thus the aim is reconciliation.[1] This can leave vulnerable people in a state of legal limbo. It is best to seek help from organizations or individuals that understand abuse dynamics better.

Domestic Violence Hotlines:

United States: 1-800-799-SAFE (7233)

Canada: 1-866-863-0511

United Kingdom: 0808 2000 247

Australia: 1800 737 732

New Zealand: 0508 744 633

South Africa: 0800 150 150

For other countries: Google your country name and "domestic violence hotline." You can also find a list of hotlines by country at FindAHelpline.com.

Resources for Those Battling Unwanted Sexual Behaviors

Books

Bauman, Andrew. *The Sexually Healthy Man: Essays on Spirituality, Sexuality, & Restoration.* Independently published, 2020. See also AndrewJBauman.com.

Cusick, Michael John. *Surfing for God: Discovering the Divine Desire Beneath Sexual Struggle.* Nashville: Thomas Nelson, 2012. See also RestoringTheSoul.com.

Jolman, Sam. *The Sex Talk You Never Got: Reclaiming the Heart of Masculine Sexuality*. Nashville: Nelson Books, 2024.

Stringer, Jay. *Unwanted: How Sexual Brokenness Reveals our Way to Healing*. Colorado Springs: NavPress, 2018. See also Jay-Stringer.com (applies to both men and women).

Wagner, Zachary. *Non-Toxic Masculinity: Recovering Healthy Male Sexuality*. Downers Grove, IL: IVP, 2023.

Other Online Resources

Omar Minwalla's Institute for Sexual Health, Minwalla Model.com.

Resources for Those Who Want Help with Their Sex Lives

If you have issues around healing from obligation messages or recovering from the idea that lust is every man's battle, please read *The Great Sex Rescue*.

For information on how sex is supposed to work and how to make it pleasurable, please read *The Good Girl's Guide to Great Sex* and/or *The Good Guy's Guide to Great Sex*.

Our team has also created an orgasm course: BareMarriage .com/the-orgasm-course.

And a libido course: BareMarriage.com/boost-your-libido.

If you find orgasm elusive, please take the orgasm course before the libido course. If sex isn't pleasurable, no wonder you have no libido!

If you are experiencing vaginismus or sexual pain, please see your physician for a diagnosis. For treatment, please see a pelvic floor physiotherapist and read *The Great Sex Rescue*.

If you experience migraines, sadness, or crying after orgasm, please see a physician. This may be a sign of a condition called postcoital dysphoria, and there are treatments that can help. Women who experience this are also at higher risk of postpartum depression, so informing your physician of this can help in your care.

If you are experiencing erectile dysfunction or premature ejaculation, please see a physician. There are treatments available, and these conditions may signal that something else is going on.

Resources about Trauma, Attachment, and Emotional Health

Allender, Dan B., and Steve Call. *The Deep-Rooted Marriage: Cultivating Intimacy, Healing, and Delight.* Nashville: W Publishing, 2025. (About working through your wounds and triggers to build intimacy.)

Kolber, Aundi. *Try Softer: A Fresh Approach to Move Us out of Anxiety, Stress, and Survival Mode—and into a Life of Connection and Joy.* Carol Stream, IL: Tyndale, 2020. (About emotional health.)

Mayfield, Krispin. *Attached to God: A Practical Guide to Deeper Spiritual Experience.* Grand Rapids: Zondervan, 2022. (Applying attachment theory to our spiritual lives.)

McBride, Hillary L., PhD. *The Wisdom of Your Body: Finding Healing, Wholeness, and Connection through Embodied Living.* Grand Rapids: Brazos, 2021. (About trauma.)

Reimersma, Jenna, LPC. *Altogether You: Experiencing Personal and Spiritual Transformation with Internal Family Systems Therapy.* Marietta, GA: Pivotal Press, 2020. (About internal family systems.)

Resources for Those Seeking the Biblical Basis for Mutuality in Marriage

Marg Mowczko hosts a wonderful website where you can look up any Scripture passage that pertains to women and see all her quick, short articles: MargMowczko.com.

Or read any of these books:

Barr, Beth Allison. *The Making of Biblical Womanhood: How the Subjugation of Women Became Gospel Truth.* Grand Rapids: Brazos, 2021.

Byrd, Aimee. *Recovering from Biblical Manhood and Womanhood: How the Church Needs to Rediscover Her Purpose.* Grand Rapids: Zondervan, 2020.

Coleman, Julie Zine. *On Purpose: Understanding God's Freedom for Women Through Scripture.* Grand Rapids: Kregel, 2022.

Payne, Philip B. *The Bible vs. Biblical Womanhood: How God's Word Consistently Affirms Gender Equality.* Grand Rapids: Zondervan, 2023.

Peppiatt, Lucy. *Rediscovering Scripture's Vision for Women: Fresh Perspectives on Disputed Texts.* Downers Grove, IL: IVP, 2019.

Williams, Terran. *How God Sees Women: The End of Patriarchy.* Cape Town: Spiritual Bakery, 2022.

Acknowledgments

There are two names on this book's cover, but there should be at least two more.

First, Joanna Sawatsky is a superstar. One March afternoon five years ago, I (Sheila) was doing the dishes and talking with Joanna on FaceTime when she gave me the idea of conducting a survey to measure how evangelical teachings are affecting marital and sexual satisfaction. That phone call put us on the road to *The Great Sex Rescue*, and this is our fifth book incorporating her research and statistical prowess. We simply couldn't have done this without Joanna. She's such a gifted and brilliant young woman, and we appreciate her dedication to accuracy and truth. And thank you, Josiah, for covering for her so she could work, and to Mari and Tali, who let us have their mommy in the early morning hours.

Next is our daughter Rebecca Lindenbach. Her name, too, is not on this book, but Rebecca has shaped our views of marriage, alerted us to peer-reviewed research, and, of course, come up with the funniest lines. Those who are familiar with her on the *Bare Marriage* podcast, or who know her writing voice from *The Great Sex Rescue* and *She Deserves Better*, will likely see many "Rebecca-isms" in this book. Of course, the rescuing seven cats idea was hers, as was much of the framework for foundation versus frills.

We're so proud of her insight and her discernment, and we're glad she's on our team.

We also want to thank our Patreon group, who helped fund the research end of this book. We are so grateful for your financial support but also for your emotional support in our Facebook group when things are tough, and for the chance to test out thoughts and ideas first before we put them on paper. You've given us a real online community, and we're tremendously grateful.

To everyone who took our marriage survey: Thank you. We are humbled. We know that it was a significant time sacrifice, and we hope that this book honors that time and does you proud.

We're grateful for those from whom we have learned and whose work has influenced our thinking on many issues, including John Gottman's marriage insights from The Gottman Institute; Eve Rodsky's conception of mental load and emotional labor and how to achieve "fair play"; Emily Nagoski's work on libido; Michael John Cusick, Andrew Bauman, and Jay Stringer on unwanted sexual behavior; Becky Castle Miller and Marc Alan Schelske on emotions; and Sarah McDugal, Gretchen Baskerville, Natalie Hoffman, and Leslie Vernick on abuse dynamics.

On the publishing end, Chip MacGregor has believed in me (Sheila) since before I was really me. I think he knew what I could go on to write, and he has stuck by me and encouraged me for almost a decade and a half. To see him now encouraging Rebecca, too, makes us, as parents, excited and proud.

This book was not originally slotted to be a Baker Book, but different circumstances moved it into the Baker camp, and we feel like that was a God thing. Quite simply, Baker is the best publisher we have ever worked with, and we're so glad we're part of the Baker family. Stephanie Duncan-Smith took a big risk with this book, and we're grateful for the belief she has in us. Kristin Adkinson, we've been through three books together now—and we're so grateful you always make sure we're clear and accurate in what we say. Thanks to Wendy Wetzel too—we love working with you!

We have such great support in our Bare Marriage team—Tammy Arseneau, Connor Lindenbach, Shari Smith, Emily Murchison. We appreciate you! Tammy, you keep our stress levels down, and we know how hard you work to take as much off our plates as possible. You're a great friend, and we're so glad you're in our lives. To my (Sheila's) mother, Elizabeth, who keeps things together at home and makes sure we're always on an even keel, thank you for your prayers and all the work you do behind the scenes. I feel as if I have fallen behind on my promise to do the cooking—I'll get better at that soon, I promise! And thank you to our rector, Brad Beale, who has shown such care for us as we do this work and has celebrated what we have already done to bring it to our local faith community. We have never felt as seen by a pastor as we do with you.

To Katie: We love you so much, and we're so happy to have just welcomed little Diana into the world! We always try to carve out time just to see your lovely family, and we hope you know in the fiber of our being that you—and Diana, Alex, Vivi, and Becca—are our hearts.

To those who have introduced our other books to your churches through hosting small groups or giving them to pastors or speaking up in youth group: Thank you for going to bat for the information we've found. To those who reach out on social media, listen to the *Bare Marriage* podcast, or read the *Bare Marriage* blog and encourage us to keep going to change the evangelical culture around marriage: Thank you for your notes, your comments, your presence. When you keep showing up, you give us energy to keep doing this work—and it's been like a whirlwind over the last five years. We're here to change the evangelical conversation about sex and marriage to something healthy, biblical, and evidence-based. You help us do that by spreading the word. There's still so much work to do, but the conversation is indeed changing, and much of that is because you're taking these ideas to your churches, your families, your neighbors. Thank you. Now let's keep building something healthy!

Notes

Introduction

1. The book was Emerson Eggerichs' bestseller *Love & Respect: The Love She Most Desires; the Respect He Desperately Needs* (Nashville: Thomas Nelson, 2004).

2. Eggerichs, *Love & Respect*, 258.

3. Eggerichs, *Love & Respect*, 249.

4. Eggerichs, *Love & Respect*, 252.

5. In fact, *Every Man's Battle* has no references of any kind, peer-reviewed or not. *The Act of Marriage* does have many references, but only one is from a peer-reviewed source (the textbook).

6. There are too many examples to quote here, but see, for example, Back to the Bible's interview "Marriage Done God's Way: An Interview with Dr. Emmerson Eggerichs," June 12, 2020, https://www.youtube.com/watch?v=VwYJDOLGCDk; Jeff and Cheryl Scruggs, "Doing it God's Way," May 12, 2022, *Focus on Marriage Podcast*, https://www.focusonthefamily.com/episodes/focus-on-marriage-podcast/doing -it-gods-way/; Jani Ortlund, "Teach Them about Marriage before the World Does," Desiring God, August 29, 2018, https://www.desiringgod.org/articles/teach-them -about-marriage-before-the-world-does. Ortlund goes on to say, "Help your children see that there are two ways to think about everything—the world's way and God's way."

7. Sheila Wray Gregoire, *The Good Girl's Guide to Great Sex: Creating a Marriage That's Both Holy and Hot*, revised and expanded ed. (Grand Rapids: Zondervan, 2022).

8. Sheila Wray Gregoire, Rebecca Gregoire Lindenbach, and Joanna Sawatsky, *The Great Sex Rescue: The Lies You've Been Taught and How to Recover What God Intended* (Grand Rapids: Baker Books, 2021); Sheila Wray Gregoire, Rebecca Gregoire Lindenbach, and Joanna Sawatsky, *She Deserves Better: Raising Girls to Resist Toxic Teachings on Sex, Self, and Speaking Up* (Grand Rapids: Baker Books, 2023).

9. Sheila Wray Gregoire and Dr. Keith Gregoire, *The Good Guy's Guide to Great Sex: Because Good Guys Make the Best Lovers* (Grand Rapids: Zondervan, 2022).

10. Our work has also been peer-reviewed, our data from our original survey for *The Great Sex Rescue* has been archived at the Association of Religion Data Archives, and a paper based on our work has been published in *The Sociology of Religion*, a peer-reviewed journal.

Chapter 1 The Unity You Want

1. In Canada, pediatrics is more of an intensivist specialty than family medicine. Think of it as an emergency physician for kids.

2. For more on how the concept of biblical womanhood and manhood has been distorted, please see Kristin Kobes Du Mez, *Jesus and John Wayne: How White Evangelicals Corrupted a Faith and Fractured a Nation* (New York: Liveright, 2020); Beth

Allison Barr, *The Making of Biblical Womanhood: How the Subjugation of Women Became Gospel Truth* (Grand Rapids: Brazos, 2021); Philip B. Payne, *The Bible vs. Biblical Womanhood: How God's Word Consistently Affirms Gender Equality* (Grand Rapids: Zondervan, 2023).

3. With thanks to Emily Nagoski, who explained the concept of overlapping bell curves so well in her book *Come as You Are*, using the example of height.

4. Ekaterina Mitricheva et al., "Neural Substrates of Sexual Arousal Are Not Sex Dependent," *Proceedings of the National Academy of Sciences* 116, no. 31 (July 2019): 15671–76, https://doi.org/10.1073/pnas.1904975116.

5. Research Department Psychometrics Canada, *Myers-Briggs Type Indicator ® (MBTI®) Instrument in French and English Canada* (Edmonton, AB: Psychometrics, 2008), https://www.psychometrics.com/wp-content/uploads/2015/02/mbti-in-canada .pdf, 6–7. We used the dataset for English Canadians; for French Canadians 72.7% of men are thinkers and 56.1% of women are feelers.

6. John M. Gottman and Nan Silver, *The Seven Principles for Making Marriage Work: A Practical Guide from the Country's Foremost Relationship Expert* (New York: Harmony Books, 1999), 116.

7. In our surveys, 78.9% of couples make decisions together, while 17.3% of marriages have the husband serving as tiebreaker. In the remaining 3.8% of marriages, she breaks the ties.

8. For more on these concepts, please see Philip B. Payne, *The Bible vs. Biblical Womanhood* or Terran Williams, *How God Sees Women: The End of Patriarchy* (Cape Town: Spiritual Bakery, 2022). Marg Mowczko's website is also a treasure trove of articles about key verses (https://margmowczko.com).

9. Gregoire, Lindenbach, and Sawatsky, *Great Sex Rescue*, 33.

10. In all our previous surveys we have used the four-question short form of the CSI. We were thrilled that we had the opportunity to use the long form version of this instrument in the matched-pair survey. Thirty-one of the thirty-two questions were included in our survey.

11. Respondents were asked to rank their marriage on a sliding scale between the two opposite words (from 0 to 5). Opposites were as follows: interesting—boring; good—bad; full—empty; friendly—lonely; sturdy—fragile; hopeful—discouraging; enjoyable—miserable.

12. In a smaller minority of marriages, she makes unilateral decisions after they talk it over. In this situation, only 10.7% of women report always feeling like their spouse really wants to hear their point of view. Point of view during arguments was evaluated with the following item from the Kansas Marital Conflict Scale: "When you and your spouse are beginning to discuss a disagreement over an important issue, how often is your spouse willing to really hear what you want to communicate?" In marriages where the husband makes unilateral decisions without consulting his wife, 9.1% of women report that their husbands really hear them during arguments.

13. Percent of respondents who reported that it is "completely true" that "I have had second thoughts about this relationship recently" as part of the Couples Satisfaction Index.

14. Christian women who make decisions collaboratively are 2.52 (2.32–2.75) times more likely to disagree that "when we have conflict, I don't feel my husband really hears me."

15. Men who report they make unilateral decisions comparison with men who report making unilateral decisions in binary logistic regression using collaborative decision-making as the reference category, p=0.498. (P-values are defined as the odds of a larger test-statistic result being obtained if the observation was repeated presuming

that the null hypothesis is true. In layman's terms, statisticians usually use a p-value less than 0.05 to mean that the result is statistically significant. We have used this as our cutoff for statistical significance in this book as well.) Men who report their wife makes unilateral decisions are also 4.8 times more likely to be dissatisfied with their sex life. However, this is a far rarer occurrence, and men don't have an entire evangelical marriage establishment telling them it is a sin for them to feel dissatisfied, as we'll look at in chapter 4.

16. Scales usually range from 0 or 1 to a number between 10 and 100 (sometimes more; it depends on how many questions were included). To make things easier to interpret, we've used a bit of arithmetic and have adjusted all scales to range from 0 to 100. Think of it this way: In high school math, if a test was out of 62, and you answered everything correctly, you scored 100%. That's how we've adjusted the scales here, too, to make them easier to interpret.

17. Blaine J. Fowers, Jean-Philippe Laurenceau, Randall D. Penfield, Laura M. Cohen, Samantha F. Lang, Meghan B. Owenz, and Elizabeth Pasipanodya, "Enhancing Relationship Quality Measurement: The Development of the Relationship Flourishing Scale," *Journal of Family Psychology* 30, no. 8 (2016): 997–1007, https://doi.org/10 .1037/fam0000263.

18. Janette L. Funk and Ronald D. Rogge, "Testing the Ruler with Item Response Theory: Increasing Precision of Measurement for Relationship Satisfaction with the Couples Satisfaction Index," *Journal of Family Psychology* 21, no. 4 (2007): 572–83, https://doi.org/10.1037/0893-3200.21.4.572. We used thirty-one of the thirty-two questions from the full version of the CSI.

19. John K. Rempel, John G. Holmes, and Mark P. Zanna, "Trust in Close Relationships," *Journal of Personality and Social Psychology* 49, no. 1 (1985), https://doi.org/10 .1037/0022-3514.49.1.95. We made a few changes to the TCRS to make the questions more readable and to streamline the survey.

20. Kenneth Eggeman, Virginia Moxley, and Walter R. Schumm, "Assessing Spouses' Perceptions of Gottman's Temporal Form in Marital Conflict," *Psychological Reports* 57, no. 1 (Aug. 1985): 171–81, https://doi.org/10.2466/pr0.1985.57.1.171. We removed questions from the KMCS regarding spouses' emotional state during arguments.

21. Endnotes also often contain statistical extras as well as test statistics, regression coefficients, and p-values, where relevant. A p-value is a measure of statistical significance and is typically (though not always) set at 0.05. In stats lingo, that means we have sufficient evidence to reject the null hypothesis if the p-value is less than 0.05. What this means in practice is that for statistics we show (where hypothesis testing is relevant), we have only shown data if the p-value is less than 0.05.

22. Mary Bell, "Complementarian Theology Pits Husbands and Wives Against Each Other," Christians for Biblical Equality, December 28, 2023, https://www.cbein ternational.org/resource/complementarian-theology-pits-husbands-and-wives-against -each-other/.

23. Bell, "Complementarian Theology."

24. This dynamic is common in conservative religious communities. Michal Gilad writes, "Abuse victims in religious communities are less likely to leave the abusive relationship, more likely to believe the abuser's promise to change his violent ways, more reluctant to seek community-based resources or shelters, and more commonly express guilt that they have failed their families and God in not being able to make the marriage work or to stop the abuse," in "In God's Shadow: Unveiling the Hidden World of Victims of Domestic Violence in Observant Religious Communities" (September 25, 2013), *11 Rutgers Journal of Law & Public Policy* 471 (2014), U of Penn Law School, Public Law Research Paper No. 13–27, http://dx.doi.org/10.2139/ssrn.2331015.

25. See, for instance, the book *The Power of a Praying Wife*, which has sold more than ten million copies, in which author Stormie Omartian claims, "You can submit to God in prayer whatever controls your husband—alcoholism, workaholic laziness, depression, infirmity, abusiveness, anxiety, fear or failure—and pray for him to be released from it" (p. 15). Throughout her book, she points to prayer as the answer to a husband's rage, abuse, and more. Many other books and movies have also done this, such as the Kendrick brothers' movie *War Room*.

26. See, for instance, Nancy DeMoss Wolgemuth, *Lies Women Believe: And the Truth That Sets Them Free* (Chicago: Moody Publishers, 2018), 262–63.

27. Paul R. Amato, Laura Spencer Loomis, and Alan Booth, "Parental Divorce, Marital Conflict, and Offspring Well-Being during Early Adulthood," *Social Forces* 73, no. 3 (March 1995): 895–916, https://doi.org/10.2307/2580551. Paul Amato was one of the groundbreaking researchers to first find that the effects of divorce on kids are not universally negative, with children from high-conflict families (including abusive ones) faring better after divorce.

28. See the appendix for suggestions of where to go for help.

29. See Eggerichs, *Love & Respect*, 49, for his use of Feldhahn's survey question to support his thesis and the footnote on p. 320 for a lengthy discussion of it; Shaunti Feldhahn, *For Women Only: What You Need to Know about the Inner Lives of Men* (Atlanta: Multnomah, 2004), 16.

30. Shauna H. Springer, "Women Need Love and Men Need Respect? A Bestseller Based on a Faulty Premise," *Psychology Today*, October 20, 2012, https://www.psychologytoday.com/ca/blog/the-joint-adventures-well-educated-couples/201210/women-need-love-and-men-need-respect.

31. Measured using the Trust in Close Relationships and the Relationship Flourishing scales.

32. R^2 for the line of best fit (LOBF) for average current Relationship Flourishing score by past belief that men need respect = 0.97. A regression model for Relationship Flourishing score by past belief was statistically significant ($p < 0.001$, $R^2 = 0.03$).

Chapter 2 The Teamwork You Want

1. This is a composite of multiple stories we've heard about the results of going to a pastor for advice about a husband's porn use.

2. A classic example of this in modern evangelical thought is the idea that husbands deserve "unconditional respect" even if they are drinking, straying, or harsh and uncaring; cf. Eggerichs, *Love & Respect*, 88.

3. Rami Tolmacz and Mario Mikulincer, "The Sense of Entitlement in Romantic Relationships—Scale Construction, Factor Structure, Construct Validity, and Its Associations with Attachment Orientations," *Psychoanalytic Psychology* 28, no. 1 (2011): 75–94, https://psycnet.apa.org/doi/10.1037/a0021479.

4. Sarah Bessey, "The (Successful) Pursuit of God: Family, Work, Ministry, and the Ghost of A. W. Tozer," *Fathom*, October 23, 2019, https://www.fathommag.com/stories/the-successful-pursuit-of-god.

5. Octav-Sorin Candel, "Sense of Relational Entitlement and Couple Outcomes: The Mediating Role of Couple Negotiation Tactics," *Behavioral Sciences* 13, no. 6 (June 3, 2023): 467, https://doi.org/10.3390/bs13060467.

Chapter 3 The Friendship You Want

1. The scale included was from 0–10. We combined respondents who ranked their responses as 1 or 0 for ease and because so few respondents chose those values.

2. For Relationship Flourishing score and sense of closeness while driving, linear regression results were $\beta = 5.21$, p<0.001, $R^2 = 0.4516$. For the LOBF $R^2 = 0.99$. Similar trends were observed using the other scales investigated in this book. Results were as follows: TCRS (regression results $\beta = 6.54$, p<0.001, $R^2 = 0.4323$; LOBF $R^2 = 0.9781$), KMCS (regression results $\beta = 5.94$, p<0.001).

3. Model results for the Relationship Flourishing score and frequency of enjoying their spouse's company were as follows: $R^2 = 0.4854$, p<0.001. For the LOBF of average RFS by frequency (shown on the graph) $R^2 = 0.9979$. Similar results were yielded for the KMCS and the TCRS. Statistics could not be conducted for the CSI as the question about frequency of fun is from the CSI itself. TCRS results for linear regression: $R^2 = 0.4589$, p<0.001. For the LOBF of average TCRS score by fun with spouse enjoyment frequency $R^2 = 0.9945$. KMCS results: $R^2 = 0.3877$, p<0.001. For LOBF of average KMCS score by fun with spouse enjoyment frequency $R^2 = 0.9954$. Additional statistical information is available at www.marriageyouwantbook.com/endnotes.

4. James Clear, *Atomic Habits: An Easy & Proven Way to Build Good Habits & Break Bad Ones* (New York: Avery, 2018).

5. Yang Du, Buyun Liu, Yangbo Sun, Linda G. Snetselaar, Robert B. Wallace, and Wei Bao, "Trends in Adherence to the Physical Activity Guidelines for Americans for Aerobic Activity and Time Spent on Sedentary Behavior among US Adults, 2007 to 2016," *JAMA Network Open* 2, no. 7 (2019): e197597, https://doi.org/10.1001/jamanetworkopen.2019.7597.

6. Saba Kheirinejad, Aku Visuri, Denzil Ferreira, and Simo Hosio, "'Leave Your Smartphone out of Bed': Quantitative Analysis of Smartphone Use Effect on Sleep Quality," *Personal and Ubiquitous Computing* 27 (2023): 447–66, https://doi.org/10.1007/s00779-022-01694-w.

7. Abdullah Muhammad Alzhrani, Khalid Talal Aboalshamat, Amal Mohammad Badawoud, Ismail Mahmoud Abdouh, Hatim Matooq Badri, Baraa Sami Quronfulah, Mahmoud Abdulrahman Mahmoud, and Mona Talal Rajeh, "The Association between Smartphone Use and Sleep Quality, Psychological Distress, and Loneliness among Health Care Students and Workers in Saudi Arabia," *PLoS One* 18, no. 1 (Jan. 26, 2023): e0280681, doi: 10.1371/journal.pone.0280681; Christine Anderl, Marlise K. Hofer, and Frances S. Chen, "Directly Measured Smartphone Screen Time Predicts Well-Being and Feelings of Social Connectedness," *Journal of Social and Personal Relationships* (Feb. 22, 2023), https://doi.org/10.25384/SAGE.22147820.v1.

8. We are aware that correlation is not necessarily causation. We are not claiming that going to bed together, in and of itself, is responsible for causing huge changes in marital flourishing. Instead, the types of couples who are more likely to go to bed together are also more likely to do other things that lead to marital flourishing—hence the huge correlation. Merely going to bed together won't magically fix a marriage, but being the kind of couple who would want to go to bed at the same time and who would prioritize that means that you are also likely the kind of couple who will flourish in other areas. The more we can adopt practices we know are correlated with better marital flourishing, the more our marriages will tend to improve. However, what works better for the "average" couple may not work best for you and your spouse. You are unique individuals at a particular stage of life, not the average statistical test. The same holds true for many of our other big correlation findings, like the effects of kinkeeping (chap. 6), making your own doctor's appointments (chap. 6), and many more.

9. Jasara N. Hogan, Alexander O. Crenshaw, Katherine J. W. Baucom, and Brian R. W. Baucom, "Time Spent Together in Intimate Relationships: Implications for Relationship Functioning," *Contemporary Family Therapy* 43, no. 3 (Sept. 2021): 226–33, https://doi.org/10.1007/s10591-020-09562-6.

10. This wording comes from a question on the Relationship Flourishing Scale.

11. Gottman and Silver, *Seven Principles*, 88.

12. Karen Bridbord, "Manage Conflict," The Gottman Institute, October 14, 2015, https://www.gottman.com/blog/manage-conflict/.

13. Orsolya Rosta-Filep, Csilla Lakatos, Barna Konkolÿ Thege, Viola Sallay, and Tamás Martos, "Flourishing Together: The Longitudinal Effect of Goal Coordination on Goal Progress and Life Satisfaction in Romantic Relationships," *International Journal of Applied Positive Psychology* 8, no. 2 (Dec. 2023): 205–25, https://doi.org/10.1007/s41042-023-00089-3.

14. Laura E. Kurtz and Sara B. Algoe, "Putting Laughter in Context: Shared Laughter as Behavioral Indicator of Relationship Well-Being," *Personal Relationships* 22, no. 4 (Dec. 2015): 573–90, https://doi.org/10.1111/pere.12095.

15. Krystyna S. Aune and Norman C. H. Wong, "Antecedents and Consequences of Adult Play in Romantic Relationships," *Personal Relationships* 9, no. 3 (Sept. 2002): 279–86, https://doi.org/10.1111/1475-6811.00019.

16. Cheryl Harasymchuk, Amy Muise, Chantal Bacev-Giles, Judith Gere, and Emily A. Impett, "Broadening Your Horizon One Day at a Time: Relationship Goals and Exciting Activities as Daily Antecedents of Relational Self-Expansion," *Journal of Social and Personal Relationships* 37, no. 6 (2020): 1910–26, https://doi.org/10.1177/0265407520911202.

17. Odds Ratio (OR) 1.77, p<0.001, 95% CI 1.57, 2.00. A confidence interval (CI) gives an interval around the point estimate such that if the observation was repeated one hundred times, 95% of 95% confidence intervals would contain the true parameter.

18. Joanna Sawatsky, Rebecca Lindenbach, Sheila Gregoire, and Keith Gregoire, "Sanctified Sexism: Effects of Purity Culture Tropes on White Christian Women's Marital and Sexual Satisfaction and Experience of Sexual Pain," *The Sociology of Religion* (Nov. 2024): srae031, https://doi.org/10.1093/socrel/srae031.

19. Samuel L. Perry, "Perceived Spousal Religiosity and Marital Quality across Racial and Ethnic Groups," *Family Relations: An Interdisciplinary Journal of Applied Family Science* 65, no. 2 (April 2016): 327–341, https://doi.org/10.1111/fare.12192.

20. Only 4.79% of women who strongly disagreed that they have a strong church family said that they can turn to their spouse and a lot of other people when they have a hard time and need support. But among women who strongly agreed that they have a strong church family, 23.20% said the same.

21. OR 2.15, p<0.001, 95% CI 1.68, 2.75.

22. OR 2.42, p<0.001, 95% CI 1.85, 3.16.

23. Sawatsky, et al., "Sanctified Sexism."

24. Patricia Homan and Amy Burdette, "When Religion Hurts: Structural Sexism and Health in Religious Congregations," *American Sociological Review* 86, no. 2 (April 2021): 234–55, https://doi.org/10.1177/0003122421996686.

25. To measure emotional intimacy, we used the Trust in Close Relationships Scale (TCRS), which incorporates a subscale looking at emotional intimacy in marriage.

26. The benefits of couples praying together were maximized for couples who prayed together daily or at least a few times a week. For other levels of prayer frequency, Relationship Flourishing scores decreased as prayer decreased. We measured relationship trust using the Trust in Close Relationships Scale (omitting some sub-items for predictability). Regressions for the impact of prayer on Relationship Flourishing scores were repeated using the faith subscale, dependability subscale, modified predictability subscale, and full modified Trust in Close Relationships Scale using alpha=0.05 as a cutoff for statistical significance.

We also found that prayer as a couple had a slightly larger effect (especially when comparing those who never pray to those who pray very frequently) among those with below average faith sub-item scores in the Trust in Close Relationship Scale.

27. In a linear regression, with the Relationship Flourishing score as the outcome variable and including respondents' gender and church attendance as controls, whether prayer as a couple and spiritual discussion as a couple were included in the same model or in different models, the coefficients for prayer were smaller than those for spiritual discussions. Additional statistical information is available at www.marriageyouwantbook.com/endnotes.

28. Additional statistical information is available at www.marriageyouwantbook.com/endnotes.

29. C. Smith, "Religious Identity and Influence Survey, 1996," August 23, 2021, https://www.thearda.com/data-archive?fid=RIIS. The survey can be freely downloaded at the Association for Religion Data Archives.

30. We restricted all analyses using the Religious Identity and Influence Survey to Christian couples. We were able to conduct these analyses on this historic data set due to its being archived at the Association of Religion Data Archives.

31. The Religious Identity and Influence Survey includes only one measure of marital satisfaction, "How satisfied are you with the way that you and your spouse make decisions in your marriage?"

32. Men odds ratios (respondent leads=ref cat) spouse leads OR=0.11, p=0.877, 95% CI -1.27, 1.48; both lead equally OR=1.55, p=0.149, 95% CI -0.55, 3.66. Women odds ratios (respondent leads=ref cat) spouse leads OR=1.16, p=0.065, 95% CI -0.07, 2.40; both lead equally OR=1.52, p=0.043, 95% CI 0.05, 2.99.

Chapter 4 The Passion You Want

1. In our survey of 20,000 women, only 39% of women who do reach orgasm do so through intercourse alone. Most women require other forms of stimulation to reach orgasm.

2. Amy Muise, Ulrich Schimmack, and Emily A. Impett, "Sexual Frequency Predicts Greater Well-Being, but More Is Not Always Better," *Social Psychological and Personality Science* 7, no. 4 (May 2016): 295–302, https://doi.org/10.1177/1948550615616462; John Gottman, "Building a Great Sex Life is Not Rocket Science," The Gottman Institute, accessed July 8, 2024, https://www.gottman.com/blog/building-great-sex-life-not-rocket-science/.

3. Josip Obradović and Mira Čudina, "Sexual Satisfaction in Long-Term Marriages: Studying the Effect of Nonsexual Predictors in Old Couples," in P. N. Claster and S. L. Blair (eds.), *Aging and the Family: Understanding Changes in Structural and Relationship Dynamics* (UK: Emerald Publishing), 209–28.

4. Gregoire, Lindenbach, and Sawatsky, *Great Sex Rescue*, 163.

5. David A. Frederick, H. Kate St. John, Justin R. Garcia, and Elisabeth A. Lloyd, "Differences in Orgasm Frequency among Gay, Lesbian, Bisexual, and Heterosexual Men and Women in a U.S. National Sample," *Archives of Sexual Behavior* 47 (2018): 273–88, https://doi.org/10.1007/s10508-017-0939-z.

6. Marieke Dewitte, Jacques Van Lankveld J, Sjouke Vandenberghe, and Tom Loeys, "Sex in Its Daily Relational Context," *Journal of Sexual Medicine* 12, no. 12 (Dec. 2015): 2436–50, https://doi.org/10.1111/jsm.13050.

7. Paul J. Wright, Robert S. Tokunaga, Ashley Kraus, and Elyssa Klann, "Pornography Consumption and Satisfaction: A Meta-Analysis," *Human Communication Research* 43, no. 3 (July 2017): 315–43, https://doi.org/10.1111/hcre.12108.

8. We found that 13% of married evangelical women have used porn at some point, and roughly 4% are currently using it. It is likely that this number will increase rapidly, as teen girls are now watching porn at higher numbers than ever before, and this will likely change the demographic makeup of porn users in the future.

9. See, for example, "Building a Dream Marriage during the Parenting Years," *Focus on the Family Broadcast*, November 5, 2019, recording, 16:21, https://www.focuson thefamily.com/episodes/broadcast/building-a-dream-marriage-during-the-parenting -years/, in which the Focus on the Family host states that the reason men often get into trouble with porn is because "that need [for sex] is not being met" at home. Book series like Every Man's Battle also have called women the "methadone" for their spouse's lust and porn problems, insinuating that if she had more sex, he wouldn't be tempted.

10. Craig S. Cashwell, Amanda L. Giordano, Kelly King, Cody Lankford, and Robin K. Henson, "Emotion Regulation and Sex Addiction among College Students," *International Journal of Mental Health and Addiction* 15 (2017): 16–27, https://doi .org/10.1007/s11469-016-9646-6.

11. Kenneth M. Adams and Donald W. Robinson, "Shame Reduction, Affect Regulation, and Sexual Boundary Development: Essential Building Blocks of Sexual Addiction Treatment," *Sexual Addiction & Compulsivity* 8, no. 1 (Jan. 2001): 23–44, https:// doi.org/10.1080/10720160127559.

12. Haley McNamara, "The Porn Industry Has Proven Itself Incapable of Verifying Consent," *Newsweek*, April 15, 2021, https://www.newsweek.com/porn-industry-has -proven-itself-incapable-verifying-consent-opinion-1583380.

13. The original version of *Every Man's Battle* actually referred to women as "methadone" for their husbands' sex addictions. Arterburn and Stoeker, *Every Man's Battle: Winning the War on Sexual Temptation One Victory at a Time* (Colorado Springs: Waterbrook, 2000), 118. We discuss this at length in *The Great Sex Rescue*, chapter 6, titled "Your Spouse Is Not Your Methadone."

14. Andrew Bauman, "A Pornographic Style of Relating," Allender Center, October 1, 2016, https://theallendercenter.org/2016/10/pornographic-style-relating/.

15. Matthew D. Johnson, Nancy L. Galambos, and Jared R. Anderson, "Skip the Dishes? Not So Fast! Sex and Housework Revisited," *Journal of Family Psychology* 30, no. 2 (2016): 203–13, https://doi.org/10.1037/fam0000161.

16. National Center for Victims of Crime, "Child Sexual Abuse Statistics," accessed July 8, 2024, https://victimsofcrime.org/child-sexual-abuse-statistics/.

17. A great resource for this is Jay Stringer's book *Unwanted: How Sexual Brokenness Reveals Our Way to Healing* (Colorado Springs: NavPress, 2018).

18. David Carr, "Gender and the Shaping of Desire in the Song of Songs and Its Interpretation," *Journal of Biblical Literature* 119, no. 2 (summer 2000): 233–48, https://doi.org/10.2307/3268485.

19. Additional statistical information is available at www.marriageyouwantbook .com/endnotes.

20. Additional statistical information is available at www.marriageyouwantbook .com/endnotes.

21. Gregoire and Gregoire, *Good Guy's Guide*, 42–43, used by permission of Zondervan.

22. Maria Uloko, Erika P. Isabey, and Blair R. Peters, "How Many Nerve Fibers Innervate the Human Glans Clitoris: A Histomorphometric Evaluation of the Dorsal Nerve of the Clitoris," *The Journal of Sexual Medicine* 20, no. 3 (March 2023): 247–52, https://doi.org/10.1093/jsxmed/qdac027.

23. Diana E. Peragine, Malvina N. Skorska, Jessica A. Maxwell, Emily A. Impett, and Doug P. VanderLaan, "A Learning Experience? Enjoyment at Sexual Debut and the

Gender Gap in Sexual Desire among Emerging Adults," *The Journal of Sex Research* 59, no. 9 (Nov. 2022): 1092–109, https://doi.org/10.1080/00224499.2022.2027855.

24. Gregoire and Gregoire, *Good Guy's Guide*, 47.

25. Additional statistical information is available at www.marriageyouwantbook.com/endnotes.

26. Gregoire, Lindenbach, and Sawatsky, *Great Sex Rescue*, 187–88.

27. Again, we were looking here only at people who waited for marriage for consensual sex.

28. Our hypothesis is that men tended to know about female orgasms at a younger age because they were also more likely to consume porn. How much better if both men and women were taught about healthy sexuality from the beginning?

29. A great write-up of the wider cultural phenomenon of her pain being the price for his pleasure is a viral article by Lili Loofbourow, "The Female Price of Male Pleasure: Let's Talk about Bad Sex," *The Week*, January 25, 2018, https://theweek.com/articles/749978/female-price-male-pleasure. Her main point is that to men, bad sex is something bland or not that fun, while to women, bad sex is dangerous, terrifying, and often painful.

30. Jimmy Evans, "The Four Major Needs of a Man," XO Marriage, accessed July 8, 2024, https://xomarriage.com/articles/the-four-major-needs-of-a-man/.

31. Kevin Leman, *Sheet Music: Uncovering the Secrets of Sexual Intimacy in Marriage* (Carol Stream, IL: Tyndale, 2003), 203.

32. See more about how we conceptualize libido in chapter 7 of *The Great Sex Rescue*.

33. Emily Nagoski, *Come As You Are: The Surprising New Science That Will Transform Your Sex Life* (New York: Simon & Schuster, 2021).

34. Gregoire, Lindenbach, and Sawatsky, *Great Sex Rescue*, 125.

35. Gregoire, Lindenbach, and Sawatsky, *Great Sex Rescue*, 133, 135.

Chapter 5 The Partnership You Want

1. This graph includes all respondents and is not restricted by employment status. The trend line fit to the graph is a polynomial (power = 2), $R^2 = 0.92$.

2. OR 0.24, p<0.001, 95% CI 0.20–0.28.

3. OR 0.26, p<0.001, 95% CI 0.19–0.35.

4. Saurabh Bhargava, "Experienced Love: An Empirical Account," *Psychological Science* 35, no. 1 (Jan. 2024): 7–20, https://doi.org/10.1177/09567976231211267.

5. Bhargava, "Experienced Love."

6. Eva Johansen, Astrid Harkin, Fionna Keating, Amelia Sanchez, and Dr. Simone Buzwell, "Fairer Sex: The Role of Relationship Equity in Female Sexual Desire," *The Journal of Sex Research* 60, no. 4 (2023): 498–507, https://doi.org/10.1080/00224499.2022.2079111.

7. Emily A. Harris, Aki M. Gormezano, and Sari M. van Anders, "Gender Inequities in Household Labor Predict Lower Sexual Desire in Women Partnered with Men," *Archives of Sexual Behavior* 51 (2022): 3847–70, https://doi.org/10.1007/s10508-022-02397-2.

8. Carolina Aragao, "Working Husbands in U.S. Have More Leisure Time Than Working Wives Do, Especially among Those with Children," Pew Research Center, October 27, 2023, https://www.pewresearch.org/short-reads/2023/10/27/working-husbands-in-the-us-have-more-leisure-time-than-working-wives-do-especially-among-those-with-children/.

9. A polynomial (power 2) trend line was fit to these data. $R^2 = 1.0$.

10. We appreciate Eve Rodsky's determination that equal downtime is the real key to whether you're dividing things fairly. We'll look at her work more in this chapter!

11. Shun Chen, David Murphy, and Stephen Joseph, "Dispositional Authenticity, Facilitativeness, Femininity Ideology, and Dyadic Relationship Functioning in Opposite-Gender Couples: Actor-Partner Interdependence Analysis," *Asian Journal of Social Psychology* 27, no. 1 (March 2024): 101–26, https://doi.org/10.1111/ajsp .12584. This study also confirmed that couples who practice egalitarianism fare best and that when one spouse adheres to stereotypical gender roles while one does not, marital flourishing suffers.

12. See *Great Sex Rescue*, 30, for more discussion on this.

13. Isabella Moody (@IsabellaMoody_), X, August 20, 2023, https://x.com/isabella moody_/status/1693388687806284165.

14. Gregoire and Gregoire, *Good Guy's Guide*, 102–4, used by permission of Zondervan.

15. Julien Laloyaux, Frank Laroi, and Marco Hirnstein, "Research: Women and Men Are Equally Bad at Multitasking," *Harvard Business Review*, September 26, 2018, https://hbr.org/2018/09/research-women-and-men-are-equally-bad-at-multitasking.

16. Matthew Fray, "She Divorced Me Because I Left Dishes by the Sink," *HuffPost*, January 25, 2016, https://www.huffpost.com/entry/she-divorced-me-i-left-dishes-by -the-sink_b_9055288.

17. $p<0.001$. There was no statistically significant difference in sexual satisfaction for men based on whether they had to remind their wives to complete recurring tasks ($p=0.052$).

18. Joe Pinsker, "Lessons from 40 Men in Egalitarian Relationships," *The Atlantic*, June 28, 2022, https://www.theatlantic.com/family/archive/2022/06/couples-gender -inequality-household-chores-caregiving-management/661404/.

19. Fray, "She Divorced Me."

20. Reece Garcia and Jennifer Tomlinson, "Rethinking the Domestic Division of Labour: Exploring Change and Continuity in the Context of Redundancy," *Sociology* 55, no. 2 (April 2021): 300–18, https://doi.org/10.1177/0038038520947311.

21. *Baroness von Sketch Show*, "Witch Trial," CBC Comedy, video, posted October 12, 2020, https://www.youtube.com/watch?v=7rGVIXt28V4.

22. OR 0.33, $p<0.001$, 95% CI 0.25–0.44; comparison to those who have equal free time. Matched respondents only.

23. OR 0.40, $p<0.001$, 95% CI 0.30–0.53; comparison to those who have equal free time. Matched respondents only.

24. OR 0.60, $p<0.001$, 95% CI 0.46–0.78; comparison to those who have equal free time. Matched respondents only.

25. OR 0.55, $p<0.001$, 95% CI 0.42–0.71; comparison to those who have equal free time. Matched respondents only.

26. The percentage of respondents agreeing in each marriage length timepoint was fit with a polynomial trend line (power = 2; $R^2 = 0.92$).

27. Trend lines were fit for both men and women based on the percentage of respondents who reported that their libido is low, very low, or nonexistent. For men: linear trend line, $R^2 = 0.67$; for women: polynomial trend line (power 2), $R^2 = 0.87$.

Chapter 6 The Dependability You Want

1. OR 7.60, $p<0.001$, 95% CI 6.17–9.36.

2. OR 16.71, $p<0.001$, 95% CI 13.59–20.54.

3. OR 1.76, $p<0.001$, 95% CI 1.45–2.14.

4. OR 4.85, $p<0.001$, 95% CI 3.95–5.95.

5. OR 2.22, p<0.001, 95% CI 1.45–3.39.

6. OR 0.51, p=0.014, 95% CI 0.31–0.87. Matched respondents only.

7. OR 0.59, p<0.001, 95% CI 0.47–0.75.

8. OR 0.55, p<0.001, 95% CI 0.49–0.61.

9. OR 0.57, p<0.001, 95% CI 0.50–0.65.

10. OR 0.60, p<0.001, 95% CI 0.49–0.72.

11. We recommend the book *How to ADHD: An Insider's Guide to Working with Your Brain (Not Against It)* (New York: Rodale, 2024) by Jessica McCabe for people looking for strategies to overcome some of the challenges they face in executive function as part of a team.

12. We measured kinkeeping by evaluating which spouse is in charge of remembering important birthdays and anniversaries for each family. Kinkeeping here was evaluated by his report of how remembering his family is split and her report of how remembering her family is split.

13. OR 1.94, p<0.001, 95% CI 1.54–2.45.

14. OR 1.37, p=0.006, 95% CI 1.10–1.70.

15. OR 1.40, p=0.005, 95% CI 1.10–1.77.

16. OR 1.28, p=0.037, 95% CI 1.01–1.61.

17. Katherine L. Fiori, Amy J. Rauer, Kira S. Birditt, Edna Brown, and Terri L. Orbuch, "You Aren't as Close to my Family as You Think: Discordant Perceptions about In-Laws and Risk of Divorce," *Research in Human Development* 17, no. 4 (2020), 258–73, https://doi.org/10.1080/15427609.2021.1874792.

Chapter 7 The Understanding You Want

1. James K. McNulty, Erin M. O'Mara, and Benjamin R. Karney, "Benevolent Cognitions as a Strategy of Relationship Maintenance: 'Don't Sweat the Small Stuff' . . . but It Is Not All Small Stuff," *Journal of Personality and Social Psychology* 94, no. 4 (April 2008): 631–46, https://doi.org/10.1037/0022-3514.94.4.631.

2. McNulty, O'Mara, and Karney, "Benevolent Cognitions."

3. Rebecca Lindenbach, quoted in Sheila Gregoire, "Iron Sharpens Iron Series: Marriage Should Make You Better People," *Bare Marriage* blog, January 8, 2020, https://baremarriage.com/2020/01/iron-sharpens-iron-series-marriage-should-make -you-better-people/.

4. Carolyn Custis James, *Half the Church: Recapturing God's Global Vision for Women* (Grand Rapids: Zondervan, 2011), 115.

5. John Piper, "Should Women Be Police Officers?" episode 661, August 13, 2015, in *Ask Pastor John* podcast, https://www.desiringgod.org/interviews/should-women -be-police-officers. Here, and in his book *Recovering Biblical Manhood and Womanhood*, Piper argues that women can never directly give a particular man instructions since that would undermine his masculinity and her femininity. She must instead be indirect, even if giving directions to the highway (pp. 61–62).

6. Nickola C. Overall and James K. McNulty, "What Type of Communication during Conflict Is Beneficial for Intimate Relationships?" *Current Opinion in Psychology* 13 (Feb. 2017): 1–5, https://doi.org/10.1016/j.copsyc.2016.03.002.

The exception was when one spouse was unwilling to listen or the couple felt the problem was unsolvable, in which case minimizing the bigger problem did tend to make the marriage more secure (although we would argue that doesn't necessarily mean healthier).

7. We understand that recognizing and naming emotions or being able to express your viewpoint, let alone your spouse's, can be especially difficult for those who are

neurodiverse or have alexithymia. Strategies for growing one's capability in these areas, and finding accommodations, are available through mental health professionals.

8. OR 0.63, p=0.017, 95% CI 0.43–0.92. Matched respondents only.

9. OR 0.31, p<0.001, 95% CI 0.21–0.45. Matched respondents only.

10. OR 0.17, p<0.001, 95% CI 0.10–0.27. Matched respondents only.

11. OR 0.07, p<0.001, 95% CI 0.03–0.19. Matched respondents only.

12. Additional statistical information is available at www.marriageyouwantbook.com/endnotes.

13. Overall and McNulty, "What Type of Communication?"

14. Dr. Henry Cloud and Dr. John Townsend, *Boundaries Updated and Expanded Edition: When to Say Yes, How to Say No to Take Control of Your Life* (Grand Rapids: Zondervan, 2017), 87; see also Galatians 6:7.

15. This is called DARVO, which stands for Deny, Attack, Reverse Victim and Offender. It's a way that the abuser can claim that they are actually the victim, and the victim is actually the aggressor. DARVO is used not just by abusers, but by abusive systems, such as a system trying to convince an abuse victim to stay in a marriage. DARVO is not necessarily intentional, but is rather the typical response when an abuse victim threatens the status quo.

16. Additional statistical information is available at www.marriageyouwantbook.com/endnotes.

17. Men: OR 0.50, p<0.001, 95% CI 0.38–0.65. Women: OR 0.30, p<0.001, 95% CI 0.24–0.39.

18. Men: OR 0.71, p=0.015, 95% CI 0.54–0.94. Women: OR 0.46, p<0.001, 95% CI 0.36–0.60.

19. See, for example, Fred and Brenda Stoeker, *Every Heart Restored: A Wife's Guide to Healing in the Wake of a Husband's Sexual Sin* (Colorado Springs: Waterbrook, 2004), 211. The Stoekers assert, "On the battlefield of broken sexual trust, your husband must become trustworthy and you must eventually choose to trust again. . . . It's self-defeating to worry about which should come first."

20. See Amato, Loomis, and Booth, "Parental Divorce, Marital Conflict, and Offspring Well-Being."

Chapter 8 The Closeness You Want

1. Quoted in "Tribute Service for Former First Lady Rosalynn Carter," CNN, November 28, 2023, 2:35 p.m. EDT, https://www.cnn.com/us/live-news/rosalynn-carter-tribute-service-tuesday-11-28-23/index.html.

2. OR 3.12, p<0.001, 95% CI 2.15–4.53. Evaluated using the item from the Trust in Close Relationships Scale: Even if I have no reason to expect my spouse to share things with me, I still feel certain that they will. Matched respondents only.

3. OR 1.52, p=0.002, 95% CI 1.16–1.98. Matched respondents only.

4. OR 5.03, p<0.0001, 95% CI 3.82–6.62. Matched respondents only.

5. OR 4.59, p<0.0001, 95% CI 3.11–6.78. Matched respondents only.

6. John Powell, *Why Am I Afraid to Tell You Who I Am?* (Grand Rapids: Zondervan, 1999).

7. For the LOBFs of average Relationship Flourishing score by male agreement that they are confident their wife will share things with them, $R^2 = 0.94$ for men and $R^2 = 0.98$ for women. Linear regression showing the impact of men's agreement that their wife will share intimate things with them showed $R^2 = 0.25$ for men (p<0.001) and $R^2 = 0.14$ for women (p<0.001).

8. For the LOBFs of average Relationship Flourishing score by female agreement that they are confident their husband will share things with them, $R^2 = 0.94$ for men

and $R^2 = 0.99$ for women. Linear regression showing the impact of women's agreement that their husband will share intimate things with them showed $R^2 = 0.16$ for men (p<0.001) and $R^2 = 0.35$ for women (p<0.001).

9. Chen, Murphy, and Joseph, "Actor-Partner Interdependence Analysis."

10. See Robert Waldinger and Mark Schulz, *The Good Life: Lessons from the World's Longest Scientific Study of Happiness* (New York: Simon & Schuster, 2023).

11. OR: 90.7, p<0.001, 95% CI 44.9–183.1.

12. While there are many different psychological and neuroscientific theories about emotions, and all see the brain constructing emotions slightly differently, all agree that emotions are cognitive.

13. Taken from an interview with Becky Castle Miller, February 10, 2024. Much of the interview can be heard on episode 224, "Lies Women Believe Part 2: Is God a Monster?" February 15, 2024, *Bare Marriage* podcast, https://baremarriage.com/2024/02/podcast-lies-women-believe-part-2-is-god-a-monster/.

14. Marc Alan Schelske, *The Wisdom of Your Heart: Discovering the God-Given Purpose and Power of Your Emotions* (Colorado Springs: David C. Cook, 2017), 30.

15. Schelske, *Wisdom of Your Heart*, 40.

16. Dan B. Allender and Steve Call, *The Deep-Rooted Marriage: Cultivating Intimacy, Healing, and Delight* (Nashville: W Publishing, 2025), 130.

17. From Schelske, *Wisdom of Your Heart*, 162–63.

18. Jay Stringer, *Unwanted: How Sexual Brokenness Reveals Our Way to Healing* (Colorado Springs: NavPress, 2018), 12.

19. In our study of 20,000 women, we also found that the obligation-sex message lowered orgasm rates, lowered libido, and increased rates of sexual pain in women.

20. Tara M. Chaplin and Amelia Aldao, "Gender Differences in Emotion Expression in Children: A Meta-Analytic Review," *Psychological Bulletin* 139, no. 4 (2013): 735–65, https://doi.org/10.1037/a0030737.

21. OR 0.57, p<0.001, 95% CI 0.45–0.72. Matched respondents only.

22. OR 0.61, p=0.001, 95% CI 0.46–0.83. Matched respondents only.

23. OR 2.1, p<0.001, 95% CI 1.6–2.7. Matched respondents only.

24. Aljoscha Dreisoerner, Nina M. Junker, Wolff Schlotz, Julia Heimrich, Svenja Bloemeke, Beate Ditzen, and Rolf van Dick, "Self-Soothing Touch and Being Hugged Reduce Cortisol Responses to Stress: A Randomized Controlled Trial on Stress, Physical Touch, and Social Identity," *Comprehensive Psychoneuroendocrinology* 8 (Nov. 2021), https://doi.org/10.1016/j.cpnec.2021.100091.

25. Gottman, *Seven Principles*, 103.

26. Jared B. Torre and Matthew D. Lieberman, "Putting Feelings into Words: Affect Labeling as Implicit Emotion Regulation," *Emotion Review* 10, no. 2 (April 2018): 116–24, https://doi.org/10.1177/1754073917742706.

27. *Shall We Dance?*, directed by Peter Chelsom (Los Angeles: Miramax, 2004).

Appendix

1. See Focus on the Family, *Should I Get a Divorce?* (Colorado Springs: Focus on the Family, 2018), 13, 15, http://media.focusonthefamily.com/fotf/pdf/channels/marriage/should-i-get-a-divorce.pdf. Pages 12 and 13 explain the reasons that Focus on the Family believes divorce is permitted, and abuse is not one of them. While Focus on the Family international organizations may not take as firm a stance, it is still best to be wary and seek out other help.

Sheila Wray Gregoire is the face behind Bare Marriage.com as well as a sought-after speaker and the award-winning author or coauthor of nine books, including *The Great Sex Rescue* and *She Deserves Better*. With her humorous, no-nonsense approach, Sheila is passionate about changing the evangelical conversation about sex and marriage to make it healthy, evidence-based, and biblical. She and her husband, Keith, live in Ontario, Canada, near their two adult daughters and three grandchildren. Sheila also knits. Even in line at the grocery store.

Dr. Keith Gregoire is a physician and the coauthor with Sheila of *The Good Guy's Guide to Great Sex*, companion to her award-winning *The Good Girl's Guide to Great Sex*. Currently, Keith spends most of his professional time providing pediatric care to remote communities in northern Ontario. Plus he birdwatches. Even during mosquito season.

Connect with Sheila and Keith:
BareMarriage.com

 BareMarriageOfficial SheilaGregoire  SheilaGregoire

Listen to the *Bare Marriage* podcast every Thursday!

Joanna Sawatsky is an epidemiologist with a research focus on the intersection of religiosity and women's health issues. As Research Coordinator at Bare Marriage, she oversees health promotion efforts by managing survey development, data collection, statistical analysis, and knowledge translation. Working alongside collaborators in sociology, medicine, and physiotherapy, Joanna leads drafting of peer-reviewed journal articles and has presented at professional conferences. A Pittsburgher turned Canadian, Joanna lives with her husband and two daughters in Edmonton, Alberta.